THE
EVERYTHING.
EASY MEDITERRANEAN
COOKBOOK

Dear Reader,

Many of us have busy lives juggling career, family, children, or even scheduling "down time" to find balance. I too have been very busy ever since *The Everything® Mediterranean Cookbook, 2nd Edition* was released in November 2013. Ever mindful of that balance, I am proud to present you with *The Everything® Easy Mediterranean Cookbook*.

It may be a challenge for you to find the time to cook. But if you're looking for quick meal solutions and don't want to sacrifice taste or nutrition, this book is for you. All of these recipes can be prepared in about 45 minutes, and chances are that many of the ingredients will already be in your pantry.

Mediterranean cooking continues to be popular for many important reasons. The ingredients are now considered to be mainstream (what was once ethnic or exotic is now found at your local supermarket), and the health benefits of these dishes have been proven over and over.

Keep it simple, cook what's in season, don't be afraid to experiment, and always make time to eat your meals with family and friends.

Peter Minaki

Welcome to the EVERYTHING® Series!

These handy, accessible books give you all you need to tackle a difficult project, gain a new hobby, comprehend a fascinating topic, prepare for an exam, or even brush up on something you learned back in school but have since forgotten.

You can choose to read an Everything® book from cover to cover or just pick out the information you want from our three useful boxes: e-facts, e-alerts, and e-ssentials. We give you everything you need to know on the subject, but throw in a lot of fun stuff along the way, too.

We now have more than 400 Everything® books in print, spanning such wide-ranging categories as weddings, pregnancy, cooking, music instruction, foreign language, crafts, pets, New Age, and so much more. When you're done reading them all, you can finally say you know Everything®!

FACT

Important snippets
of information

ALERT

Urgent
warnings

ESSENTIAL

Quick
handy tips

PUBLISHER Karen Cooper

MANAGING EDITOR, EVERYTHING® SERIES Lisa Laing

COPY CHIEF Casey Ebert

ASSISTANT PRODUCTION EDITOR Alex Guarco

ACQUISITIONS EDITOR Lisa Laing

DEVELOPMENT EDITOR Brett Palana-Shanahan

EVERYTHING® SERIES COVER DESIGNER Erin Alexander

THE
EVERYTHING®
EASY MEDITERRANEAN COOKBOOK

Peter Minaki

Adams Media

New York London Toronto Sydney New Delhi

This book is dedicated to the mothers and grandmothers who fed us and nurtured us with food memories that inspire the cook in each one of us. A special thank you to my mother, Chrissanthi.

Adams Media
An Imprint of Simon & Schuster, Inc.
57 Littlefield Street
Avon, Massachusetts 02322
Copyright © 2015 by Simon & Schuster, Inc.

An Everything® Series Book.
Everything® and everything.com® are registered trademarks of Simon & Schuster, Inc.

ADAMS MEDIA and colophon are trademarks of Simon and Schuster.

For information about special discounts for bulk purchases, please contact Simon & Schuster Special Sales at 1-866-506-1949 or business@simonandschuster.com.

The Simon & Schuster Speakers Bureau can bring authors to your live event. For more information or to book an event contact the Simon & Schuster Speakers Bureau at 1-866-248-3049 or visit our website at www.simonspeakers.com.

Nutritional statistics by Nicole Cormier, RD, LDN.

Manufactured in the United States of America

6 2021

Library of Congress Cataloging-in-Publication Data has been applied for.

ISBN 978-1-4405-9240-9
ISBN 978-1-4405-9241-6 (ebook)

Always follow safety and commonsense cooking protocol while using kitchen utensils, operating ovens and stoves, and handling uncooked food. If children are assisting in the preparation of any recipe, they should always be supervised by an adult.

Contains material adapted from *The Everything® Mediterranean Cookbook* by Dawn Altomari-Rathjen, LPN, BPS, and Jennifer M. Bendelius, MS, RD, copyright © 2003 by Simon & Schuster, Inc., ISBN 978-1-58062-869-3; *The Everything® Mediterranean Cookbook, 2nd Edition* by Peter Minaki, copyright © 2013, 2003 by Simon & Schuster, Inc., ISBN 978-1-4405-6855-8; *The Everything® Mediterranean Diet Book* by Connie Diekman, MEd, RD, LD, FADA, and Sam Sotiropoulos, copyright © 2010 by Simon & Schuster, Inc., ISBN 978-1-4405-0674-1; and *The Everything® Mediterranean Slow Cooker Cookbook* by Brooke McLay and Launie Kettler, copyright © 2014 by Simon & Schuster, Inc., ISBN 978-1-4405-6852-7.

Contents

Introduction

THE MEDITERRANEAN REGION IS known for its beauty, diversity, variety of seafoods, and the diet that takes its name from the region. The region encompasses the countries that ring the Mediterranean Sea. On the northern and western side of the sea are Albania, Bosnia-Herzegovina, Croatia, France, Greece, Italy, Malta, Monaco, Serbia (considered Mediterranean because of its weather), Slovenia, and Spain. The southern and eastern part of the region includes Algeria, Cyprus, Egypt, Israel, Lebanon, Libya, Morocco, Palestinian Authority, Syria, Tunisia, and Turkey. Despite the wide range of countries that comprise the Mediterranean region, the Mediterranean diet is most commonly associated with Spain, Southern France, Italy, Greece (the isle of Crete in particular), and the Middle East. There are regional differences in what constitutes the Mediterranean diet, but all share an essential common trait: a focus on whole grains, fruits, vegetables, and fish.

Although the Mediterranean diet has been enjoyed for centuries, within the last sixty years it has been the subject of much interest by dietitians, medical professionals, and consumers. People in the southern Mediterranean countries tend to have less heart disease compared to those in western Europe and North America, even though they consume more fat than many dietary guidelines recommend and drink a relatively large amount of wine. These two factors together seem to contradict the concept of healthful eating, but for people in the Mediterranean this diet is a part of life. Another factor that characterizes this diet is the use of oils, nuts, and seeds. The use of oils in place of animal fats not only produces a diet with more healthful fats but also provides a variety of phytonutrients, which help in the prevention of disease.

Mediterranean cuisine focuses on food that is in season. People cook what they find at their local farmers' market. Vegetables such as eggplants and peppers are consumed in the summer months while cabbage and cauliflower are enjoyed in the winter. When preparing the recipes in this book, try to use local ingredients that are in season. You can create authentic Mediterranean dishes by buying seasonal local ingredients and by stocking your pantry with some specialty items that are central to Mediterranean cooking, such as grape leaves. Most of the specialty items mentioned in this book can be found at Greek or Middle Eastern grocers, but many supermarkets carry these items, too. Just look for them in the international-product aisles.

Most of the recipes in this book can be made easily on a weeknight. In no more than 45 minutes, you can get a healthful, delicious dinner on the table—try Skillet Chicken Parmesan (Chapter 9) for a quick take on a classic family dinner or easy, elegant Grilled Salmon with Lemon and Lime (Chapter 10).

Make-ahead recipes are denoted with **MA**. These dishes require a little hands-off time for marinating, precooking, or an overnight stay in the refrigerator. That little extra preparation means you can impress your guests with Lemon Verbena Rack of Lamb (Chapter 8) and Lemon-Coconut Ice Cream (Chapter 13) while still having time to enjoy the party.

No "easy" cookbook is complete without the ultimate "set-it-and-forget-it" appliance, the slow cooker. Slow cooker recipes are called out with a **SC**. Prep your ingredients in the morning, and this kitchen workhorse will do the rest—greeting you with the aroma of a long-simmered meal when you get home from work. When you use a slow cooker, you can add dishes like Risotto and Greens (Chapter 6), Tuscan Chicken and Sausage Stew (Chapter 4), and Short Ribs of Beef with Red Wine (Chapter 8) to your regular weeknight rotation.

Whether you're headed to the grocery store, fixing a new recipe, or trying a new type of whole grain, this book will provide you with the help you need to make Mediterranean eating your way of eating.

CHAPTER 1

The Mediterranean Kitchen

Thoughts of the Mediterranean create visions of youth, vitality, and, of course, delicious food. With a diet full of lean meats and crisp vegetables, people who live in the Mediterranean region are fortunate enough to enjoy some of the freshest, most vibrant foods available. In addition, research indicates that the people in these regions have the lowest rates of chronic diseases and one of the highest life expectancies in the world. Once you start preparing your own Mediterranean dishes, you'll begin to understand why the Mediterranean lifestyle is believed to be one of the healthiest.

Stocking Your Pantry with the Basics

Mediterranean food is flavorful and simple to prepare. Having a well-stocked pantry will make planning and preparing a Mediterranean meal even simpler. Here are some items you should always have on hand so that you are ready to cook many different Mediterranean meals.

Olive Oil

Extra-virgin olive oil is a staple of Mediterranean cooking. Most countries surrounding the Mediterranean Sea produce their own olive oil. Ripe olives are pressed and the oil is filtered and then bottled or canned for consumer use.

Olive oil is used in cooking, baking, dressings, and for frying. The smoke point for olive oil is 410°F, which is well above the ideal frying temperature of 365°F–375°F, so go ahead and fry with olive oil! Spend some time trying out different kinds of olive oil to discover which ones you like the most. A good-quality olive oil can make a simple dish outstanding.

Spices and Herbs

Mediterranean cuisine uses a variety of herbs and spices. The recipes in this book feature common Mediterranean herbs such as parsley, dill, rosemary, thyme, sage, mint, fennel fronds, bay leaf, tarragon, lemon verbena, and oregano. Whenever possible, it's best to use fresh herbs in their fresh state, with one exception—oregano. Oregano is more pungent in its dried state and goes wonderfully with meats, fish, and seafood. Herbs are also good for making teas. The most popular ones are chamomile, mint, sage, and lemon verbena.

ALERT

In order to consume fresh, less-processed foods, try the following tip: Make a grocery list once a week that always includes fresh foods that have long shelf lives. These foods include apples, oranges, baby carrots, and romaine lettuce. All are readily available, inexpensive, and most people like them.

Spices add warmth to many dishes. Some common Mediterranean spices to keep on hand include cinnamon, cloves, allspice, nutmeg, anise, saffron, red pepper flakes, and mastiha. Mastiha is a spice that comes from the island of Chios, Greece, in the Eastern Mediterranean. Mastiha is harvested from the sap of the local *Pistacia lentiscus* tree at specific times in the year. It has a unique woody, slightly piney, and incense-like flavor. It is traditionally used in Christmas and Easter breads and desserts, but you can also use it in savory dishes as well. Buy spices in small amounts as they tend to get stale when stored for too long.

Dairy Products

Dairy products play an important role in Mediterranean dishes. Although olive oil is the main fat used in cooking, it is not the only one. Butter is used, though sparingly. Since olive trees do not grow in high-altitude or mountainous regions, the people in those areas traditionally use animal fat or butter for cooking.

When using phyllo, most Mediterranean cooks brush the sheets with butter rather than with oil. Other cooks use oil. Try both and see which you prefer. You may also try a combination of 50 percent oil and 50 percent butter.

Folks in the Mediterranean love cheese. Most of the cheese is made from sheep's and goat's milk. These cheeses are easier to digest and have a more complex texture and flavor than the cheeses made from cow's milk that are common in North America. For example, a true feta cheese is only made in Greece, and it is made from sheep's or goat's milk or a blend of the two. Buy feta made in Greece; otherwise, it is not true feta.

Other Greek cheeses referenced in this book are kefalotyri, which is a sharp sheep's milk cheese; Graviera, which is similar to a Gruyère; and kasseri, which is a mild table cheese. Halloumi is a wonderful cheese from Cyprus that holds up well on a grill. Romano, Parmesan, ricotta, and mascarpone cheeses are all more familiar cheeses from the Mediterranean region.

FACT

All foods from animal sources (fish, poultry, egg, and meat) are to be eaten sparingly if one hopes to achieve the benefits of this healthy lifestyle.

Unless otherwise noted, the recipes that use yogurt in this book call for full-fat Greek yogurt. Yes, it is higher in fat than most yogurts, but many low-fat yogurts sold today are full of chemicals or gelatins so as to mimic the thickness that naturally occurs in Greek yogurt. Try using Greek yogurt as a healthier alternative to sour cream in your dishes.

Other Diet Staples

Mediterranean cuisine includes beans, lentils, tomatoes, potatoes, and, of course, olives, among its staple ingredients. Even though some of these ingredients are new additions to the Mediterranean pantry, they have been seamlessly incorporated into many modern and traditional dishes.

Beans and Lentils

The Mediterranean diet is one of the most healthful in the world because it includes a large amount of beans and legumes. Most beans and lentils you purchase in the store are dried, meaning they will keep for a long time in your pantry. Make sure you have plenty of navy beans, butter beans, lentils, and chickpeas. Dried beans require soaking overnight before they can be used, so having canned beans on hand is good for those days when you're in a hurry. Chickpeas and navy beans are good choices.

Stocks

A good stock will elevate any dish. Making your own stock lets you choose what flavors to add, and most important how much salt to add. Keep your freezer well "stocked" with quart-sized containers of chicken, turkey, beef, veal, lamb, fish, seafood, and vegetable stocks.

Tomatoes, Potatoes, and Citrus Fruits

Although tomatoes, potatoes, lemons, and oranges are more recent additions to the Mediterranean pantry, it is hard to imagine cooking Mediterranean dishes without them. Buy tomatoes when they are in season. If you must use them in the winter, cherry tomatoes are a good choice. Always have cans of tomato paste and plum tomatoes on hand. They are great for flavoring sauces, soups, and stews.

Citrus fruit are widely available all year but you can also use preserved lemons, a great pantry staple. Potatoes are varied in colors, texture, and size. Experiment with the varieties and discover your favorites.

Olives

Have a variety of green and black olives in your pantry. They are wonderful for garnishing salads, making dips, or just eating as a snack.

Vinegars, Honey, and Molasses

Balsamic, red-wine, white-wine, and cider vinegars are a must in a Mediterranean pantry. They are used to flavor stews, soups, salads, and even desserts. Honey has been a part of Mediterranean cooking for centuries, and it continues to be an essential ingredient in sweet and savory dishes. You will also find sweeteners such as pomegranate molasses and grape molasses in desserts and in dressings for salads.

Kitchen Equipment

Most Mediterranean kitchens aren't full of fancy gadgets—just a few trusty tools can take care of most cooking tasks. Invest in a good chef's knife. Choose one that fits your hand properly and has a good quality blade. If you invest wisely, this knife will last you a lifetime.

A mortar and pestle is necessary for grinding spices, making pastes, and mixing dips. Don't bother getting a small one. Find one that holds at least 3 cups. You want a strong, sturdy mortar and pestle. Avoid ceramic or glass varieties. Wood or hard-stone mortar and pestles are the best.

Cheese, vegetables, garlic, and onions can be grated by hand using a box grater. A microplane grater is indispensable for zesting citrus and grating spices. A food processor is also handy for puréeing and mixing dough. And immersion blenders are an efficient way to blend soups.

Every kitchen should have a meat thermometer and a candy thermometer. The meat thermometer will help you determine when your meat is cooked to a safe temperature. Candy thermometers give you accurate temperatures for frying and making sugar desserts.

If you want to make pizzeria-grade crusts, you'll need to use a pizza stone. This is not an expensive item and you can find one in any cooking store. The stone gets very hot and distributes the heat evenly across the pizza base, creating a wonderfully crispy crust. It is also provides a good surface for baking bread.

Easy Mediterranean Cooking at Home

Now that you've learned the basics of Mediterranean cuisine, it's time to experiment in your own kitchen. Refer back to this chapter for tips and guidance as you start your own culinary adventures.

The 300 recipes in this book are broken down into easy-to-follow steps, and call for fresh ingredients that you can find in any grocery store. You'll discover that vibrant, healthy meals don't have to take all day to cook. In fact, these easy recipes make for perfect weeknight fare or stress-free entertaining on the weekends. Most of these dishes can be made in 45 minutes or less. Some need a little prep time for marinating or soaking. And others require more time because they are made in the slow cooker, the ultimate "hands-off appliance."

ESSENTIAL

Have fun with the recipes, and get creative. For example, you can turn the vegetarian side dish options into main courses and make the meat and fish dishes sides, inverting the ratio of proteins and vegetables. This way, you'll eat leaner without denying yourself anything.

Don't get too hung up on specific ingredients. If you can't find a specific ingredient, you can substitute with something similar. Dried herbs work in place of fresh, canned lentils and beans are great pantry items, and there are many substitution options for olive oil and cheeses . . . too many to mention! When it comes to fish, meat, and poultry, you can even switch your proteins in the recipes. Because the best option is the freshest option (especially fish and seafood), sometimes it makes sense to substitute.

In the cold months, all-in-one-pan meals can be made in a skillet, pot, or deep baking dish in your oven. In the summer months, get outdoors and use your grill. The grill offers quick and healthy cooking alternatives, and with a bit of practice most anyone can become a grill master!

Of course, the easiest way to make your weeknight dinners even easier is not to cook at all. But you don't have to resort to fast food and take out. When you have time, make double or triple batches of soups, entrées, and sauces and then freeze them in meal-sized containers. On those hectic nights when everyone is hungry and no one wants to cook, you'll have a selection of healthful, delicious meals just waiting to be defrosted and reheated.

CHAPTER 2

Breakfast

Fig, Apricot, and Almond Granola

Cardamom is a wonderful earthy spice that lends a citrusy note to this granola.

INGREDIENTS | SERVES 16

Nonstick vegetable-oil spray
⅓ cup vegetable oil
⅓ cup honey
2 tablespoons white sugar
1 teaspoon vanilla extract
4 cups old-fashioned oats
1¼ cups sliced almonds
½ cup chopped dried apricots
½ cup chopped dried figs
½ cup packed brown sugar
½ teaspoon salt
½ teaspoon ground cardamom

Dried Fruits

Dried fruits such as figs, raisins, dates, and apricots have been part of the Mediterranean diet for centuries. Drying fruit is one of the oldest forms of preservation and is still popular today.

1. Preheat oven to 300°F. Lightly spray two large baking sheets with nonstick spray.

2. In a small saucepan over medium heat, add oil, honey, sugar, and vanilla. Cook 5 minutes or until sugar is dissolved. Remove pan from heat and let it cool 2 minutes.

3. In a large bowl, combine oats, almonds, apricots, figs, brown sugar, salt, and cardamom. Mix with your hands to combine.

4. Pour honey mixture over the oat mixture. Using your hands (if it is too hot, use a wooden spoon), toss ingredients together to make sure everything is well coated. Spread granola evenly over two baking sheets. Bake 30 minutes, stirring every 10 minutes.

5. Let granola cool completely on the baking sheets then break it up into pieces. Store in an airtight container up to 3 weeks.

Per Serving: Calories: 235 | Fat: 9g | Protein: 5g | Sodium: 78mg | Fiber: 4g | Carbohydrates: 35g

Greek Yogurt Smoothie

*Add whatever fruit you like to this smoothie. Use what is fresh
and in season. Try blueberries, peaches, or kiwi.*

INGREDIENTS | SERVES 4

2 cups plain Greek yogurt

2 cups orange or apple juice

2 large ripe bananas, peeled
and chopped

1 cup fresh or frozen mango slices

½ cup fresh or frozen sliced strawberries

½ cup pineapple chunks

⅓ cup honey

1. Put all ingredients into a food processor.

2. Process until smooth and all ingredients are well
   incorporated. Serve cool.

   Per Serving: Calories: 306 | Fat: 4.5g | Protein: 6g | Sodium:
   59mg | Fiber: 5g | Carbohydrates: 66g

Greek Yogurt with Honey and Granola

*Use your favorite store-bought granola or try Fig, Apricot, and
Almond Granola (see recipe in this chapter).*

INGREDIENTS | SERVES 4

1⅓ cups plain Greek yogurt

1 cup granola

1 cup fresh berries (raspberries,
blueberries, or strawberries)

½ cup honey

1. Divide yogurt into four small bowls and top with
   granola and berries.

2. Drizzle honey over each bowl and serve.

   Per Serving: Calories: 348 | Fat: 10g | Protein: 9g | Sodium:
   47mg | Fiber: 3g | Carbohydrates: 55g

Fresh Fruit and Yogurt

Use fruits that are in season. Mix and match the ripest.

INGREDIENTS | SERVES 6

6 cups plain nonfat yogurt

¼ medium cantaloupe, seeded and chopped

¼ medium honeydew melon, seeded and chopped

2 medium kiwis, peeled and sliced

1 medium peach, pitted and sliced into wedges

1 large plum, pitted and sliced into wedges

½ pint fresh raspberries

6 mint sprigs

Spoon the yogurt into serving bowls and arrange fruit decoratively around each rim. Garnish with mint.

Per Serving: Calories: 154 | Fat: 2g | Protein: 15g | Sodium: 214mg | Fiber: 11g | Carbohydrates: 38g

Yogurt Cheese and Fruit M A

This breakfast is worth the extra effort of making the yogurt cheese. If you don't have the time or inclination, use farmer's cheese instead.

INGREDIENTS | SERVES 6

3 cups plain nonfat yogurt

1 teaspoon fresh lemon juice

½ cup orange juice

½ cup water

1 large Golden Delicious apple, peeled, cored, and cut into thin wedges

1 large pear, peeled, cored, and cut into thin wedges

¼ cup honey

¼ cup dried cranberries

1. Prepare yogurt cheese the day before by lining a colander or strainer with cheesecloth. Spoon yogurt into cheesecloth and place the strainer over a pot or bowl to catch the whey. Refrigerate at least 8 hours.

2. In a large bowl, mix together lemon juice, orange juice, and water. Place apple and pear wedges in the juice mixture and let sit at least 5 minutes. Strain off liquid.

3. Remove yogurt cheese from refrigerator, slice, and place on plates. Arrange fruit wedges around yogurt. Drizzle with honey and sprinkle with cranberries just before serving.

Per Serving: Calories: 183 | Fat: 4g | Protein: 5g | Sodium: 59mg | Fiber: 2g | Carbohydrates: 35g

Breakfast Bruschetta

It's not unusual for a Mediterranean breakfast dish to be dominated by vegetables.

INGREDIENTS | SERVES 4

4 slices Italian or French bread

3 tablespoons olive oil, divided

¼ cup pesto

2 large eggs

2 large egg whites

1 medium tomato, diced

½ cup chopped roasted red pepper

¼ cup shredded mozzarella cheese

1. Heat grill pan over medium-high heat. Brush both sides of bread slices with 2 tablespoons of the olive oil and grill until lightly browned, about 3 minutes per side.

2. Place toasted bread on a baking sheet and spread with pesto.

3. Preheat broiler. In a medium bowl, lightly beat eggs and egg whites. Stir in tomato.

4. Heat the remaining oil in a medium skillet pan over medium heat. Add egg mixture and stir once. Continuously move the pan, using a spatula to push the edges inward slightly to allow the egg mixture to pour outward and solidify. Cook until mixture is firm, about 6 minutes, then use a spatula to fold it in half. Remove from pan and cut into 4 pieces. Place on top of bread slices and top with peppers and cheese. Broil until cheese melts, about 2 minutes.

Per Serving: Calories: 341 | Fat: 20g | Protein: 11g | Sodium: 481mg | Fiber: 4g | Carbohydrates: 27g

Eggs in Italian Bread

Use the best crusty bread you can find for this classic Italian breakfast.

INGREDIENTS | SERVES 6

6 (2") slices crusty Italian bread

1 tablespoon olive oil, divided

2 medium red bell peppers, seeded and thinly sliced

1 small shallot, peeled and minced

6 large eggs

1 teaspoon salt

½ teaspoon ground black pepper

1. Using a cookie cutter or glass, cut out large circles from the center of each bread slice. Discard center pieces and set hollowed-out bread slices aside.

2. Heat 1 teaspoon oil in a medium skillet over medium heat. Sauté bell peppers and shallot 5–7 minutes or until tender. Remove from skillet and drain on paper towel; keep warm.

3. Heat remaining oil over medium-high heat in a large skillet. Place bread slices in pan. Crack 1 egg into hollowed-out center of each bread slice. Cook 5 minutes, then flip carefully and cook 3 minutes more. Transfer to plates and top with bell pepper mixture.

4. Season with salt and black pepper before serving.

Per Serving: Calories: 198 | Fat: 8g | Protein: 10g | Sodium: 672mg | Fiber: 2g | Carbohydrates: 21g

Pancetta on Baguette

This Mediterranean version of bacon and cheese is incredibly delicious! The salty spice of the pancetta is a perfect foil for the sweet fruit.

INGREDIENTS | SERVES 6

1 medium baguette, sliced diagonally into 6 slices

1 teaspoon extra-virgin olive oil

6 ounces pancetta, very thinly sliced

3 ounces goat cheese, crumbled

½ teaspoon ground black pepper

¼ cantaloupe, seeded and diced

¼ honeydew melon, seeded and diced

1. Preheat broiler.

2. Place baguette slices on a baking sheet. Brush each slice with oil, then toast 1 minute on each side.

3. Place pancetta slices on each baguette slice and return under broiler. Broil 1 minute. Transfer to plates. Top with cheese and pepper.

4. Mix cantaloupe and melon in a small bowl. Divide melon mixture among serving plates.

Per Serving: Calories: 252 | Fat: 19g | Protein: 9g | Sodium: 362mg | Fiber: 1g | Carbohydrates: 12g

Strapatsatha

Strapatsatha is a dish brought to Greece by the Sephardic Jews from Spain. It's a kind of omelet with fresh tomatoes and feta. There are many variations of this classic dish.

INGREDIENTS | SERVES 6

1 tablespoon extra-virgin olive oil

⅔ cup sliced chorizo sausage

4 large ripe tomatoes, passed through a box grater

½ cup diced sweet banana pepper

3 scallions, ends trimmed, sliced

1 cup crumbled feta cheese

8 large eggs, beaten

½ teaspoon ground black pepper

1. Add oil to a large skillet over medium-high heat and heat 30 seconds. Add sausage and cook 2 minutes. With a slotted spoon, remove sausage from the skillet and set aside. Take skillet off heat and let it cool 5 minutes.

2. Return the skillet to medium heat and add tomatoes. Cook 5 minutes or until most of the liquid is evaporated. Add banana peppers and scallions and cook 2 more minutes. Add feta and cook 1 minute.

3. Add eggs, black pepper, and cooked sausage. Carefully stir the egg mixture as it cooks until just set. Serve immediately or at room temperature.

Per Serving: Calories: 250 | Fat: 18g | Protein: 15g | Sodium: 469mg | Fiber: 2g | Carbohydrates: 7g

Mushroom Strapatsatha with Halloumi and Crispy Bacon

Any type of mushrooms can be used in this dish. Experiment with your own combinations.

INGREDIENTS | SERVES 4

3 tablespoons extra-virgin olive oil, divided

⅓ cup chopped onions or scallions

1 clove garlic, peeled and minced

1 cup sliced cremini mushrooms

1 teaspoon salt, divided

½ teaspoon ground black pepper, divided

1 cup sliced oyster mushrooms

4 (¼") slices halloumi cheese, roughly chopped

8 large eggs, beaten

¼ cup heavy cream or evaporated milk

1 teaspoon fresh thyme leaves

1 teaspoon chopped fresh tarragon

4 strips crispy cooked bacon, crumbled and divided

2 tablespoons chopped fresh chives

¼ cup jarred or homemade salsa

1. In a large skillet over medium heat, add 2 tablespoons oil and heat 30 seconds. Add onions and garlic and cook 5 minutes or until onions are softened.

2. Add cremini mushrooms and ½ teaspoon salt and ¼ teaspoon pepper. Cook 5 minutes or until mushrooms are lightly browned.

3. Add oyster mushrooms and cook 2 minutes. Stir in halloumi and cook 1 more minute.

4. In a medium bowl, whisk together eggs, cream or milk, thyme, tarragon, and remaining salt and pepper. Add eggs to mushroom mixture and stir until the eggs are cooked, about 5 minutes. Stir in bacon.

5. Serve topped with chives and salsa. Drizzle with remaining oil and serve immediately.

Per Serving: Calories: 504 | Fat: 26g | Protein: 14g | Sodium: 740mg | Fiber: 1g | Carbohydrates: 6g

Frittata

This Italian egg dish is like a quiche without a crust. It's a great way to use leftover potatoes and any vegetables in your refrigerator. Frittata is both a terrific breakfast dish and an easy weeknight supper.

INGREDIENTS | SERVES 6

1 pound Idaho potatoes, peeled and thickly sliced

2 medium yellow bell peppers, seeded and sliced

2 medium red bell peppers, seeded and sliced

2 medium green bell peppers, seeded and sliced

1 large red onion, peeled and sliced

2 teaspoons extra-virgin olive oil

1 teaspoon salt, divided

½ teaspoon ground black pepper, divided

3 large eggs

6 large egg whites

1 cup plain yogurt

1 cup whole milk

3 ounces fontina or Gouda cheese, grated

1 tablespoon chopped fresh oregano leaves

1. Preheat oven to 375°F.

2. Toss potatoes, bell peppers, and onion in oil and place on a baking sheet. Season with ½ teaspoon salt and ¼ teaspoon black pepper. Roast 10 minutes.

3. In a medium baking dish, add roasted vegetables in one layer.

4. In a medium bowl, whisk eggs, egg whites, yogurt, milk, cheese, and remaining salt and pepper. Pour egg mixture into the baking dish over vegetables.

5. Bake until eggs are completely set, approximately 30 minutes. Sprinkle with oregano and serve.

Per Serving: Calories: 259 | Fat: 11g | Protein: 16g | Sodium: 639mg | Fiber: 3g | Carbohydrates: 25g

For the Meat Lover

If you think a breakfast just isn't breakfast without pork, consider adding chopped bacon, sausage, or ham to this recipe.

Gypsy's Breakfast

This hearty breakfast is infused with Spanish flavors. The traditional sausage for this dish is a smoky chorizo, but you can use your favorite type. You can switch up the types of vegetables and cheese as well.

INGREDIENTS | SERVES 8

1 cup diced cured sausage

¼ cup water

3 large potatoes, peeled and diced

1 large onion, peeled and sliced

1 large green bell pepper, seeded and sliced

1 large red bell pepper, seeded and sliced

1 teaspoon smoked paprika

¾ teaspoon salt, divided

½ teaspoon ground black pepper

½ teaspoon fresh thyme leaves

1 cup grated Graviera or Gruyère cheese

4 tablespoons extra-virgin olive oil, divided

8 large eggs

1. In a large skillet over medium-high heat, add sausage and water. Cook 3 minutes or until water evaporates and sausage is crispy. Add potatoes and stir to coat in the sausage drippings. Reduce heat to medium and cook another 5 minutes.

2. Add onions, bell peppers, and smoked paprika. Cook 3 more minutes. Season with ½ teaspoon salt, black pepper, and thyme. Reduce heat to medium-low and cook 10–15 minutes or until potatoes are fork-tender. Sprinkle with cheese and take the pan off the heat. The residual heat will melt the cheese.

3. In another skillet, add 2 tablespoons oil and fry each egg to your liking (sunny-side up or over easy). Season eggs with remaining salt.

4. To serve, place a scoop of sausage-onion mixture onto each plate and a fried egg on top. Drizzle with remaining oil. Serve hot.

Per Serving: Calories: 334 | Fat: 19g | Protein: 14g | Sodium: 456mg | Fiber: 4.5g | Carbohydrates: 26g

Baked Eggs with Spinach and Cheese SC

This is an excellent brunch, lunch, or supper. Everyone loves it. Even better, after a tough day it's easy to put together.

INGREDIENTS | SERVES 4

Nonstick olive oil cooking spray

1½ cups cornbread crumbs

3 (10-ounce) packages frozen spinach, thawed, moisture squeezed out

2 tablespoons butter, melted

½ cup shredded Swiss cheese

½ teaspoon nutmeg

1 teaspoon salt

½ teaspoon ground black pepper

1 cup heavy cream

8 large eggs

Herbs and Spices

People often confuse herbs with spices. Herbs are green and come from plant leaves. Lavender is the only herb (in Western cooking) that is a flower. Frequently used herbs include parsley, basil, oregano, thyme, rosemary, cilantro, and mint. Spices are roots, tubers, barks, berries, or seeds. These include black pepper, cinnamon, nutmeg, allspice, cumin, turmeric, ginger, cardamom, and coriander.

1. Grease a 4- to 5-quart slow cooker with cooking spray. Sprinkle cornbread crumbs on the bottom of slow cooker.

2. In a medium bowl, mix spinach, butter, cheese, nutmeg, salt, and pepper together. Stir in cream. Spread spinach-cheese mixture on top of cornbread crumbs.

3. Using the back of a tablespoon, make 8 depressions in spinach mixture. Break open eggs and place one egg in each hole.

4. Cover and cook on low 3 hours or on high 1½–2 hours until yolks are cooked through but not hard.

Per Serving: Calories: 578 | Fat: 43g | Protein: 26g | Sodium: 935mg | Fiber: 7g | Carbohydrates: 26g

Mediterranean Omelet

This simple omelet is light and fluffy. It's a quick but sophisticated breakfast.

INGREDIENTS | SERVES 6

2 large eggs
6 large egg whites
¼ cup plain nonfat yogurt
2 teaspoons olive oil, divided
2 ounces pancetta, sliced paper thin
3 ounces Swiss cheese, shredded
¼ cup chopped parsley
½ teaspoon ground black pepper

Season the Pan

When making omelets, always make sure your pan is properly seasoned. A properly seasoned pan is worth its weight in gold. To season, generously coat the pan with oil, and put it in a warm oven, then wipe clean.

1. In a medium bowl, beat eggs and egg whites, then whisk in the yogurt.

2. Heat 1 teaspoon oil in a small skillet over medium-high heat. Quickly sauté the pancetta until crisp, about 2 minutes, then remove and drain on paper towel.

3. Heat remaining oil in a large sauté pan over medium heat. Pour in egg mixture, then sprinkle in pancetta and cheese. Stir once only. Continuously move the pan, using a spatula to push the edges inward slightly to allow the egg mixture to pour outward and solidify. Cook until mostly firm, about 5 minutes, then use a spatula to fold it in half.

4. Reduce heat to low, cover, and cook approximately 3 minutes more. Sprinkle with parsley and pepper and serve.

Per Serving: Calories: 128 | Fat: 8g | Protein: 12g | Sodium: 242mg | Fiber: 0g | Carbohydrates: 2g

Pastina and Egg

Pasta for breakfast? Why not—this hearty breakfast is great on a cold morning to fortify you for the day.

INGREDIENTS | SERVES 6

1 large egg
2 large egg whites
3 cups fat-free chicken broth
1½ cups pastina
¼ cup grated Parmesan cheese
½ teaspoon ground black pepper
¼ cup chopped parsley

1. Beat egg and egg whites in a small bowl.

2. Bring the broth to a slow boil in a medium saucepan over medium-high heat then add the pastina. Cook 3 minutes, stirring frequently, until almost al dente.

3. Whisk in egg mixture, stirring constantly until eggs are completely cooked and the pasta is al dente, about 2 minutes. Remove from heat and ladle into bowls. Top with cheese, pepper, and parsley.

Per Serving: Calories: 294 | Fat: 5g | Protein: 14g | Sodium: 622mg | Fiber: 2g | Carbohydrates: 48g

Roasted Potatoes with Vegetables

This dish serves double duty as a treat for breakfast or as a side dish at dinner.

INGREDIENTS | SERVES 6

2 tablespoons olive oil
3 medium baking potatoes, peeled and chopped
1 medium sweet potato, peeled and chopped
3 large carrots, peeled and chopped
1 medium yellow onion, peeled and chopped
½ pound button mushrooms
1 teaspoon salt
1 teaspoon ground black pepper

1. Preheat oven to 400°F.

2. In a large bowl, combine oil, potatoes, carrots, onions, and mushrooms. Stir to mix. Transfer vegetables to a large roasting pan and sprinkle with salt and pepper.

3. Roast until tender, about 30–45 minutes. Serve warm or at room temperature.

Per Serving: Calories: 174 | Fat: 5g | Protein: 4g | Sodium: 438mg | Fiber: 4g | Carbohydrates: 30g

Tomato and Goat Cheese Breakfast Casserole

Tomatoes and oregano pair elegantly with goat cheese to create a luscious casserole that works just as well on a midweek morning as it does for a weekend breakfast party.

INGREDIENTS | SERVES 6

8 large eggs
1 cup whole milk
1 teaspoon salt
1 teaspoon ground black pepper
2 cups halved cherry tomatoes
¼ cup chopped oregano
4 ounces goat cheese, diced
1 teaspoon olive oil

1. Whisk eggs, milk, salt, and pepper together in a medium bowl. Stir in tomatoes, oregano, and goat cheese and mix well again.

2. Grease a 4- to 5-quart slow cooker with olive oil.

3. Pour egg mixture into slow cooker and cook on low 4–6 hours or on high 2–3 hours. The casserole is done when a knife inserted into the center comes out clean. Serve hot.

Per Serving: Calories: 227 | Fat: 15g | Protein: 16g | Sodium: 558mg | Fiber: 1g | Carbohydrates: 7g

Breakfast Risotto

Serve this as you would cooked oatmeal: topped with additional brown sugar, raisins or other dried fruit, and milk.

INGREDIENTS | SERVES 6

Nonstick olive oil cooking spray
¼ cup butter, melted
1½ cups Arborio rice
3 small apples, peeled, cored, and sliced
1½ teaspoons ground cinnamon
⅛ teaspoon nutmeg
⅛ teaspoon ground cloves
⅛ teaspoon salt
⅓ cup packed light brown sugar
1 cup apple juice
3 cups whole milk

1. Spray the inside of a 4- to 5-quart slow cooker with cooking spray. Add butter and rice to the slow cooker; stir to coat rice in butter.

2. Add remaining ingredients and stir to combine. Cover and cook on low 6–7 hours or on high 2–3 hours until rice is cooked through and is firm but not mushy. Serve immediately.

Per Serving: Calories: 419 | Fat: 12g | Protein: 7g | Sodium: 108mg | Fiber: 2.5g | Carbohydrates: 71g

Breakfast Baklava French Toast

Use a firm bread like challah or sourdough for this special-occasion French toast.

INGREDIENTS | SERVES 2

3 large eggs

2 tablespoons orange juice

1 teaspoon grated orange zest

⅛ teaspoon vanilla extract

¼ cup plus 1 tablespoon honey, divided

2 tablespoons whole milk

¾ teaspoon ground cinnamon, divided

¼ cup chopped walnuts

¼ cup chopped blanched almonds

¼ teaspoon ground cloves

1 tablespoon sugar

2 tablespoons white bread crumbs or ground melba toast

4 slices bread

2 tablespoons unsalted butter

1 teaspoon confectioners' sugar

1. In a large bowl, whisk together eggs, orange juice, zest, vanilla, ¼ cup honey, milk, and ¼ teaspoon cinnamon. Reserve.

2. Pulse walnuts and almonds in a food processor until they are finely crumbled. Transfer nuts to a small bowl and add cloves, ¼ teaspoon cinnamon, sugar, and bread crumbs. Stir to combine.

3. Sandwich half the walnut-and-almond mixture between 2 slices of bread. Repeat with the remaining 2 slices. Carefully dunk both sides of the sandwiches into egg mixture. Make sure egg mixture soaks into the bread.

4. Add butter to a large skillet over medium heat and heat 30 seconds. Add sandwiches and fry 2 minutes per side or until golden.

5. Place each sandwich on a plate and cut them diagonally. Dust with confectioners' sugar. Top with remaining honey and sprinkle with ¼ teaspoon cinnamon. Serve immediately.

Per Serving: Calories: 815 | Fat: 36g | Protein: 22g | Sodium: 569mg | Fiber: 5g | Carbohydrates: 97g

Fruit-Stuffed French Toast

The rich eggy flavor of challah is perfect for this easy special-occasion French toast.

INGREDIENTS | SERVES 6

½ teaspoon olive oil

3 medium loaves challah bread, sliced into 6 thick (3") slices

½ cup sliced strawberries

½ cup blueberries

1 cup diced peaches

2 large eggs

4 large egg whites

¼ cup skim milk

1 cup orange juice

¼ cup nonfat plain yogurt

¼ cup confectioners' sugar

1. Preheat oven to 375°F. Grease a baking sheet with oil.

2. Cut a slit into the bottom crust of each bread slice to form a pocket.

3. Mix strawberries, blueberries, and peaches in a medium bowl. Fill each pocket with about ⅓ cup fruit mixture. Press the pocket closed.

4. In a large shallow bowl, beat eggs, egg whites, and milk. Dip bread into egg mixture, letting it fully absorb the mixture. Place bread on prepared baking sheet. Bake 20 minutes, flipping bread halfway through.

5. While bread is baking, boil orange juice in a small saucepan over medium heat until reduced by half and mixture is syrupy, about 15 minutes.

6. Remove French toast from oven, transfer to plates, and cut each slice in half diagonally. Serve each with dollop of yogurt, a drizzle of juice, and a sprinkling of sugar.

Per Serving: Calories: 294 | Fat: 4g | Protein: 13g | Sodium: 486mg | Fiber: 3g | Carbohydrates: 52g

Tiganites

Tiganites are the Greek equivalent of pancakes. Instead of maple syrup, drizzle them with honey or petimezi, a grape molasses found in Greek, Turkish, and Middle Eastern specialty grocery shops.

INGREDIENTS | SERVES 6

2 cups all-purpose flour

2 tablespoons sugar

2 teaspoons baking powder

¾ teaspoon salt

2 large eggs

2 cups whole milk

¼ cup vegetable oil

4 tablespoons unsalted butter, divided

¼ cup honey or petimezi

Petimezi

Petimezi is a grape molasses that has its origins in ancient Greece. It is made by reducing grape must (freshly pressed juice) into thick syrup. Petimezi can be found in Greek, Turkish, or Middle Eastern grocery stores. Try it on toast or as a topping for ice cream.

1. In a medium bowl, combine flour, sugar, baking powder, and salt.

2. In another medium bowl, whisk together eggs, milk, and oil.

3. Add flour mixture to egg mixture and stir to combine.

4. In a large skillet over medium heat, add 2 tablespoons butter and heat 30 seconds. Pour ¼ cup batter into the pan. Cook until you see bubbles forming on the top side of the pancake (about 2 minutes), then flip the pancake over and cook another 2 minutes. Remove pancake from the pan and keep warm. Repeat with the remaining batter.

5. Serve hot topped with honey and remaining butter.

Per Serving: Calories: 299 | Fat: 17g | Protein: 9g | Sodium: 511mg | Fiber: 1g | Carbohydrates: 52g

Beet and Walnut Muffins

Greeks use beets in both savory and sweet dishes. This quirky muffin recipe will have your guests guessing!

INGREDIENTS | SERVES 12

2 cups plus ¼ cup all-purpose flour, divided
1 tablespoon baking powder
¾ cup sugar
½ teaspoon salt
2 teaspoons ground cinnamon
2 large eggs, beaten
1 cup whole milk
¼ cup extra-virgin olive oil
2 cups grated beets, peeled
¾ cup chopped walnuts

Sinking Feeling

Tossing solid ingredients (chocolate chips, fruits, or nuts) in a little flour before adding them to a batter ensures they do not sink to the bottom of the muffins while baking. Try this trick with your next batch.

1. In a medium bowl, combine 2 cups flour, baking powder, sugar, salt, and cinnamon.

2. In another medium bowl, whisk together eggs, milk, and oil.

3. In a third medium bowl, combine beets, walnuts, and remaining flour. Toss to coat beets and walnuts in flour.

4. Preheat oven to 375°F. Add flour mixture to egg mixture and stir to combine. Stir in walnuts and beets until just combined. Don't overmix the batter or the muffins will be tough.

5. Line a 12-muffin tin with paper cups and divide the batter evenly among the 12 cups. Bake on middle rack 15–20 minutes, or until a toothpick inserted into a muffin comes out clean.

6. Transfer muffins to a cooling rack. Cool 10 minutes before removing from pan and serving.

Per Serving: Calories: 257 | Fat: 11g | Protein: 6g | Sodium: 259mg | Fiber: 2g | Carbohydrates: 35g

Baklava Oatmeal S C

If you've ever enjoyed baklava—sweet, nutty dessert bars found at many Greek restaurants—you're going to love this simple recipe. Baked with cinnamon and topped with a sweet baklava streusel and a drizzle of honey, this healthful oatmeal is a delicious breakfast choice any morning of the week.

INGREDIENTS | SERVES 4

Nonstick olive oil cooking spray

4 cups plus ½ teaspoon water, divided

1 cup steel-cut oats

1½ teaspoons cinnamon, divided

½ cup walnuts, crushed

1 teaspoon sugar

4 tablespoons honey

About Steel-Cut Oats

Steel-cut oats are the whole-grain, inner parts of the oat kernel that have been cut into pieces. They generally take longer to cook than traditional rolled oats, so preparing them in the slow cooker is the perfect way to bake them for breakfast!

1. Spray the bottom of a small (1½- to 3-quart) slow cooker with cooking spray.

2. Place 4 cups water, oats, and 1 teaspoon cinnamon in slow cooker. Stir until combined. Cover and cook on low 7–8 hours.

3. Just before serving, place walnuts in a large skillet over medium heat. Sprinkle with remaining cinnamon, sugar, and ½ teaspoon water. Cook just until sugar begins to bubble and walnuts turn a light, toasted golden brown color.

4. Spoon walnut mixture over hot bowls of oatmeal.

5. Drizzle with honey before serving.

Per Serving: Calories: 242 | Fat: 11g | Protein: 5g | Sodium: 2.5mg | Fiber: 3.5g | Carbohydrates: 34g

CHAPTER 3

Appetizers and Dips

Baked Oysters with Tomatoes, Capers, and Feta

A fresh raw oyster topped with a squeeze of lemon is a great treat. But if you're trying oysters for the first time, baking them is a good introduction.

INGREDIENTS | SERVES 4

1 tablespoon extra-virgin olive oil
½ cup thinly sliced scallion
2 cloves garlic, sliced
3 medium plum tomatoes, chopped
½ teaspoon smoked paprika
¼ cup dry white wine
2 teaspoons capers
1 teaspoon fresh thyme leaves
¼ teaspoon crushed red pepper
½ cup bread crumbs
1 cup crumbled feta cheese
12 medium fresh oysters, shucked and bottom shells reserved
1 large lemon, cut into wedges

1. Preheat oven to 450°F.

2. In a large skillet over medium heat, add oil and heat 30 seconds. Add scallions, garlic, and tomatoes and sauté 5–6 minutes.

3. Add paprika and wine and cook another 2–3 minutes or until most of the liquid evaporates.

4. Add capers, thyme, and crushed red pepper. Take skillet off the heat and allow ingredients to cool 15 minutes.

5. Add bread crumbs and feta to cooled tomato mixture. Line a baking sheet with oysters in their bottom shells. Divide topping mixture evenly over oysters.

6. Bake oysters on middle rack 15–20 minutes or until tops are golden brown. Serve oysters hot or warm with lemon wedges.

Per Serving: Calories: 242 | Fat: 13g | Protein: 11g | Sodium: 654mg | Fiber: 2g | Carbohydrates: 18g

Cheese Saganaki

This dish is made using kefalotyri, a firm sheep's milk cheese from Greece. If you can't find it, you can substitute any aged sheep's milk cheese. Ask your grocer to suggest one for you.

INGREDIENTS | SERVES 2

1 (4" × 4" × ½") piece of kefalotyri cheese, rind removed
½ cup all-purpose flour
1½ tablespoons extra-virgin olive oil
1 ounce Metaxa (or other) brandy, or ouzo
1 large lemon wedge

1. Heat a medium cast-iron pan over medium-high heat 5 minutes. Dip cheese in a bowl of water and then dredge in flour. Shake off excess flour.

2. Add oil to the pan and heat 30 seconds. Add cheese and fry 2 minutes. Carefully flip with a spatula and fry another 2 minutes.

3. Turn off heat, pour brandy from a cup over cheese, and carefully ignite brandy with a lighter. Squeeze lemon wedge over cheese to douse the flame. Serve immediately.

Per Serving: Calories: 440 | Fat: 25g | Protein: 18g | Sodium: 482mg | Fiber: 2g | Carbohydrates: 27g

Baked Feta

Roma tomatoes are perfect for this appetizer because they have less water, fewer seeds, and are usually sweeter than other tomato varieties. Don't forget to serve lots of crusty bread with it to sop up all the tasty juices.

INGREDIENTS | SERVES 4

1 (4" × 4" × 1") slab feta cheese
2 tablespoons extra-virgin olive oil, divided
1 large Roma tomato, thinly sliced
1 large banana or sweet pepper, seeded and thinly sliced
¼ teaspoon crushed red pepper
¼ teaspoon dried oregano

1. Preheat oven to 400°F. Place feta and 1 tablespoon oil in a small baking dish. Top with alternating layers of tomato and pepper slices. Drizzle remaining oil and sprinkle crushed red pepper and oregano over tomato and pepper slices.

2. Cover baking dish tightly with foil and bake 20 minutes. Serve immediately.

Per Serving: Calories: 224 | Fat: 18g | Protein: 9g | Sodium: 528mg | Fiber: 1.5g | Carbohydrates: 6g

Fried Calamari

Frozen, cleaned calamari (squid) is readily found in most major supermarkets and will work well for this dish. If using frozen calamari, thaw it in the refrigerator overnight.

INGREDIENTS | SERVES 4

1 pound squid, tubes and tentacles cleaned and quill removed

1 cup all-purpose flour

½ cup fine cornmeal

1½ teaspoons salt, divided

¾ teaspoon ground black pepper

Extra-virgin olive oil for frying

1 large lemon, cut into wedges

How to Clean a Squid

To clean a squid, pull the head and tentacles away from the body. Remove the thin, clear quill and innards. Peel the skin from the body. Cut the tentacles away from the head just below the eyes and beak. Discard the quill, innards, skin, and head. Rinse the squid pieces well and pat dry with a paper towel.

1. Cut calamari tubes into ½" rings. Pat rings and tentacles dry with paper towels.

2. In a medium bowl, combine flour, cornmeal, 1 teaspoon salt, and pepper. Dredge calamari in the flour mixture. Shake off excess flour.

3. Add 2 inches oil to a deep frying pan over medium-high heat. Bring oil temperature to 365°F. Adjust heat to keep the temperature at 365°F while frying. Fry calamari (in batches) 3–4 minutes until they are lightly golden. Place calamari on a tray lined with paper towels to soak up excess oil. Sprinkle remaining salt over calamari immediately after frying.

4. Serve warm or at room temperature with lemon wedges.

Per Serving: Calories: 311 | Fat: 5.5g | Protein: 22g | Sodium: 835mg | Fiber: 2g | Carbohydrates: 41g

Fried Peppers

Using a variety of different colored peppers makes this simple dish spectacular.

INGREDIENTS | SERVES 4

1 pound long, slender red or green peppers (sweet or hot)

¼ cup extra-virgin olive oil, divided

1 teaspoon salt

1 tablespoon red or white wine vinegar

Eat More Peppers

Did you know peppers are fruits, not vegetables? Peppers originated in Mexico and South America and were introduced to Spain in the late 1400s. They were quickly adopted by and grown in other European countries. From there, peppers spread to Africa and Asia.

1. Poke peppers with a fork a few times all over. Heat 2 tablespoons oil in a large skillet over medium-high heat. Fry peppers (in batches) 3–4 minutes per side until skins are lightly golden.

2. Transfer peppers to a tray lined with paper towels and season with salt. Serve on a plate with a drizzle of vinegar and the remaining oil. Serve warm or at room temperature.

Per Serving: Calories: 142 | Fat: 13g | Protein: 1g | Sodium: 583mg | Fiber: 2g | Carbohydrates: 5g

Roasted Red Peppers

Roasted peppers can be stored in the freezer for up to 6 months. To protect the peppers from freezer burn, leave the charred skin on. Thaw the peppers overnight in the refrigerator and peel the charred skin off the peppers before using.

INGREDIENTS | SERVES 4

6 large red bell peppers

¼ cup extra-virgin olive oil

½ teaspoon salt

1. Preheat a gas or charcoal grill to medium-high. Place peppers on grill and char them on all sides. Place the peppers in a bowl and cover tightly with plastic wrap. Cool 20 minutes. Remove charred skins and discard. Slit the peppers in half; remove and discard the seeds and stem.

2. Place peppers on a serving tray. Drizzle with oil and season with salt. Serve at room temperature.

Per Serving: Calories: 56 | Fat: 1g | Protein: 2g | Sodium: 302mg | Fiber: 4g | Carbohydrates: 11g

Cretan Dakos

Dakos, or rusks, are hard twice-baked slices of bread. You can find rusks at Greek or Middle Eastern grocers.

INGREDIENTS | SERVES 4

4 medium rusks
1 clove garlic
¼ cup extra-virgin olive oil
1 large tomato, peeled and grated
¼ cup crumbled feta cheese
1 teaspoon dried oregano

1. Sprinkle some water over each rusk to soften it slightly. Then firmly rub the garlic clove over each rusk to infuse it with garlic flavor.

2. Drizzle oil evenly over rusks and let them absorb the oil for 4–5 minutes.

3. Top rusks with tomato, feta, and a sprinkle of oregano. Serve at room temperature.

Per Serving: Calories: 246 | Fat: 16g | Protein: 5.5g | Sodium: 310mg | Fiber: 1.5g | Carbohydrates: 20g

Deep-Fried Zucchini

These zucchini chips are perfect with Tzatziki (see recipe in this chapter).

INGREDIENTS | SERVES 6

Sunflower oil for frying
¾ cup all-purpose flour
¼ cup cornstarch
1 teaspoon salt, divided
¼ teaspoon ground black pepper
4 medium zucchini, trimmed and thinly sliced (⅛" thick)

1. In a deep skillet over medium-high heat, bring 3 inches oil to 370°F.

2. In a large bowl, combine flour, cornstarch, ½ teaspoon salt, and pepper. Lightly dredge zucchini in flour mixture and shake off excess flour.

3. Fry zucchini (in batches) about 2 minutes or until golden. Place fried zucchini on a tray lined with paper towels to soak up excess oil. Season with remaining salt and serve immediately.

Per Serving: Calories: 120 | Fat: 3g | Protein: 3.5g | Sodium: 379mg | Fiber: 2g | Carbohydrates: 20g

Grilled Halloumi with Roasted Red-Pepper Sauce

You can buy halloumi cheese in most cheese shops and Greek grocery stores.
If you have any leftover sauce, serve it with pasta and shrimp.

INGREDIENTS | SERVES 6

¼ cup extra-virgin olive oil

⅓ cup chopped red onions

1 clove garlic, smashed

1 Roasted Red Pepper (see recipe in this chapter), diced

½ cup crushed canned tomatoes

½ teaspoon salt

⅛ teaspoon crushed red pepper

½ teaspoon dried oregano

12 (¼") slices halloumi cheese

3 medium pitas, cut into 4 triangles big enough to hold a slice of cheese

Halloumi Cheese

Halloumi cheese comes from Cyprus. It's made from sheep's milk and is known as the "squeaky" cheese because of the sound it makes when you chew it.

1. Heat oil in a small skillet over medium heat 30 seconds. Add onions and garlic and cook 2–3 minutes or until onions are softened. Add roasted pepper and tomatoes, increase heat to medium-high, and bring to a boil. Reduce heat to medium, add salt, and simmer 7–10 minutes or until sauce has thickened.

2. Cool sauce 10 minutes and then process it in a food processor until smooth. Stir in crushed red pepper and oregano.

3. Preheat a gas or charcoal grill to medium-high. Place cheese slices on the grill and cook 1–1½ minutes per side. The cheese should be soft but still intact.

4. Place each piece of grilled cheese over a pita triangle and top with a dollop of the warm sauce. Serve immediately.

Per Serving: Calories: 296 | Fat: 18g | Protein: 11g | Sodium: 588mg | Fiber: 2g | Carbohydrates: 21g

Crispy Fried Atherina (Smelts)

Greeks love to eat smelts. If you can't find them, substitute with fresh anchovies.

INGREDIENTS | SERVES 4

2 pounds small whole smelts, heads and guts removed

2 teaspoons salt, divided

½ teaspoon ground black pepper

1 teaspoon sweet paprika

½ cup rice flour

1 cup all-purpose flour

Sunflower oil for frying

1 tablespoon grated lemon zest

1 tablespoon grated lime zest

1 large lemon, cut into wedges

1 large lime, cut into wedges

Smelts

Did you know smelts are found in both the ocean and in fresh water? Although the smelts of the Mediterranean are a slightly different species from the freshwater fish found in the Great Lakes, both work wonderfully in this dish. Choose the small ones as those can be eaten whole!

1. Pat smelts with paper towels to dry. In a large bowl, combine 1 teaspoon salt, pepper, and paprika, and then add smelts and toss.

2. Combine flours in a medium bowl and then add to the large bowl; toss again to coat smelts in flour mixture. Shake off excess flour from smelts.

3. In a deep skillet over medium-high heat, bring 3 inches oil to 360°F. Adjust heat to keep temperature at 360°F while frying.

4. Fry smelts (in batches) 3 minutes or until golden. Place them on a tray lined with paper towels to soak up excess oil. Season with remaining salt.

5. Sprinkle lemon and lime zests over smelts. Serve immediately with lemon and lime wedges.

Per Serving: Calories: 448 | Fat: 9g | Protein: 44g | Sodium: 1,078mg | Fiber: 2.5g | Carbohydrates: 44g

Spicy Chicken Wings   MA

Be sure to have a cool drink on hand when serving these wings. Try a Greek beer! Serve with some lemon wedges for a fresh hit of citrus.

INGREDIENTS | SERVES 4

4 cloves garlic, minced

1 small onion, peeled and grated

1 tablespoon grated lemon zest

1 tablespoon lemon juice

¼ teaspoon ground cinnamon

¼ teaspoon smoked paprika

½ teaspoon ground allspice

1 teaspoon ground black pepper

2 teaspoons salt

2 tablespoons fresh thyme leaves

¼ cup extra-virgin olive oil

2 pounds chicken wings, patted dry

1. In a large bowl, combine all ingredients except chicken wings. Add chicken wings and stir to coat.

2. Marinate wings at least 4 hours or overnight in the refrigerator. Remove wings from refrigerator 20 minutes before grilling so they come up to room temperature. Remove excess marinade from the wings.

3. Preheat a gas or charcoal grill to medium-high. Place wings on grill and cook 4–5 minutes per side or until juices run clear. Serve immediately.

Per Serving: Calories: 634 | Fat: 49g | Protein: 42g | Sodium: 1,345mg | Fiber: 1g | Carbohydrates: 4g

Tyropita Cheese Filling

For a change, try adding some of your favorite chopped fresh herbs to this cheese filling. The filling can be used immediately in dishes like Phyllo Triangles (see recipe in this chapter), or it can be refrigerated. If refrigerated, bring the filling to room temperature before using it.

INGREDIENTS | SERVES 12

2 cups ricotta cheese

2 cups crumbled feta cheese

3 large eggs, beaten

½ teaspoon ground black pepper

Put all ingredients in a large bowl and stir well to combine.

Per Serving: Calories: 155 | Fat: 12g | Protein: 10g | Sodium: 330mg | Fiber: 0g | Carbohydrates: 2g

Phyllo Triangles

These easy-to-make flaky triangles of phyllo are popular at parties.

INGREDIENTS | SERVES 40

1 pound unsalted butter, melted

1 package phyllo pastry, thawed, at room temperature

1 recipe Tyropita Cheese Filling or Spanokopita Filling (see recipes in this chapter)

1. Preheat oven to 350°F. Brush melted butter on the bottom of a large baking tray. Open package of phyllo and lay sheets flat. Cover sheets with a slightly damp tea towel.

2. Place one sheet of phyllo on the work surface. Brush sheet with butter, and then place another sheet on top of it. Brush top sheet with butter. Place a third sheet on top of the second sheet. Cut the stack of phyllo sheets lengthwise into four equal strips.

3. To form a triangle, place a tablespoon of filling on a strip of phyllo, 1 inch from the bottom. Fold the end over the filling at a 45-degree angle. Continue folding right to the top to form a triangle that completely encloses the filling. Repeat the process with remaining three strips. Place triangles on baking sheet and brush tops with butter. Repeat these steps with remaining phyllo and filling.

4. Bake phyllo triangles 30 minutes or until golden. Allow to cool 10 minutes and serve warm.

Per Serving: Calories: 79 | Fat: 3g | Protein: 7g | Sodium: 120mg | Fiber: 1g | Carbohydrates: 15g

Spanokopita Filling

This is a spinach-and-ricotta filling that can be used for Phyllo Triangles (see recipe in this chapter). It's also delicious as a filling for stuffed chicken breasts. The filling can be used immediately or it can be refrigerated. If you refrigerate the filling, bring it to room temperature before using.

INGREDIENTS | SERVES 12

¼ cup extra-virgin olive oil

4 scallions, ends trimmed, thinly sliced

1½ cups blanched and drained spinach, excess water removed, chopped

1 cup ricotta cheese

1 cup crumbled feta cheese

½ teaspoon ground black pepper

2 large eggs, beaten

½ cup chopped fresh dill

1. Heat oil in a large skillet over medium heat 30 seconds. Add scallions and cook 5 minutes or until scallions are soft. Remove skillet from heat, and allow scallions to cool.

2. In a large bowl, combine scallions, spinach, ricotta, feta, pepper, eggs, and dill. Stir well to combine.

Per Serving: Calories: 122 | Fat: 10g | Protein: 5g | Sodium: 172mg | Fiber: 0g | Carbohydrates: 1.7g

Marinated Portobello Mushrooms Ⓜ Ⓐ

Portobello mushrooms have a meaty flavor, and they are used in place of meat in many recipes.

INGREDIENTS | SERVES 6

6 portobello mushrooms

1 teaspoon extra-virgin olive oil

2 teaspoons balsamic vinegar

⅛ teaspoon salt

¼ teaspoon ground black pepper

¼ cup roughly chopped marjoram

¼ cup roughly chopped oregano

1. Remove the stems from the caps of the mushrooms and scrape out the black membrane. Slice the stems in half and reserve for later use in a stock.

2. Mix together remaining ingredients in a large bowl or zip-top bag. Add mushroom caps, cover or seal bag, and marinate at least 3 hours at room temperature.

3. Preheat oven to 400°F.

4. Transfer mushrooms to a baking sheet lined with foil. Roast mushrooms 15–20 minutes. Cut the caps into small wedges before serving.

Per Serving: Calories: 35 | Fat: 1g | Protein: 2g | Sodium: 59mg | Fiber: 2g | Carbohydrates: 6g

Sfougato

For Greeks, eggs are not limited to breakfast. This omelet often makes an appearance at the lunch or dinner table as an appetizer or a main course.

INGREDIENTS | SERVES 6

1 medium onion, peeled and finely diced
4 tablespoons all-purpose flour
¼ cup dried bread crumbs
2 tablespoons finely chopped fresh mint
½ cup crumbled feta cheese
1 teaspoon salt
½ teaspoon ground black pepper
1 tablespoon dried thyme
8 large eggs
2 tablespoons extra-virgin olive oil

1. Preheat oven to 350°F.

2. Combine onion, flour, bread crumbs, mint, cheese, salt, pepper, and thyme in a medium bowl; mix well.

3. In a large bowl, add eggs and beat well. Stir in onion mixture.

4. Add oil to a large oven-safe skillet over medium-high heat. When oil is hot, add egg mixture. Cook 4–5 minutes or until thickened, stirring constantly. Flip omelet, reduce heat to medium, and cook another 4–5 minutes until eggs are set.

5. Transfer skillet to oven and bake 5 minutes. Serve immediately.

Per Serving: Calories: 190 | Fat: 13g | Protein: 9g | Sodium: 235mg | Fiber: 1g | Carbohydrates: 10g

Olive Cheese Bread

Your guests will love the strong and unique flavor of this appetizer.

INGREDIENTS | SERVES 6

¼ pound pitted cured olives

1 clove garlic

2 tablespoons pine nuts

1½ tablespoons olive oil

1 large loaf crusty French or Italian bread, sliced into 12 (¼"-thick) slices

¼ pound Gorgonzola cheese, crumbled

1. Preheat broiler.

2. Pulse olives, garlic, pine nuts, and olive oil in a food processor until smooth. Place bread slices on a baking sheet. Spread olive mixture on bread and top with cheese.

3. Broil 2 minutes, or until cheese begins to bubble. Serve hot.

Per Serving: Calories: 150 | Fat: 14g | Protein: 5g | Sodium: 504mg | Fiber: 1g | Carbohydrates: 3g

Bruschetta with Marinated Red Pepper MA

You probably have all of the ingredients for this appetizer in your kitchen right now. This bruschetta is simple but elegant.

INGREDIENTS | SERVES 6

1 (12-ounce) jar roasted red peppers, drained

1 teaspoon balsamic vinegar

¼ cup chopped oregano

12 (1½"-thick) slices baguette

1 teaspoon extra-virgin olive oil

1½ ounces grated manchego, Romano, or Parmesan cheese

½ teaspoon ground black pepper

1. Purée roasted peppers in a blender or food processor. Add vinegar and oregano and continue to process into a smooth paste. Let stand at least 1 hour or refrigerate up to 1 day.

2. Preheat oven to 400°F.

3. Brush bread slices with oil. Place on baking sheet and toast until lightly golden brown.

4. Spread puréed pepper on toasted bread and sprinkle with cheese and black pepper. Serve immediately.

Per Serving: Calories: 251 | Fat: 5g | Protein: 11g | Sodium: 529mg | Fiber: 3g | Carbohydrates: 43g

Fig, Prosciutto, and Brie Bruschetta

A tiny piece of dark chocolate would be a nice addition to the cheese and figs in this recipe. Though it may not sound all too appealing at first, chocolate and cheese go extremely well together. A bit of fruit rounds off the combination.

INGREDIENTS | SERVES 6

6 thin slices Italian bread

2 tablespoons olive oil

12 ounces Brie cheese, sliced

6 thin slices prosciutto

3 fresh figs, sliced

1. Preheat broiler. Brush both sides of bread with olive oil and place on a baking sheet. Broil slices until lightly toasted, about 2 minutes per side.

2. Top each slice of bread with 2 slices Brie, 1 slice prosciutto, and 2 or 3 fig slices. Serve immediately.

Per Serving: Calories: 441 | Fat: 31g | Protein: 18g | Sodium: 749mg | Fiber: 1g | Carbohydrates: 23g

Tzatziki

Ouzo is an anise-flavored aperitif that Greeks enjoy drinking with appetizers. It is also the secret ingredient in this tzatziki.

INGREDIENTS | SERVES 8

½ long English cucumber, seeded and grated

1¼ teaspoons salt, divided

18 ounces plain Greek yogurt

2 cloves garlic, minced

2 tablespoons red wine vinegar

1 ounce ouzo

2 tablespoons chopped fresh dill

¼ cup extra-virgin olive oil

1. In a fine-mesh strainer over a medium bowl, add cucumber and ¼ teaspoon salt. Strain cucumber 30 minutes. Hand-squeeze remaining water from the cucumber.

2. In a large bowl, stir together cucumber, remaining salt, yogurt, garlic, vinegar, ouzo, and dill.

3. Slowly stir in oil until thoroughly combined. Refrigerate or serve at room temperature.

Per Serving: Calories: 110 | Fat: 8g | Protein: 4g | Sodium: 348mg | Fiber: 0.5g | Carbohydrates: 4g

Roasted Red Pepper Dip

If you don't have time to roast peppers, use drained jarred roasted red peppers. You can find them in most grocery stores.

INGREDIENTS | SERVES 8

2 large red bell peppers

1 medium hot banana pepper

1 scallion, ends trimmed

1 clove garlic

4 sun-dried tomatoes, packed in olive oil, drained and rinsed

1 cup crumbled feta cheese

1 cup coarsely chopped fresh basil

⅓ cup extra-virgin olive oil

1. Preheat a gas or charcoal grill to medium-high heat. Place all peppers on hot grill and char them on all sides. Place peppers in a bowl and cover tightly with plastic wrap. Cool 20 minutes. Remove charred skins and discard. Slit peppers in half; remove and discard seeds and stem.

2. Add peppers and the next 5 ingredients to a food processor and pulse until smooth. With the processor running, slowly add oil. Serve at room temperature.

Per Serving: Calories: 143 | Fat: 13g | Protein: 4g | Sodium: 227mg | Fiber: 1g | Carbohydrates: 4g

Bouyiourdi

This dish is a hot, cheesy Greek fondue that's perfect with crusty bread.

1 large tomato, diced, divided

½ cup grated kasseri or Gouda cheese, divided

½ cup crumbled feta cheese

1 small banana pepper, sliced into ¼" slices, seeded and stem removed

1 tablespoon extra-virgin olive oil

¼ teaspoon crushed red pepper

½ teaspoon oregano

1. Preheat oven to 400°F. Place half of the diced tomatoes on the bottom of a medium-sized ramekin. Top tomatoes with ¼ cup kasseri and then feta. Top cheeses with remaining diced tomatoes. Top with pepper slices and remaining kasseri. Drizzle with oil, then sprinkle with crushed red pepper and oregano.

2. Cover ramekin tightly with foil and bake 20 minutes or until cheese is bubbling. Serve immediately.

Per Serving: Calories: 182 | Fat: 14g | Protein: 10g | Sodium: 415mg | Fiber: 1g | Carbohydrates: 4.5g

Melitzanosalata

You will need either a charcoal or a gas grill, as well as a mortar and pestle, to prepare this eggplant dip with finesse.

INGREDIENTS | SERVES 8

1 large eggplant, skin pierced several times with a fork

1 clove garlic

1 teaspoon salt

1 tablespoon red wine vinegar

½ cup extra-virgin olive oil

2 tablespoons finely chopped fresh parsley

1. Preheat grill to medium-high heat. Place eggplant on the grill and cook 20–30 minutes or until skin is charred and inside is soft. Let eggplant cool 10 minutes. Cut eggplant open lengthwise and scoop out the softened flesh, discarding the charred skin.

2. Place garlic and salt in a mortar and mash with a pestle into a fine paste. Add eggplant and vinegar. Mash until smooth.

3. Slowly add oil to eggplant mixture and continue to mash until oil is completely incorporated. Stir in parsley. Serve at room temperature.

Per Serving: Calories: 137 | Fat: 13g | Protein: 1g | Sodium: 282mg | Fiber: 2.5g | Carbohydrates: 4g

Taramosalata

Resist the temptation to use extra-virgin olive oil in this dip because the strong flavor of the oil will interfere with the delicate flavor of the tarama.

INGREDIENTS | SERVES 12

9 slices white bread
5 ounces carp roe caviar
½ cup chopped onion
1½ cups light olive oil, divided
¼ cup fresh lemon juice
¼ cup cold water

1. In a large bowl, soak bread in room-temperature water for 10 seconds and then squeeze the water out with your hands. Reserve bread and discard water.

2. In a food processor, process caviar and onion 2 minutes to combine. Add bread and process 2–3 minutes or until the mixture is smooth.

3. With the processor running, slowly add ¾ cup oil. Add lemon juice and cold water and process to combine.

4. With the processor running, slowly add remaining oil. Serve cold or at room temperature. Leftovers can be stored in a sealed container in the refrigerator for up to 4 weeks.

Per Serving: Calories: 238 | Fat: 28g | Protein: 6g | Sodium: 169mg | Fiber: 1g | Carbohydrates: 15g

Olive and Red-Pepper Dip

Serve this lovely dip with flatbread or toasted pita.

INGREDIENTS | SERVES 8

½ cup pitted green olives

1 Roasted Red Pepper (see recipe in this chapter), chopped

1 teaspoon balsamic vinegar

⅔ cup soft bread crumbs

2 cloves garlic, smashed

½ teaspoon crushed red pepper

⅓ cup extra-virgin olive oil

1. In a food processor, combine all ingredients except oil. Pulse to combine but leave the mixture chunky.

2. With the processor running, slowly add oil until it is well combined. Refrigerate or serve at room temperature.

Per Serving: Calories: 130 | Fat: 10g | Protein: 1.5g | Sodium: 140mg | Fiber: 1g | Carbohydrates: 8g

Hummus

Chickpeas are full of protein and zinc, and they are low in fat. They make this dish both tasty and healthful.

INGREDIENTS | SERVES 12

2 cups canned chickpeas, drained and rinsed

4 cloves garlic, smashed

2 scallions, ends trimmed, chopped

1 Roasted Red Pepper (see recipe in this chapter)

½ cup tahini

2 tablespoons lemon juice

¼ teaspoon crushed red pepper

½ cup extra-virgin olive oil

2 teaspoons salt

1 teaspoon paprika

1. In a food processor, add chickpeas, garlic, scallions, roasted pepper, tahini, lemon juice, and crushed red pepper. Process until smooth.

2. With the processor running, slowly add oil until completely incorporated. Season with salt and sprinkle with paprika. Refrigerate or serve at room temperature.

Per Serving: Calories: 191 | Fat: 15g | Protein: 4g | Sodium: 475mg | Fiber: 3g | Carbohydrates: 12g

Santorini Fava

Fava, in the Greek food sense, has nothing to do with fava beans. Rather, it's a dip made from split peas. Serve it with toasted pita bread or sturdy crackers.

INGREDIENTS | SERVES 8

3 cups water

1 cup dried yellow split peas, rinsed

½ cup chopped onions

2 cloves garlic, smashed

2 bay leaves

1 teaspoon red wine vinegar

½ cup plus 1 tablespoon extra-virgin olive oil, divided

2 teaspoons fresh thyme leaves

1 teaspoon salt

½ teaspoon ground black pepper

2 tablespoons thinly sliced red onions

½ teaspoon dried oregano

Split Peas

Split peas are very high in dietary fiber and protein. They are an excellent and healthy alternative to meat proteins. Unlike other dried beans, you don't need to presoak them before cooking. Just give them a rinse and pick out any shriveled or broken beans, stones, or debris, and they are ready to cook.

1. In a medium pot over medium-high heat, add water, peas, onions, garlic, and bay leaves. Cover pot and bring mixture to a boil. Reduce heat to medium-low and simmer 15–20 minutes or until peas are tender.

2. Strain peas and remove bay leaves. Reserve a few whole peas for garnish. Combine pea mixture and vinegar in a food processor and process until the mixture is smooth. With the processor running, slowly add ½ cup oil.

3. Remove the dip from the processor and stir in thyme, salt, and pepper.

4. Garnish with reserved peas, red onions, and oregano. Drizzle with remaining oil. Serve warm or at room temperature.

Per Serving: Calories: 225 | Fat: 16g | Protein: 6g | Sodium: 225mg | Fiber: 6g | Carbohydrates: 16g

Htipiti

This spicy feta dip is pronounced "Huh'tee-pee-tee" in Greek. It's fun to say and delicious to eat.

INGREDIENTS | SERVES 8

2 medium hot banana peppers
1 cup crumbled feta cheese
1 cup ricotta cheese
3 tablespoons plain Greek yogurt
¼ cup extra-virgin olive oil

1. Preheat a gas or charcoal grill to medium-high. Place peppers on grill and char them on all sides. Place peppers in a large bowl and cover tightly with plastic wrap. Cool 20 minutes. Remove charred skins and discard. Slit peppers in half; remove and discard seeds and stem. Finely mince peppers.

2. In a medium bowl, thoroughly combine feta, ricotta, yogurt, and oil. Stir in minced peppers. Refrigerate or serve at room temperature.

Per Serving: Calories: 170 | Fat: 15g | Protein: 6g | Sodium: 226mg | Fiber: 0.5g | Carbohydrates: 3g

Baba Ganoush 🆂🅲

Serve this dish with pita bread and fresh vegetables.

INGREDIENTS | SERVES 12

1 (1-pound) eggplant
2 tablespoons tahini
2 tablespoons lemon juice
2 cloves garlic

Tahini Tips

Tahini is a paste made from ground sesame seeds. The most common type of tahini uses seeds that have been toasted before they are ground, but "raw" tahini is also available. The two can be used interchangeably in most recipes, but occasionally a recipe will specify one or the other.

1. Pierce eggplant with a fork. Cook 2 hours on high in a 4- to 5-quart slow cooker.

2. Allow to cool. Peel off skin, slice in half, and remove seeds. Discard skin and seeds.

3. Place pulp in a food processor and add remaining ingredients. Pulse until smooth.

Per Serving: Calories: 25 | Fat: 1.5g | Protein: 1g | Sodium: 4mg | Fiber: 1.5g | Carbohydrates: 3g

Eggplant Caponata SC

Serve this on small slices of Italian bread as an appetizer or use as a filling in sandwiches or wraps.

INGREDIENTS | SERVES 8

2 (1-pound) eggplants
1 teaspoon olive oil
1 medium red onion, peeled and diced
4 cloves garlic, minced
1 stalk celery, diced
2 medium tomatoes, diced
2 tablespoons nonpareil capers
2 tablespoons toasted pine nuts
1 teaspoon crushed red pepper
¼ cup red wine vinegar

Little Dippers

Slice a baguette into ⅛"-thick slices. Brush lightly with olive oil and sprinkle with dried tarragon and rosemary. Bake at 350°F for 10 minutes or until crisp.

1. Pierce eggplants with a fork. Cook 2 hours on high in a 4- to 5-quart slow cooker.

2. Allow to cool. Peel off skin, slice each in half, and remove the seeds. Discard skin and seeds.

3. Place pulp in a food processor. Pulse until smooth. Set aside.

4. Heat oil in a large nonstick skillet. Sauté onion, garlic, and celery until onion is soft, about 5–7 minutes. Add eggplant and tomatoes. Sauté 3 minutes.

5. Return to slow cooker and add capers, pine nuts, crushed red pepper, and vinegar. Stir. Cook on low 30 minutes. Stir prior to serving.

Per Serving: Calories: 54 | Fat: 1.5g | Protein: 2g | Sodium: 73mg | Fiber: 5g | Carbohydrates: 10g

Eggplant-Herb Dip S C

This herby eggplant dip is filled with a fresh and smoky flavor that is as delicious with pita chips as it is with crudités.

INGREDIENTS | SERVES 12

1 (1-pound) eggplant

1 clove garlic, diced

1 small onion, peeled and chopped

1 teaspoon cumin

½ teaspoon hot smoked paprika

1 (14½-ounce) can diced tomatoes

½ cup chopped parsley

2 tablespoons chopped cilantro

¼ cup olive oil

1. Trim and cube eggplant into 1" pieces. Place eggplant in slow cooker with garlic, onion, cumin, smoked paprika, and tomatoes.

2. Cover and cook on low heat 6–8 hours. Turn heat off and remove cover. Let sit 30 minutes to cool.

3. Place eggplant mixture in food processor fitted with a metal blade. Add parsley, cilantro, and olive oil. Process to desired consistency.

4. Serve at room temperature or chill for 2 hours.

Per Serving: Calories: 59 | Fat: 5g | Protein: 1g | Sodium: 51mg | Fiber: 2g | Carbohydrates: 4g

Scorthalia

This dip is a cousin to the famous garlic yogurt dip known as tzatziki and is an excellent accompaniment for vegetable and fish dishes.

INGREDIENTS | SERVES 8

1¼ teaspoons salt, divided

3 large potatoes, peeled and cut into eighths

6 garlic cloves, finely shredded

⅓ cup extra-virgin olive oil

⅓ cup vinegar

1 tablespoon dried oregano

½ teaspoon ground black pepper

1. Fill a medium saucepan with water and ¼ teaspoon salt. Bring to boil over high heat. Add potatoes and boil until soft, 15–20 minutes. Drain and transfer to a large mixing bowl.

2. Using a potato masher or large fork, thoroughly mash potatoes. Add garlic, oil, vinegar, oregano, pepper, and remaining salt. Stir well to incorporate all ingredients.

3. Set aside to cool. Serve at room temperature.

Per Serving: Calories: 171 | Fat: 12g | Sodium: 4mg | Carbohydrates: 15g | Fiber: 1.5g | Protein: 1.5g

Piquante Feta and Roasted Pepper Dip

This dip ought to be spicy but not red hot, so adjust the amount of crushed red pepper accordingly. Serve it with some warm pita bread.

INGREDIENTS | SERVES 8

½ pound feta cheese, crumbled

1 tablespoon crushed red pepper

2 large Roasted Red Peppers (see recipe in this chapter), chopped

4 tablespoons extra-virgin olive oil

1 teaspoon ground black pepper

Pulse all ingredients in a food processor until smooth. Refrigerate or serve at room temperature.

Per Serving: Calories: 93 | Fat: 9g | Protein: 3g | Sodium: 214mg | Fiber: 0g | Carbohydrates: 1.5g

Love of Olive Oil

The most characteristic aspect of the Mediterranean diet is the ubiquitous presence of the olive and its oil in the foods that comprise the traditional cuisines that evolved under its influence.

Feta and Pepper Spread

For a spicy variation, you can add a teaspoon of crushed red pepper to this recipe. Serve this spread hot with fresh crusty bread or warm pita bread.

INGREDIENTS | SERVES 8

2 tablespoons extra-virgin olive oil

1 medium onion, peeled and sliced

1 large green bell pepper, seeded and chopped

1 large red bell pepper, seeded and chopped

½ pound feta cheese (1 thick slice)

1 teaspoon dried oregano

½ teaspoon ground black pepper

1. Preheat oven to 350°F.

2. Heat oil in a large skillet over medium-high heat. Sauté onion and bell peppers until soft, about 8 minutes.

3. Place feta in a small baking dish and top with onion-pepper mixture. Sprinkle oregano and black pepper over top. Cover dish and bake 15 minutes. Serve hot.

Per Serving: Calories: 117 | Fat: 10g | Protein: 4.5g | Sodium: 320mg | Fiber: 0.5g | Carbohydrates: 4g

Garlic Feta Spread

This fresh-tasting dip is lovely with some fresh crusty bread or warm pita bread.

INGREDIENTS | SERVES 6

½ pound feta cheese, crumbled

3garlic cloves, pressed

2 tablespoons extra-virgin olive oil

2 tablespoons finely chopped
   fresh parsley

1 teaspoon dried oregano

½ teaspoon ground black pepper

Combine all ingredients in a medium bowl. Mash with a fork and mix well until combined. Refrigerate or serve at room temperature.

Per Serving: Calories: 108 | Fat: 9g | Protein: 4g | Sodium: 320mg | Fiber: 0g | Carbohydrates: 2g

Parsley Spread

This unusual spread is a refreshing change of pace for summer parties.
Use it on crostini or pita chips.

INGREDIENTS | SERVES 8

4 slices stale bread, crusts removed

2 cups chopped fresh parsley leaves

3 scallions, ends trimmed, chopped

½ cup extra-virgin olive oil

¼ cup fresh lemon juice

1 tablespoon vinegar

1 teaspoon dried oregano

1 teaspoon salt

½ teaspoon ground black pepper

1. In a medium bowl moisten bread with a little water. Squeeze to drain excess water.

2. Pulse parsley and scallions in a food processor to combine. Slowly add bread, oil, lemon juice, vinegar, oregano, salt, and pepper. Continue pulsing until smooth. Refrigerate or serve at room temperature.

Per Serving: Calories: 152 | Fat: 14g | Protein: 1g | Sodium: 39mg | Fiber: 0.5g | Carbohydrates: 7g

CHAPTER 4

Soups and Stews

Cold Cucumber Soup MA

Make this soup when you have an abundance of cucumbers from your garden. It comes together quickly using a food processor.

INGREDIENTS | SERVES 6

2 cloves garlic, minced

1 tablespoon red wine vinegar

2 slices white bread, crusts removed

1 large English cucumber, ends trimmed and grated

1½ cups plain yogurt

1½ cups cold water

4 tablespoons extra-virgin olive oil, divided

¼ cup plus 2 tablespoons chopped fresh dill, divided

¾ teaspoon salt

1 cup cubed English cucumber

1. In a food processor, add garlic, vinegar, and bread. Process until mixture becomes a paste. Add grated cucumber and yogurt and process again.

2. With the processor running, slowly add water in a steady stream. Add 2 tablespoons oil, ¼ cup dill, and salt. Pulse a few times to blend into the soup.

3. Transfer soup into a container with lid. Cover it and refrigerate until chilled.

4. Before serving, stir the soup. Serve cold and top with the cubed cucumber, remaining dill, and remaining oil.

Per Serving: Calories: 163 | Fat: 11g | Protein: 4g | Sodium: 313mg | Fiber: 0.5g | Carbohydrates: 12g

Gazpacho

This soup makes a great showcase from your summer garden! Use only the freshest ingredients and remove the seeds from the vegetables.

INGREDIENTS | SERVES 6

2 large sweet onions, chopped

3 medium cucumbers, peeled and chopped

1½ pounds plum tomatoes, chopped

3 cloves garlic, minced

½ cup chopped cilantro

1 chipotle chili pepper (canned in adobo sauce), drained and chopped

Zest and juice of 1 large lime

¼ teaspoon hot pepper sauce

½ teaspoon ground black pepper

1½ quarts vegetable broth

1. In a large bowl, mix together all ingredients except broth. Purée all but a quarter of this mixture in a blender.

2. Add broth to puréed mixture in blender and continue to purée until smooth. To serve, ladle into serving bowls. Garnish with reserved vegetable mixture.

Per Serving: Calories: 87 | Fat: 1g | Protein: 5g | Sodium: 799mg | Fiber: 3g | Carbohydrates: 17g

Greek Gazpacho MA

Roasted peppers add a sweetness and smokiness to a typical gazpacho recipe. Olive-oil ice cubes provide a unique garnish.

INGREDIENTS | SERVES 8

2 slices day-old white bread

1 tablespoon dried oregano

3 cloves garlic, smashed

2 tablespoons chopped fresh parsley

¼ cup red wine vinegar

¼ cup extra-virgin olive oil

1 large Roasted Red Pepper (see recipe in Chapter 3)

1 large roasted green bell pepper (prepared in the same way as red pepper)

2 medium red onions, roughly chopped

1 large English cucumber, seeded and chopped

4 large ripe tomatoes, roughly chopped

¾ cup pitted sun-dried black olives

6 cups vegetable cocktail beverage

1 teaspoon ground black pepper

1 cup cubed feta cheese

4 Olive-Oil Ice Cubes (see sidebar)

1. Place bread, oregano, garlic, and parsley into a food processor. Process until a wet paste is formed. Add vinegar and oil and pulse until incorporated. Empty the contents of the processor into a large bowl. Reserve.

2. Add roasted peppers, onions, cucumber, tomatoes, and olives to the food processor. Pulse until the ingredients are coarsely chopped. Add this mixture to the reserved bread mixture.

3. Stir in vegetable cocktail beverage and black pepper. Cover with plastic wrap and chill at least 3 hours.

4. Serve cold, topped with feta and olive-oil ice cubes.

Per Serving: Calories: 230 | Fat: 13g | Protein: 6g | Sodium: 619mg | Fiber: 4g | Carbohydrates: 25g

Olive-Oil Ice Cubes

Fill an ice-cube tray's compartments half-way with extra-virgin olive oil. Place the tray in the freezer to harden. Use them as a garnish for any cold savory soups.

Spring Vegetable Soup S C

This delicious vegetable-packed soup is perfect for springtime, when fresh asparagus is readily available and affordable at local grocers.

INGREDIENTS | SERVES 6

Nonstick olive oil cooking spray

3 pounds asparagus

1 pound cauliflower

½ pound carrots, peeled and sliced

½ pound turnips, peeled and cut into 2" strips

½ pound string beans, cut diagonally

1 cup green peas

2 cups low-sodium chicken broth

¼ teaspoon salt

¼ teaspoon ground black pepper

½ cup chopped cilantro

1. Spray a 4- to 5-quart slow cooker with cooking spray. Cut 2" tips from asparagus and florets from cauliflower and place in slow cooker; set aside asparagus stalks and cauliflower stems for use in other recipes.

2. Stir in carrots, turnips, beans, peas, broth, salt, and pepper. Cover and cook on low 3½ hours.

3. Stir in cilantro and cook 30 minutes more.

Per Serving: Calories: 153 | Fat: 2g | Protein: 10g | Sodium: 228mg | Fiber: 10g | Carbohydrates: 28g

Avgolemono Soup with Chicken and Rice

Try substituting rice with orzo or hand-crushed nests of vermicelli pasta. You can also use leftover roast chicken in this recipe.

INGREDIENTS | SERVES 8

10 cups chicken stock

⅓ cup finely diced carrot

⅓ cup finely diced celery

⅓ cup Arborio or Carolina rice

2½ teaspoons salt

2 large eggs

3 tablespoons fresh lemon juice

2 cups cooked and chopped skinless chicken, at room temperature

1. Add stock to a large pot over medium-high heat and bring to a boil. Add carrots, celery, and rice. Boil 10–15 minutes then remove from heat. Season with salt.

2. In a large bowl, whisk together eggs and lemon juice. Continuing to whisk vigorously, slowly add a ladle of soup liquid into egg-lemon mixture. Continue whisking and slowly add another 3–4 ladles of soup (one at a time) into egg-lemon mixture.

3. Slowly stir egg-lemon mixture back into soup. Stir in chicken.

4. Let the soup cool 5 minutes before serving.

Per Serving: Calories: 355 | Fat: 9g | Protein: 44g | Sodium: 1,118mg | Fiber: 0.5g | Carbohydrates: 18g

Leek and Potato Soup

This soup never goes out of style. When served hot, it's a satisfying and comforting cold-weather soup. But you can also chill it and serve it cold.

INGREDIENTS | SERVES 8

¼ cup extra-virgin olive oil

3 medium leeks, trimmed, cleaned, cut lengthwise, and sliced

2 bay leaves

1 teaspoon dried thyme

3 large russet potatoes, peeled and grated

8 cups chicken or vegetable stock

½ cup heavy cream or evaporated milk

2½ teaspoons salt

1 teaspoon ground black pepper

½ cup chopped fresh chives

1. Add the oil to a large pot over medium heat and heat 30 seconds. Add the leeks, bay leaves, and thyme. Cook 10–15 minutes or until the leeks soften.

2. Add the potatoes and cook another 5 minutes. If the mixture gets dry or gluey, add some water or stock.

3. Add the stock and increase heat to medium-high. Bring soup to a boil, reduce heat to medium-low, and cook 30–40 minutes. Remove the bay leaves.

4. Using an immersion blender or a regular blender, carefully purée the soup until it is smooth. Add the cream, salt, and pepper.

5. Serve hot and topped with chives.

Per Serving: Calories: 236 | Fat: 13g | Protein: 8g | Sodium: 725mg | Fiber: 2g | Carbohydrates: 23g

Roasted Yellow Bell Pepper Soup

Try using orange or red bell peppers to make a brilliant-colored soup.
Garnish with Greek yogurt and cubed roasted beets.

INGREDIENTS | SERVES 6

¼ cup extra-virgin olive oil

1 large leek (white part only), trimmed, cleaned, and sliced

1 medium carrot, peeled and diced

½ stalk celery, diced

4 cloves garlic, smashed

1½ teaspoons salt, divided

½ teaspoon ground black pepper, divided

2 medium Yukon gold potatoes, peeled and diced

1 teaspoon sweet paprika

1 teaspoon fresh thyme leaves

4 large roasted yellow bell peppers (see recipe for Roasted Red Peppers in Chapter 3)

1 small hot banana pepper, stemmed, seeded, and chopped

4 cups vegetable or chicken stock

½ cup sliced fresh basil leaves

½ cup heavy cream

½ cup grated Graviera or Gruyère cheese

1. Add oil to a large pot over medium heat and heat 30 seconds. Add leeks, carrot, celery, and garlic. Season with ½ teaspoon salt and ¼ teaspoon black pepper. Reduce heat to medium-low and cook 10 minutes or until leeks soften.

2. Add potatoes, paprika, and thyme. Cook 2 minutes. Add roasted peppers, banana pepper, and stock. Increase heat to medium-high and bring soup to a boil. Reduce heat to medium-low, cover, and cook another 20 minutes.

3. Add the basil. Using an immersion blender or a regular blender, carefully purée the soup until it is smooth. Add cream, cheese, and remaining salt and black pepper. Stir until the cheese is melted and the soup is smooth.

4. Serve hot.

Per Serving: Calories: 302 | Fat: 18g | Protein: 10g | Sodium: 693mg | Fiber: 4.5g | Carbohydrates: 23g

Stracciatella

Stracciatella, or Italian Egg-Drop Soup, is hearty enough to stand on its own as a main dish.

INGREDIENTS | SERVES 6

1 tablespoon extra-virgin olive oil

1 large onion, peeled and chopped

1 medium shallot, peeled and finely chopped

6 cloves garlic, minced

8 cups chicken stock

½ cup chopped fresh parsley

2 teaspoons fresh thyme leaves

1 pound fresh spinach, finely sliced

2 large eggs

4 large egg whites

1 teaspoon salt

½ teaspoon ground black pepper

¼ cup grated Parmesan cheese

1. Heat oil in a large pot over medium heat 30 seconds. Add onion, shallot, and garlic. Cook 3 minutes or until onion is softened.

2. Add stock, parsley, and thyme; simmer 30–45 minutes. Add spinach and cook 5 minutes or until wilted.

3. In a small bowl, whisk eggs and egg whites. Stir eggs into soup and cook 5 minutes. Season with salt and pepper. Serve topped with a sprinkle of Parmesan.

Per Serving: Calories: 223 | Fat: 9g | Protein: 17g | Sodium: 937mg | Fiber: 2.5g | Carbohydrates: 18g

Greek-Style Orzo and Spinach Soup S C

Lemon zest adds a bright, robust flavor to this simple soup.

INGREDIENTS | SERVES 6

2 cloves garlic, minced

3 tablespoons lemon juice

1 teaspoon lemon zest

5 cups low-sodium chicken broth

1 small onion, peeled and thinly sliced

1 cup cubed cooked chicken breast

⅓ cup dried orzo

4 cups baby spinach

1. Add garlic, lemon juice, zest, broth, and onion to a 4- to 5-quart slow cooker. Cover and cook on low 6–8 hours.

2. Stir in chicken and cook 30 minutes on high. Add orzo and spinach. Stir and continue to cook on high an additional 15 minutes. Stir before serving.

Per Serving: Calories: 90 | Fat: 1g | Protein: 9g | Sodium: 237mg | Fiber: 1g | Carbohydrates: 10g

Bakaliaros Avgolemono

This version of the famous avgolemono (egg-lemon) soup includes chunks of cod. If you're using salted cod, soak it in water for at least 24 hours to remove the salt, making sure to change the water several times.

INGREDIENTS | SERVES 8

4 cups water

⅓ cup olive oil

2 celery stalks, sliced

1 medium onion, peeled and diced

3 medium potatoes, peeled and cubed

1 teaspoon salt

½ teaspoon ground black pepper

½ tablespoon corn flour

½ cup warm water

1½ pounds fresh or salted cod (cut into 1" thick pieces)

2 large eggs, separated

Juice of 2 medium lemons

A "Good" Fat

Olive oil is a monounsaturated fat that has been shown to raise HDL levels ("good" cholesterol) in blood.

1. In a large pot, bring 4 cups water to a boil over high heat. Add oil, celery, onion, potatoes, salt, and pepper. Cover, reduce heat to medium-low, and simmer 15 minutes.

2. Dilute corn flour in ½ cup of warm water. Add to pot and stir well. Immediately add cod to pot. Cover, return heat to high, and boil 5–6 minutes.

3. Whisk egg whites in a large bowl until stiff. Add yolks while continuing to whisk. Slowly add lemon juice while stirring mixture constantly with whisk.

4. Slowly mix 2 ladlefuls of hot broth from pot into egg mixture while continually whisking to achieve a uniform creamy consistency.

5. Remove pot from heat and stir in egg mixture. Cover and let stand a few minutes before serving.

Per Serving: Calories: 274 | Fat: 11g | Protein: 19g | Sodium: 90mg | Fiber: 4g | Carbohydrates: 26g

Classic Minestrone   SC

A traditional vegetarian Italian soup, minestrone can withstand long cooking periods. It tastes even better on the second day.

INGREDIENTS | SERVES 12

3 tablespoons olive oil

1 cup minced onion

3 stalks celery, chopped

4 cloves garlic, minced

1 small zucchini, trimmed and chopped

4 cups vegetable broth

2 (14-ounce) cans diced tomatoes, drained

2 (15-ounce) cans red kidney beans, drained

2 (15-ounce) cans cannellini (white) beans, drained

1 (28-ounce) can Italian-style green beans

½ cup diced carrots

1 cup red wine (Chianti or Cabernet Sauvignon)

2 (6-ounce) cans tomato paste

2 tablespoons minced parsley

1½ teaspoons dried oregano

2 teaspoons salt

½ teaspoon ground black pepper

1 teaspoon garlic powder

½ teaspoon Italian seasoning

4 cups baby spinach

1 cup cooked small pasta

1. In a large skillet, heat oil over medium heat. Sauté onion, celery, garlic, and zucchini 3–5 minutes until onion is translucent.

2. Add sautéed vegetables and vegetable broth to a 6-quart slow cooker, along with tomatoes, red and white beans, green beans, carrots, wine, tomato paste, parsley, oregano, salt, pepper, garlic powder, and Italian seasoning. Cover and cook on high 8 hours.

3. One hour prior to serving, stir in spinach. Pour into soup bowls and add 1 tablespoon cooked pasta to each bowl of soup.

Per Serving: Calories: 245 | Fat: 4g | Protein: 11g | Sodium: 1,214mg | Fiber: 11g | Carbohydrates: 38g

Tahini Soup

Tahini is a ground sesame paste that has been used in cooking throughout the eastern regions of the Mediterranean for many centuries. Most supermarkets carry at least one brand of tahini. Or you can visit a Middle Eastern grocery store, where they are sure to have it in stock.

INGREDIENTS | SERVES 6

8 cups water
2 cups orzo
1 teaspoon salt
½ teaspoon ground black pepper
½ cup tahini
Juice of 2 large lemons

1. Bring water to boil in large pot over high heat. Add orzo, salt, and pepper and stir well. Cover and simmer until cooked, about 10 minutes. Remove pot from heat.

2. Place tahini in a small bowl. Slowly add lemon juice while whisking constantly. Once lemon juice is incorporated, take about ½ cup hot pasta water from pot and slowly add to tahini-lemon mixture while whisking until smooth.

3. Pour mixture into pot with pasta and mix well. Serve immediately.

Per Serving: Calories: 249 | Fat: 10g | Protein: 8g | Sodium: 15mg | Fiber: 3g | Carbohydrates: 34g

Seafood and Cilantro Soup

This quick-to-make soup is full of lively, fresh summertime flavors.

INGREDIENTS | SERVES 6

2 quarts seafood broth or fat-free chicken broth
1 teaspoon olive oil
1 medium red onion, peeled and chopped
6 large bay scallops
4 ounces lobster meat, roughly chopped
6 small (35/45) shrimp, peeled and deveined
¼ cup dry white wine
¼ cup chopped cilantro
1 teaspoon lime juice
1 teaspoon ground black pepper

1. In a large stockpot, heat the broth over medium-high heat 30 minutes.

2. Meanwhile, heat oil in a large skillet over medium heat. Sauté onion 5 minutes or until softened, then add scallops, lobster, and shrimp. Add wine. Cook until seafood is firm and opaque, about 10 minutes. Remove from heat and transfer to a bowl.

3. Add cilantro, lime juice, and pepper to bowl with seafood and mix thoroughly.

4. Ladle hot stock into 6 bowls and add seafood mixture to each.

Per Serving: Calories: 190 | Fat: 6g | Protein: 14g | Sodium: 1,485mg | Fiber: 0g | Carbohydrates: 18g

Giouvarlakia Soup

This hearty soup is a one-pot meal.
The tiny meatballs cook quickly, so it's perfect for a weeknight supper.

INGREDIENTS | SERVES 8

1 pound lean ground beef

1 medium onion, peeled and grated

3 large eggs, divided

⅓ cup plus ½ cup Arborio rice, divided

1 teaspoon ground allspice

⅛ teaspoon grated nutmeg

1½ teaspoons salt, divided

1½ teaspoons ground black pepper, divided

8 cups chicken stock

1 tablespoon flour

2 tablespoons water

3 tablespoons fresh lemon juice

1. In a large bowl, combine beef, onion, 1 egg, ⅓ cup rice, allspice, nutmeg, ½ teaspoon salt, and ½ teaspoon pepper. Roll the mixture into 1" balls. Reserve.

2. Add stock to a large pot over medium-high heat and bring to a boil. Reduce heat to medium. Add meatballs and remaining rice, salt, and pepper. Cover and cook 20 minutes. Take the pot off the heat.

3. In a large bowl, whisk together flour and water until smooth. Whisk in remaining eggs and lemon juice. Continuing to whisk vigorously, slowly add a ladle of soup liquid into egg-lemon mixture. Continue whisking and slowly add another 3–4 ladles of soup (one at a time) into egg-lemon mixture.

4. Slowly stir egg-lemon mixture back into soup.

5. Allow soup to cool 5 minutes and then serve it immediately.

Per Serving: Calories: 229 | Fat: 6g | Protein: 21g | Sodium: 525mg | Fiber: 1g | Carbohydrates: 22g

Hearty Winter Vegetable Soup

Serve this soup with crusty bread and a glass of red wine. It's wonderful when eaten by a warm fire.

INGREDIENTS | SERVES 8

¼ cup extra-virgin olive oil

1 large leek, trimmed, cleaned, cut lengthwise, and sliced

5 cloves garlic, minced

2 large carrots, peeled and diced

3 stalks celery, diced

1 large red bell pepper, seeded and diced

3 bay leaves

3 sprigs thyme

2 teaspoons salt, divided

1 teaspoon ground black pepper, divided

1 medium sweet potato, peeled and grated

1 cup shredded white cabbage

1 cup halved broccoli florets

1 cup halved cauliflower florets

9–10 cups vegetable stock

2 cups chopped romaine lettuce

1 cup small pasta

1. Add oil to a large pot over medium heat and heat 30 seconds. Add leeks, garlic, carrots, celery, bell pepper, bay leaves, and thyme. Season with ½ teaspoon salt and ¼ teaspoon black pepper. Cover and cook 10 minutes or until vegetables are softened.

2. Add sweet potato and cook 2 minutes. Add cabbage, broccoli, and cauliflower. Cook another minute.

3. Add stock, increase heat to medium-high, and bring the soup to a boil. Reduce heat to medium-low and cook 15 minutes. Add lettuce and pasta and cook another 20–25 minutes.

4. Season with remaining salt and black pepper. Remove thyme stems and bay leaves. Serve hot.

Per Serving: Calories: 130 | Fat: 2.5g | Protein: 8g | Sodium: 618mg | Fiber: 4g | Carbohydrates: 20g

Leeks

Leeks are part of the onion family and are wonderful for making soups. They do need thorough cleaning, as dirt often gets in between the layers. To clean them properly, cut the ends off the leeks, and cut them in half lengthwise. Run them under cold water while running your fingers back and forth between the layers to remove grit.

Spanish Beef Stew SC

*For extra flavor use wrinkled Turkish olives (or other olives) instead of
the standard stuffed olives found in the grocery store.*

INGREDIENTS | SERVES 8

Nonstick olive oil cooking spray
1 tablespoon olive oil
2 cloves garlic, sliced
1 medium onion, peeled and sliced
3 slices bacon, cut into 1" pieces
1 pound stew beef, cubed
3 large Roma tomatoes, diced
1 bay leaf, crumbled
¼ teaspoon sage
¼ teaspoon marjoram
½ teaspoon paprika
½ teaspoon curry powder
1 teaspoon salt
2 tablespoons vinegar
1 cup beef stock
½ cup white wine
4 medium potatoes, peeled and sliced
⅓ cup pitted, sliced olives
2 tablespoons chopped parsley

1. Spray a 4- to 5-quart slow cooker with cooking spray.

2. Heat oil in a large skillet over medium heat. Sauté garlic, onion, bacon, and beef until bacon and beef are done and onion is softened, about 7–8 minutes. Drain and transfer meat mixture to slow cooker.

3. Add tomatoes, bay leaf, sage, marjoram, paprika, curry powder, salt, vinegar, stock, and wine to slow cooker. Cover and cook on low 5 hours.

4. Add potatoes, olives, and parsley to slow cooker and cook 1 hour more.

Per Serving: Calories: 250 | Fat: 10g | Protein: 16g | Sodium: 467mg | Fiber: 4g | Carbohydrates: 22g

Tuscan Chicken and Sausage Stew

You don't need a lot of ingredients to create a stew full of hearty and warm Tuscan flavors.

INGREDIENTS | SERVES 8

Nonstick olive oil cooking spray

1 pound boneless, skinless chicken thighs, cut into bite-sized pieces

8 ounces turkey sausage, cut into ½" slices

1 (26-ounce) jar pasta sauce

1 (14.5-ounce) can green beans, drained

1 teaspoon dried oregano

Change It Up

Don't like green beans or don't have them available in your pantry? Use navy beans, cannellini beans, or even black beans.

1. Spray a 4- to 5-quart slow cooker with cooking spray.

2. Place all ingredients in slow cooker and stir to combine. Cook on high 4 hours or on low 8 hours.

Per Serving: Calories: 209 | Fat: 8g | Protein: 20g | Sodium: 202mg | Fiber: 3g | Carbohydrates: 14g

CHAPTER 5

Salads and Dressings

Tuna Salad with Toasted Pine Nuts

Tarragon has a delicate anise flavor. It's often used in fish and chicken dishes in Southern France.

INGREDIENTS | SERVES 6

1 (5-ounce) can tuna packed in olive oil, drained and flaked

1 medium shallot, peeled and diced

3 tablespoons chopped fresh chives

1 tablespoon chopped fresh tarragon

1 stalk celery, finely diced

2–3 tablespoons mayonnaise, depending on your preference

1 teaspoon Dijon mustard

¼ teaspoon salt

⅛ teaspoon ground black pepper

¼ cup toasted pine nuts

1. In a medium bowl, toss tuna, shallot, chives, tarragon, and celery.

2. In a small bowl, combine the mayonnaise, mustard, salt, and pepper. Stir the mayonnaise mixture into the tuna mixture.

3. Stir in the pine nuts. Refrigerate or serve at room temperature.

Per Serving: Calories: 134 | Fat: 10g | Protein: 8g | Sodium: 172mg | Fiber: 0.5g | Carbohydrates: 1.5g

Bulgur Salad with Nuts, Honey, and Cheese

Bulgur is a whole-wheat grain that has been cracked and parboiled. You can find pomegranate molasses in Greek or Middle Eastern grocery stores.

INGREDIENTS | SERVES 8

1 cup coarse (#3) bulgur wheat

1 teaspoon salt

½ cup extra-virgin olive oil

¼ cup chopped toasted almonds

¼ cup chopped toasted walnuts

¼ teaspoon ground allspice

¼ cup pomegranate molasses

2 teaspoons red wine vinegar

2 teaspoons honey

2 scallions, ends trimmed, thinly sliced

1½ cups baby arugula, washed and dried

¼ cup chopped fresh mint

1 cup crumbled goat cheese

¼ teaspoon ground black pepper

1. Fill a medium pot two-thirds with water and set it over medium-high heat. Bring water to a boil. Add bulgur and salt. Boil 6 minutes. Drain the bulgur and transfer to a large bowl.

2. Add oil, nuts, allspice, molasses, vinegar, and honey to the bowl. Mix well.

3. Add the scallions, arugula, mint, cheese, and pepper. Toss to combine. Serve at room temperature.

Per Serving: Calories: 307 | Fat: 28g | Protein: 8g | Sodium: 300mg | Fiber: 4g | Carbohydrates: 20g

Arugula, Pear, and Goat Cheese Salad

Arugula is a peppery salad green that is sometimes called "rocket" in grocery stores.

INGREDIENTS | SERVES 6

2 medium pears, cored and cut into wedges

2 tablespoons fresh lemon juice, divided

1 tablespoon balsamic vinegar

⅓ cup extra-virgin olive oil

¼ cup chopped fresh chives

½ teaspoon salt

⅛ teaspoon ground black pepper

3 cups arugula

½ cup chopped unsalted pistachios

½ cup crumbled goat cheese

1. In a small bowl, toss pears with 1 tablespoon lemon juice.

2. In a large bowl, whisk remaining lemon juice, vinegar, oil, chives, salt, and pepper.

3. Add arugula to the large bowl and toss to coat. Transfer to a serving platter.

4. Arrange pears over arugula and sprinkle with pistachios and cheese.

5. Drizzle any remaining dressing over the salad and serve.

Per Serving: Calories: 247 | Fat: 23g | Protein: 6g | Sodium: 234mg | Fiber: 3g | Carbohydrates: 13g

Strawberry and Feta Salad

Sweet strawberries complement the tart and briny feta very well.

INGREDIENTS | SERVES 4

1 teaspoon Dijon mustard

2 tablespoons balsamic vinegar

1 clove garlic, minced

¼ cup extra-virgin olive oil

½ teaspoon salt

⅛ teaspoon ground black pepper

4 cups salad greens, rinsed and dried

1 pint ripe strawberries, hulled and halved

1½ cups crumbled feta cheese

1. In a small bowl, whisk mustard, vinegar, garlic, oil, salt, and pepper to make the dressing.

2. In a large bowl, combine salad greens and dressing. Transfer salad to a serving platter and top with the strawberries and feta.

3. Drizzle any remaining dressing over the salad and serve.

Per Serving: Calories: 310 | Fat: 25g | Protein: 9g | Sodium: 751mg | Fiber: 2g | Carbohydrates: 11g

Greek Village Salad

An authentic Greek salad contains no lettuce of any kind. Use the best extra-virgin olive oil in your pantry for this salad. You don't need any kind of vinegar; the acidity from the tomatoes is enough.

INGREDIENTS | SERVES 6

4 medium ripe tomatoes, cut into wedges

½ English cucumber, halved and sliced into ½" slices

1 medium green Cubanelle pepper, seeded and sliced

1 small red onion, peeled and thinly sliced

⅛ teaspoon salt

⅓ cup extra-virgin olive oil

1½ cups cubed feta cheese

1 teaspoon dried oregano

8 kalamata olives

1. On a serving plate, arrange tomatoes and cucumbers. Next add peppers and onions. Season vegetables with salt.

2. Drizzle oil over vegetables. Top with feta and sprinkle with oregano.

3. Top salad with olives and serve at room temperature.

Per Serving: Calories: 239 | Fat: 17g | Protein: 7g | Sodium: 407mg | Fiber: 2g | Carbohydrates: 9g

Politiki Cabbage Salad

This dish comes from the Byzantine city of Constantinople, or modern-day Istanbul. Because cabbage is so plentiful in the Mediterranean, cabbage salads are common fare.

INGREDIENTS | SERVES 6

1 teaspoon sugar

1½ teaspoons salt, divided

¼ cup red wine vinegar

4 cups shredded white cabbage

½ cup grated carrot

½ cup thinly sliced red bell pepper

¼ cup diced celery

¼ cup extra-virgin olive oil

⅛ teaspoon crushed red pepper

½ teaspoon ground black pepper

1. In a large bowl, whisk sugar, 1 teaspoon salt, and vinegar. Add cabbage, carrot, bell pepper, and celery and toss to combine. Let vegetables sit 15–20 minutes.

2. Using your hands, squeeze out excess liquid from the vegetables and place the vegetables in a separate large bowl.

3. Add oil, crushed red pepper, black pepper, and remaining salt and toss to coat vegetables. Refrigerate or serve at room temperature.

Per Serving: Calories: 123 | Fat: 10g | Protein: 2g | Sodium: 415mg | Fiber: 3g | Carbohydrates: 8g

Creamy Caesar Salad

This recipe makes more dressing than you'll need for the salad. Leftover dressing can be stored in the refrigerator for up to 1 week.

INGREDIENTS | SERVES 6

2 cloves garlic, chopped

3 large egg yolks

1 tablespoon Dijon mustard

3 tablespoons Worcestershire sauce

1 tablespoon anchovy paste or 2 anchovy fillets

½ cup grated Parmesan cheese, divided

2 tablespoons fresh lemon juice, divided

½ teaspoon salt

1 teaspoon ground black pepper

1 tablespoon water

1 cup light olive oil

1 head romaine lettuce, washed, dried, and chopped

½ cup chopped cooked bacon

1 cup croutons

1. Place garlic, egg yolks, mustard, Worcestershire sauce, anchovy paste, ¼ cup Parmesan cheese, 1 tablespoon lemon juice, salt, pepper, and water into a food processor. Process until dressing is combined and thick. With the processor running, slowly add oil until well incorporated.

2. In a large bowl, combine lettuce and remaining lemon juice. Add just enough dressing to coat lettuce (add more if you want to make it creamier). Toss in bacon and croutons. Top salad with remaining Parmesan. Serve with extra dressing.

Per Serving: Calories: 444 | Fat: 28g | Protein: 8g | Sodium: 653mg | Fiber: 3g | Carbohydrates: 10g

Make Your Own Croutons

Croutons are easy to make and add a delicious crunch to any salad. All you need is leftover bread, some olive oil, and an oven. Cut up leftover bread into cubes or chunks. Toss them with just enough olive oil to lightly coat the bread but not soak it. Lay the bread on a baking sheet and bake it in a preheated 350°F oven for 30 minutes or until the croutons are crunchy.

Asparagus Salad

Top this salad with your favorite cheese or finely chopped nuts.

INGREDIENTS | SERVES 6

1 pound asparagus, rinsed and woody ends trimmed

1 teaspoon salt

1 tablespoon fresh lemon juice

1 clove garlic, minced

1 tablespoon grated lemon zest

1 teaspoon fresh thyme leaves

2 tablespoons chopped fresh parsley

½ teaspoon ground black pepper

¼ cup extra-virgin olive oil

1. Using a vegetable peeler, shave asparagus into long thin strips. In a medium bowl, combine shaved asparagus, salt, and lemon juice. Set aside 15 minutes.

2. In a small bowl, whisk garlic, zest, thyme, parsley, pepper, and oil.

3. Add dressing to asparagus and toss to coat. Refrigerate or serve at room temperature.

Per Serving: Calories: 97 | Fat: 9g | Protein: 2g | Sodium: 329mg | Fiber: 2g | Carbohydrates: 3g

Arugula Salad with Figs and Goat Cheese

Don't worry if you can't find fresh figs—dried ones also work well for this recipe. Or you can use any seasonal fruit instead.

INGREDIENTS | SERVES 8

1 tablespoon honey

1 teaspoon Dijon mustard

3 tablespoons balsamic vinegar

1 small clove garlic, minced

1 teaspoon salt

½ teaspoon ground black pepper

⅔ cup extra-virgin olive oil

5 cups arugula leaves

12 fresh (ripe) figs, stemmed and quartered

1 cup roughly chopped walnuts

¼ cup crumbled goat cheese

1. In a large bowl, whisk honey, mustard, vinegar, garlic, salt, and pepper. Slowly whisk in the oil until well incorporated.

2. Add arugula and figs. Toss salad to coat with dressing.

3. Sprinkle salad with walnuts and cheese before serving.

Per Serving: Calories: 341 | Fat: 28.5g | Protein: 4.5g | Sodium: 342mg | Fiber: 3g | Carbohydrates: 20g

Spinach Salad with Apples and Mint

Use any variety of apples you like for this salad, but make sure you include at least one tart apple.

INGREDIENTS | SERVES 8

⅓ cup extra-virgin olive oil

10 fresh mint leaves, chopped

1 large orange, peeled and segmented, juice reserved

1 large grapefruit, peeled and segmented, juice reserved

1 tablespoon fresh lime juice

¾ teaspoon salt

¼ teaspoon ground black pepper

1 large red apple, cored and cut into thin slices

1 large green apple, cored and cut into thin slices

⅓ cup finely chopped red onion

1 stalk celery, chopped

4 cups baby spinach

1. Process oil and mint in a food processor until well incorporated. Set aside and let the mint infuse the oil.

2. In a large bowl, whisk together reserved orange and grapefruit juices, lime juice, salt, pepper, and olive oil–mint infusion. Add apple slices, onion, and celery and toss to coat.

3. Add spinach and toss again to combine. Top salad with orange and grapefruit segments and serve.

Per Serving: Calories: 140 | Fat: 9g | Protein: 1.5g | Sodium: 215mg | Fiber: 2.5g | Carbohydrates: 15g

Tomato Salad with Roasted Garlic Dressing

This easy-to-make salad is a nice addition to any summer meal.

INGREDIENTS | SERVES 8

½ medium red onion, peeled and thinly sliced

4 large ripe tomatoes, cut into wedges

1 teaspoon salt

½ teaspoon ground black pepper

6 cloves roasted garlic

⅓ cup pine nuts, toasted

½ cup sliced fresh basil

¼ cup extra-virgin olive oil

¼ cup sliced kalamata olives

1. In a large bowl, gently toss onion, tomatoes, salt, and pepper.

2. Place garlic, pine nuts, and basil in a mortar. Using a pestle, grind ingredients to make a paste. Add oil and mix to combine.

3. Add dressing to onions and tomatoes. Gently toss to coat. Top salad with olives and serve.

Per Serving: Calories: 120 | Fat: 10g | Protein: 2g | Sodium: 254mg | Fiber: 2g | Carbohydrates: 7g

Tomato Salad with Fried Feta

Keep the fried cheese warm in a preheated 280°F oven until you are ready to serve.

INGREDIENTS | SERVES 4

1 large egg
1 teaspoon whole milk
¼ cup all-purpose flour
1½ cups cubed feta cheese
1 tablespoon lemon juice
1⅔ cups extra-virgin olive oil, divided
1 teaspoon Dijon mustard
1 tablespoon balsamic vinegar
1 teaspoon honey
2 teaspoons dried oregano
1 teaspoon salt
¼ teaspoon ground black pepper
2 medium tomatoes, sliced into
  ½" slices
4 cups salad greens
1 small red onion, peeled and
  thinly sliced
½ cup kalamata olives

1. In a small bowl, beat egg and milk. Put flour into another small bowl. Dip feta cubes in egg mixture and then dredge with flour. Shake off excess flour. Refrigerate dredged feta at least 30 minutes.

2. Into a small jar with a lid, put lemon juice, ⅔ cup oil, mustard, vinegar, honey, oregano, salt, and pepper. Close jar and shake vigorously until dressing is well incorporated.

3. Add remaining oil to a medium nonstick frying pan and heat on medium 1 minute. Add feta (in batches) and fry until cubes are lightly golden on all sides (20–30 seconds per side). Place feta on a tray lined with paper towels to absorb excess oil.

4. In a large bowl, place tomatoes, greens, onions, and olives. Shake dressing and then add it to salad. Toss to combine ingredients.

5. Top salad with fried feta. Serve immediately.

Per Serving: Calories: 803 | Fat: 55g | Protein: 12g | Sodium: 1,168mg | Fiber: 2.5g | Carbohydrates: 20g

Potato Salad

This salad is ideal for serving in the summer. It comes together easily and can be made ahead of time. It's delicious served with grilled fish.

INGREDIENTS | SERVES 12

6 large Yukon gold potatoes, skins on

1½ teaspoons salt

½ teaspoon ground black pepper

½ cup extra-virgin olive oil

¼ cup Dijon mustard

2 tablespoons capers, drained and chopped

¼ cup red wine vinegar

2 tablespoons chopped fresh parsley

3 scallions, ends trimmed, finely chopped

½ cup chopped fresh dill

1 tablespoon fresh lemon juice

1. Place a large pot of water over medium-high heat. Add potatoes and bring to a boil. Cook 30 minutes. Let potatoes cool 10 minutes, and then peel them. Cut potatoes into chunks.

2. In a large bowl, whisk remaining ingredients until well incorporated.

3. Add potatoes to dressing and toss to coat. Serve salad warm or at room temperature.

Per Serving: Calories: 213 | Fat: 9g | Protein: 3g | Sodium: 359mg | Fiber: 5g | Carbohydrates: 29g

Creamy Coleslaw

This version of coleslaw uses a little mayonnaise combined with healthful, protein-rich Greek yogurt. Leftover coleslaw can be covered and stored for up to 5 days in a refrigerator.

INGREDIENTS | SERVES 12

1 tablespoon sugar

2 teaspoons salt, divided

¼ cup red wine vinegar

½ large head cabbage, cored and thinly sliced

1 large carrot, peeled and grated

2 scallions, ends trimmed, thinly sliced

2 cloves garlic, minced

½ cup extra-virgin olive oil

¼ cup mayonnaise

½ cup plain Greek yogurt

½ teaspoon ground black pepper

1. In a large bowl, whisk together sugar, 1½ teaspoons salt, and vinegar. Add cabbage, carrots, scallions, and garlic. Toss to combine. Let vegetables sit 5 minutes.

2. To the vegetables, add oil, mayonnaise, yogurt, pepper, and remaining salt. Stir to combine and coat the vegetables in the dressing.

3. Refrigerate or serve at room temperature.

Per Serving: Calories: 136 | Fat: 13g | Protein: 1g | Sodium: 272mg | Fiber: 1g | Carbohydrates: 4.5g

Artichoke Salad

For a variation, try topping this salad with fried calamari or grilled shrimp.

INGREDIENTS | SERVES 8

2 medium onions, chopped, divided

1 medium carrot, peeled and diced, divided

1 tablespoon finely chopped celery

2 tablespoons fresh lemon juice

1 teaspoon salt

8 canned or jarred artichoke hearts, rinsed and halved

½ cup extra-virgin olive oil, divided

1 medium red bell pepper, seeded and chopped

2 medium zucchini, trimmed and diced

½ cup fresh peas or thawed frozen peas

1 teaspoon salt

½ teaspoon ground black pepper

10 pitted kalamata olives, sliced

¼ cup finely chopped capers

½ cup chopped fresh mint

1. Have a large bowl of ice water ready.

2. Add 3 inches water to a large deep skillet and bring to a boil over medium-high heat. Add 2 tablespoons onions, 1 tablespoon carrots, celery, lemon juice, and salt. Return to a boil.

3. Add artichokes and reduce heat to medium-low. Cook artichokes 3 minutes or until tender. Remove artichokes with a slotted spoon and place them in an ice bath to stop the cooking process. Discard the cooking liquid. When the artichokes have cooled, remove them from the ice bath and reserve.

4. In a large skillet over medium-high heat, add ¼ cup oil and heat 30 seconds. Add remaining onions, remaining carrots, and bell pepper. Reduce heat to medium and cook 5–6 minutes. Add zucchini and cook 2 minutes. Add peas and cook another 2 minutes. Season with salt and black pepper. Remove from heat and cool 10–15 minutes.

5. In a medium bowl, combine onion-carrot mixture, remaining oil, olives, capers, and mint.

6. To serve, place 3–4 artichokes on each plate and top with onion-carrot mixture. Serve at room temperature.

Per Serving: Calories: 174 | Fat: 13g | Protein: 2g | Sodium: 633mg | Fiber: 2.5g | Carbohydrates: 12g

Chickpea Salad with Roasted Red Peppers and Green Beans

Try using a combination of red, green, yellow, or orange peppers for a more colorful salad.

INGREDIENTS | SERVES 6

3 cloves garlic, minced

1 teaspoon Dijon mustard

2 tablespoons red wine vinegar

1 teaspoon salt, divided

½ teaspoon ground black pepper, divided

½ cup extra-virgin olive oil

1 cup canned chickpeas, drained and rinsed

1 pound green beans, trimmed and blanched for 5–6 minutes

2 Roasted Red Peppers (see recipe in Chapter 3), sliced

1 cup pickled cauliflower florets, halved

2 cups salad greens, washed and dried

¼ cup chopped fresh parsley

2 teaspoons dried oregano

12 kalamata olives, pitted

1. In a large bowl, whisk garlic, mustard, vinegar, ½ teaspoon salt, and ¼ teaspoon black pepper. Slowly whisk in oil until it is well incorporated.

2. Add chickpeas, beans, roasted peppers, and cauliflower. Toss to coat.

3. Add greens, parsley, oregano, olives, and remaining salt and pepper. Toss to combine the ingredients and serve immediately.

Per Serving: Calories: 254 | Fat: 18g | Protein: 5g | Sodium: 529mg | Fiber: 5g | Carbohydrates: 19g

Kalamata Olives

Kalamata is a region in Greece that is famous for its olives and its olive oil. Kalamata olives have a distinct brown-green color and are briny and meaty.

Warm Mushroom Salad

This is a wonderful hearty winter salad. King mushrooms, used in many Mediterranean dishes, are thick and meaty. If you can't find them, use portobello mushrooms instead.

INGREDIENTS | SERVES 8

⅔ cup extra-virgin olive oil, divided

2 cups sliced cremini mushrooms

2 cups sliced king mushrooms

6 cloves garlic, smashed

2 bay leaves

1 teaspoon chopped fresh rosemary

1 teaspoon fresh thyme leaves

1 teaspoon salt, divided

½ teaspoon ground black pepper, divided

1 teaspoon Dijon mustard

2 tablespoons balsamic vinegar

1 tablespoon fresh lemon juice

4 cups salad greens, washed and dried

¼ cup pumpkin seeds

½ cup crumbled goat cheese

¼ cup Crispy Fried Onions (see sidebar)

1. Heat ⅓ cup oil in a large cast-iron pan over medium-low heat 30 seconds. Add mushrooms, garlic, bay leaves, rosemary, thyme, ½ teaspoon salt, and ¼ teaspoon pepper. Stirring occasionally, cook 20 minutes. Remove bay leaves.

2. In a small jar with a lid, place remaining oil, mustard, vinegar, lemon juice, and remaining salt and pepper. Close the jar and shake vigorously until dressing is well incorporated.

3. In a large bowl, add greens and dressing and toss to combine. Divide and plate greens, and then top with mushrooms. Sprinkle salad with pumpkin seeds, cheese, and crispy fried onions. Serve warm or at room temperature.

Per Serving: Calories: 219 | Fat: 20g | Protein: 5g | Sodium: 285mg | Fiber: 1g | Carbohydrates: 4g

Crispy Fried Onions

Crispy fried onions are tasty and easy to make. Use them as a topping for salads, potatoes, and meats. Slice a medium onion as thinly as possible. Toss the onion slices in a little cornstarch; shake off any excess. Heat ¼ cup olive oil in a pan, place the onions in the hot oil, and fry until they are golden and crispy. Sprinkle the onions with salt and allow them to cool.

Grilled Halloumi Salad

Halloumi cheese holds its shape well when heated. It's usually served grilled or fried, and it adds a wonderful chewy texture to any salad.

INGREDIENTS | SERVES 4

12 kalamata olives, pitted and
   finely chopped
¼ cup extra-virgin olive oil
2 tablespoons balsamic vinegar
1 tablespoon dried oregano
1 medium carrot, peeled and shredded
¼ small head green cabbage, shredded
1 large tomato, chopped
4 cups chopped arugula
3 cups chopped romaine
2 scallions, ends trimmed, finely sliced
1 thick slice (½ pound) halloumi cheese

1. In a small bowl, combine olives, oil, vinegar, and oregano. Mix well and set aside.

2. In a large salad bowl, combine carrot, cabbage, tomato, arugula, romaine, and scallions.

3. Preheat a gas or charcoal grill to medium-high heat. Place cheese slices on the grill and cook 1–1½ minutes per side. The cheese should be soft but still intact.

4. Cut cheese into cubes and add to salad. Pour dressing over salad and mix well. Serve immediately.

Per Serving: Calories: 362 | Fat: 33g | Protein: 13g | Sodium: 613mg | Fiber: 2g | Carbohydrates: 13g

Grilled Banana Pepper Salad

If you don't like hot peppers, this salad can be made with any type of sweet pepper.

INGREDIENTS | SERVES 6

6 medium hot banana peppers
½ cup crumbled feta cheese
2 tablespoons extra-virgin olive oil
2 tablespoons wine vinegar
1 teaspoon dried oregano

1. Preheat a gas or charcoal grill to medium-high heat. Grill peppers until soft and peels are charred, approximately 8–10 minutes. Transfer to a large bowl and cover. Cool 15 minutes then remove charred peels.

2. After seeding, spread peppers flat on a serving dish. Top with feta. Drizzle with oil and wine vinegar. Sprinkle with oregano and serve.

Per Serving: Calories: 82 | Fat: 7g | Protein: 2g | Sodium: 143mg | Fiber: 1g | Carbohydrates: 2.5g

Sliced Tomato Salad with Feta and Balsamic Vinaigrette

This dish is all about presentation, so take your time with it. Your guests will be pleased with the way it looks as well as how it tastes!

INGREDIENTS | SERVES 6

4 large tomatoes, cut into ¼"-thick slices
¼ pound crumbled feta cheese
1 teaspoon dried oregano
¼ cup extra-virgin olive oil
2 tablespoons balsamic vinegar
1 teaspoon ground black pepper

1. Arrange tomato slices in a slightly overlapping circle pattern on a large serving platter. Cover tomatoes with layer of feta cheese then sprinkle oregano over cheese.

2. In a small bowl, whisk oil and vinegar. Pour over cheese and tomatoes. Sprinkle with pepper and serve.

Per Serving: Calories: 101 | Fat: 9g | Protein: 2g | Sodium: 145mg | Fiber: 0.5g | Carbohydrates: 4g

Everything Has Its Time

Traditional eating patterns are based on seasonal availability of fresh ingredients and do not rely on canning, preservatives, and refrigeration.

Baby Greens with Chickpea Dressing

Puréed chickpeas are the base for this creamy, unusual salad dressing.

INGREDIENTS | SERVES 6

¼ cup canned chickpeas, drained and rinsed
2 cloves garlic, minced
1 small shallot, peeled and minced
¼ cup chopped parsley
½ teaspoon ground black pepper
½ cup balsamic vinegar
¼ cup extra-virgin olive oil
6 cups baby salad greens

1. In a food processor, purée chickpeas. Add garlic, shallots, parsley, pepper, and vinegar; pulse until well incorporated.

2. With processor running, slowly add oil and process until mixture emulsifies.

3. Place greens in a large salad bowl. Top with chickpea dressing and toss. Serve immediately.

Per Serving: Calories: 140 | Fat: 10g | Protein: 3g | Sodium: 33g | Fiber: 2g | Carbohydrates: 11g

Marinated Artichoke Hearts

Serve these artichoke hearts as part of an antipasto platter, in a pasta dish, or as an easy side dish.

INGREDIENTS | SERVES 6

3 large fresh artichokes

1 tablespoon lemon juice

2 tablespoons dry white wine

1½ cups vegetable broth

1 tablespoon extra-virgin olive oil

½ teaspoon dried thyme

1 teaspoon dried oregano

1 teaspoon dried marjoram

1 teaspoon dried basil

½ teaspoon ground black pepper

1. Peel stems and remove the leaves from artichokes. Discard leaves or reserve for another use. Slice artichokes in half lengthwise, then place in a large skillet. Pour in lemon juice, wine, and broth. Bring to a boil over high heat. Boil 10 minutes or until artichokes are fork tender. Remove from heat, strain, and transfer artichokes to a medium bowl.

2. Add oil, thyme, oregano, marjoram, basil, and pepper. Cool to room temperature or cover and refrigerate until ready to serve.

Per Serving: Calories: 68 | Fat: 3g | Protein: 3g | Sodium: 273mg | Fiber: 5g | Carbohydrates: 9g

Bean and Olive Salad

Olives add a Mediterranean twist to a traditional three-bean salad.

INGREDIENTS | SERVES 6

1 cup trimmed green beans

1 large red onion, peeled and thinly sliced

2 tablespoons chopped marjoram

¼ cup kalamata olives, roughly chopped

½ cup cooked red kidney beans

½ cup cooked chickpeas or cannellini beans

2 tablespoons extra-virgin olive oil

½ cup balsamic vinegar

1 teaspoon ground black pepper

1. Have large bowl of ice water ready.

2. Bring 1 quart of water to a boil in a large stockpot. Blanch the green beans in boiling water 2 minutes, then immediately drain in a colander and shock in ice-water bath. Drain thoroughly.

3. Mix together all ingredients in a large bowl. Refrigerate or serve at room temperature.

Per Serving: Calories: 118 | Fat: 5g | Protein: 3g | Sodium: 71mg | Fiber: 4g | Carbohydrates: 16g

Watermelon and Feta Salad

Purslane is a green, crisp, and slightly tangy herb popular in Greece and other countries of the Eastern Mediterranean. If you can't find purslane, substitute pea shoots or watercress.

INGREDIENTS | SERVES 4

4¼ cups cubed (¾")
   watermelon, divided
⅓ cup sliced red onions
⅓ cup purslane leaves
1½ cups cubed (¾") feta
¼ cup fresh mint leaves
1 teaspoon honey
1 tablespoon fresh lemon juice
2 tablespoons extra-virgin olive oil

1. In a large bowl, combine 4 cups watermelon, onions, purslane, and feta.

2. Place remaining watermelon, mint, honey, lemon juice, and oil in a food processor. Process until dressing is well incorporated.

3. Pour dressing over watermelon mixture and toss gently with your fingers to combine. Refrigerate or serve at room temperature.

Per Serving: Calories: 277 | Fat: 19g | Protein: 10g | Sodium: 640mg | Fiber: 2g | Carbohydrates: 19g

Grapefruit-Pomegranate Salad

This refreshing salad is a lovely way to incorporate fruit into your wintertime diet.

INGREDIENTS | SERVES 6

2 large ruby red grapefruits
1 large pomegranate
6 cups mixed baby greens
¼ cup vegetable broth
3 ounces Parmesan cheese

1. Peel grapefruits with a knife, completely removing pith (the white layer under the skin). Cut out each section with the knife, again ensuring that no pith remains. Set aside. Slice pomegranate in half and remove all arils.

2. Toss greens with broth in a large salad bowl.

3. Top with grapefruit sections and pomegranate arils. Use a vegetable peeler or sharp knife to shave Parmesan over salad.

Per Serving: Calories: 137 | Fat: 4g | Protein: 7g | Sodium: 282mg | Fiber: 4g | Carbohydrates: 19g

Creamy Feta Dressing

Spoon this dressing over fries, a baked potato, or a vegetable tray.

INGREDIENTS | SERVES 8

⅓ cup crumbled feta cheese

2 teaspoons water

¾ cup plain yogurt

2 tablespoons mayonnaise

2 tablespoons evaporated milk

1 teaspoon dried oregano

1 clove garlic, minced

2 tablespoons chopped fresh chives

⅛ teaspoon ground black pepper

1. Place feta and water in a medium bowl. Using a fork, mash into a paste.

2. Add remaining ingredients and mix until well incorporated. Keep dressing refrigerated until needed.

Per Serving: Calories: 60 | Fat: 5g | Protein: 2g | Sodium: 99mg | Fiber: 0g | Carbohydrates: 2g

Sun-Dried Tomato Vinaigrette

Use this dressing with spinach or peppery salad greens.

INGREDIENTS | SERVES 8

⅓ cup sun-dried tomatoes, packed in olive oil, rinsed and finely chopped

2 tablespoons balsamic vinegar

1 teaspoon garlic powder

1 teaspoon dried oregano

¼ teaspoon ground black pepper

½ teaspoon salt

⅓ cup extra-virgin olive oil

1. In a small bowl, whisk all ingredients until well incorporated.

2. Keep dressing refrigerated until needed.

Per Serving: Calories: 73 | Fat: 8g | Protein: 0.5g | Sodium: 160mg | Fiber: 0g | Carbohydrates: 2g

Cucumber and Dill Dressing

This dressing pairs wonderfully with salad greens, ripe tomatoes, and some peppery radish slices.

INGREDIENTS | SERVES 8

½ medium English cucumber, grated

¾ teaspoon salt, divided

½ cup plain Greek yogurt

¼ cup whole milk

2 tablespoons mayonnaise

2 teaspoons fresh lemon juice

1 scallion (white part only), ends trimmed and thinly sliced

1 clove garlic, minced

2 tablespoons chopped fresh dill

¼ teaspoon ground black pepper

1. Place cucumber and ¼ teaspoon salt in a fine-mesh strainer over a medium bowl. Strain 30 minutes. Squeeze remaining water from the cucumber.

2. Combine cucumber and remaining ingredients in a medium bowl. Stir well to incorporate the ingredients.

3. Refrigerate dressing in a tightly covered jar up to 1 week.

Per Serving: Calories: 43 | Fat: 3.5g | Protein: 1g | Sodium: 202mg | Fiber: 0g | Carbohydrates: 2g

Pomegranate Dressing

Toss this dressing with baby dandelion greens and top with crumbled feta or goat cheese. Pomegranate molasses can be found in Greek and Middle Eastern grocers.

INGREDIENTS | SERVES 8

½ cup unsweetened pomegranate juice

1 clove garlic, minced

1 cup extra-virgin olive oil

¾ teaspoon salt

⅓ teaspoon ground black pepper

1 teaspoon Dijon mustard

2 tablespoons pomegranate molasses

1. Combine all ingredients in a jar with a lid. Close the jar and shake it vigorously until ingredients are well incorporated.

2. Serve dressing at room temperature.

Per Serving: Calories: 228 | Fat: 21g | Protein: 0g | Sodium: 201mg | Fiber: 0g | Carbohydrates: 4g

Kalamata Olive Dressing

This dressing is wonderful with romaine lettuce, cherry tomatoes, and grilled halloumi cheese.

INGREDIENTS | SERVES 8

¼ cup chopped red onions

1 clove garlic, smashed

½ cup pitted kalamata olives

2 sun-dried tomatoes, packed in olive oil, rinsed and chopped

½ teaspoon dried oregano

2 tablespoons red wine vinegar

1 tablespoon balsamic vinegar

1 teaspoon Dijon mustard

½ teaspoon ground black pepper

⅔ cup extra-virgin olive oil

1. Add all ingredients to a food processor and process until well incorporated.

2. Refrigerate dressing until needed.

Per Serving: Calories: 124 | Fat: 14g | Protein: 0g | Sodium: 20mg | Fiber: 0g | Carbohydrates: 3g

CHAPTER 6

Pasta and Rice

Spaghetti with Tomato and Basil

This pasta dish tastes like summer in a bowl. Use ripe summer tomatoes and fresh basil from the garden for best results.

INGREDIENTS | SERVES 6

1 tablespoon plus 1½ teaspoons salt, divided

1 pound spaghetti

¼ cup plus 2 tablespoons extra-virgin olive oil, divided

8 cloves garlic, minced

1 (28-ounce) can whole tomatoes, hand crushed

½ teaspoon ground black pepper

1 cup sliced fresh basil leaves

1 cup grated Romano cheese, divided

Al Dente

Al dente means "to the tooth" in Italian. It refers to pasta that is cooked but not soft. The cooked pasta should be slightly firm and still hold its shape. Perfectly cooked pasta is the best vehicle for a delicious sauce.

1. Fill a large pot two-thirds with water and place over medium-high heat. Add 1 tablespoon salt and bring water to a boil. Add pasta and cook about 6–7 minutes or until al dente (follow the package's cooking times).

2. In a large skillet over medium heat, heat ¼ cup oil for 30 seconds. Add garlic and cook 2 minutes, or until fragrant. Add tomatoes (including liquid) and increase heat to medium-high. Bring to a boil, then reduce heat to medium-low. Season sauce with remaining salt and pepper and cook 10–12 minutes or until thickened.

3. Reserve ¼ cup pasta cooking water and drain pasta. Add pasta to sauce and stir to combine. If sauce is a little thin or dry, stir in reserved pasta water. Add basil and stir to combine.

4. Add ¾ cup cheese and toss to combine.

5. Serve pasta topped with remaining cheese and a drizzle of remaining oil.

Per Serving: Calories: 445 | Fat: 16g | Protein: 13g | Sodium: 2,017mg | Fiber: 4g | Carbohydrates: 63g

Linguine Carbonara

Try a new type of pasta today. The Italians have hundreds of different pasta shapes. The possibilities are endless!

INGREDIENTS | SERVES 6

1 tablespoon salt

1 pound linguine pasta

4 large egg yolks

2 teaspoons ground black pepper

1 cup grated Romano cheese, divided

¾ cup diced bacon or pancetta

3 tablespoons water

¼ cup extra-virgin olive oil

¼ cup diced red onion

2 cloves garlic, smashed

¼ cup dry white wine

Pasta Water

Adding a little of the pasta cooking water to the sauce helps the sauce thicken (because of the starches in the water). It also helps the sauce stick to the pasta.

1. Fill a large pot two-thirds with water and place it over medium-high heat. Add salt and bring the water to a boil. Add pasta and cook 6–7 minutes or until al dente (follow the package's cooking times).

2. In a small bowl, whisk egg yolks, pepper, and ¾ cup Romano. Set aside.

3. Add bacon and 3 tablespoons water to a large skillet over medium-high heat. Cook bacon until crispy but not hard. Remove bacon with a slotted spoon and set aside. Discard all but 1 tablespoon bacon fat from the skillet.

4. Add oil to skillet and heat 30 seconds over medium heat. Add onions and garlic and cook 1–2 minutes. Add wine and deglaze the pan for 2 minutes. Remove from heat and stir in reserved bacon.

5. Reserve ¼ cup pasta cooking water and drain pasta. Add pasta, pasta water, and egg mixture to the skillet. The residual heat of the hot pasta and pasta water should cook and bind the egg mixture into a thick and creamy sauce. Serve topped with remaining cheese.

Per Serving: Calories: 529 | Fat: 24g | Protein: 16g | Sodium: 1,436mg | Fiber: 3g | Carbohydrates: 58g

Penne all'Arrabbiata

This dish is zesty from the crushed red pepper and gooey from the melted mozzarella. It is a quick and easy dinner to pull together.

INGREDIENTS | SERVES 6

1 tablespoon plus 1 teaspoon salt, divided

1 pound penne rigate

¼ cup extra-virgin olive oil

1 medium onion, peeled and diced

6 cloves garlic, minced

2 cups canned whole tomatoes, hand crushed

½ teaspoon ground black pepper

1 cup grated mozzarella cheese

1 teaspoon crushed red pepper

1 cup torn fresh basil

½ cup grated Romano or Parmesan cheese

Penne Rigate

Penne rigate is a short, thick, ridged, hollow pasta. It is perfect for a thick tomato sauce because the sauce sticks to the outside ridges and fills the inside. Every bite is a burst of flavor!

1. Fill a large pot two-thirds with water and place it over medium-high heat. Add 1 tablespoon salt and bring to a boil. Add pasta and cook 8–9 minutes or until al dente (follow the package's cooking times).

2. Heat oil in a large skillet over medium heat 30 seconds. Add onions and garlic. Reduce heat to medium-low and cook 5 minutes or until onions soften. Add tomatoes (including liquid), black pepper, and remaining salt. Cook 20 minutes or until the sauce has thickened.

3. Reserve ¼ cup pasta cooking water and drain pasta. Add pasta to sauce and stir to combine. If sauce is a little thin or dry, stir in reserved pasta water. Add mozzarella, crushed red pepper, and basil. Stir until mozzarella has melted.

4. Top with grated cheese and serve.

Per Serving: Calories: 447 | Fat: 15g | Protein: 16g | Sodium: 1,727mg | Fiber: 4g | Carbohydrates: 62g

Pasta with Cherry Tomatoes, Cheese, and Basil

Use any ripe chopped tomato if you can't find cherry tomatoes.

INGREDIENTS | SERVES 8

1 tablespoon plus ½ teaspoon salt, divided

1 pound broad egg noodles

¼ cup extra-virgin olive oil

1 pint ripe cherry tomatoes, halved

¼ teaspoon ground black pepper

6 cloves garlic, minced

1 cup diced halloumi cheese

1 cup sliced fresh basil leaves

1½ cups crumbled feta cheese, divided

½ cup plain Greek yogurt

½ teaspoon crushed red pepper

Basil

The word *basil* in Greek is *basilikos*, which means king. In the Mediterranean, there's no doubt that basil is the king of herbs. There are many varieties to be found, so try as many as you can to find your favorite.

1. Fill a large pot two-thirds with water and place it over medium-high heat. Add 1 tablespoon salt and bring water to a boil. Add noodles and cook 6–7 minutes or until al dente (follow the package's cooking times).

2. In a large skillet over medium heat, add oil and heat 30 seconds. Add tomatoes, remaining salt, and black pepper. Cover the skillet and cook 5 minutes. Uncover and mash tomatoes slightly to release their juices. Add garlic and cook 10 minutes or until sauce thickens.

3. Reserve ¼ cup pasta cooking water and then drain pasta. Add pasta to sauce and stir to combine. If the sauce is a little thin or dry, stir in reserved pasta water. Stir in halloumi and basil.

4. In a medium bowl, combine 1 cup feta, yogurt, and crushed red pepper. Mash everything together with a fork. Add feta mixture to pasta and stir until sauce is creamy.

5. Top with remaining feta and serve immediately.

Per Serving: Calories: 508 | Fat: 20g | Protein: 14g | Sodium: 1,688mg | Fiber: 3g | Carbohydrates: 37g

Spaghetti with Brown Butter and Feta

Brown butter has a lovely nutty taste. This recipe can be easily doubled or tripled.

INGREDIENTS | SERVES 4

1¼ teaspoons salt, divided

½ pound spaghetti

¼ cup unsalted butter

3 tablespoons extra-virgin olive oil, divided

2 cloves garlic, smashed

2 tablespoons grated kefalotyri or Romano cheese

2 tablespoons crumbled feta cheese, divided

¼ teaspoon ground black pepper

1. Fill a large pot two-thirds with water and place it over medium-high heat. Add 1 teaspoon salt and bring water to a boil. Add pasta and cook 6–7 minutes or until al dente (follow the package's cooking times).

2. Add butter, 2 tablespoons oil, and garlic to a small skillet over medium heat. Whisk constantly until butter turns a chestnut brown color, about 1–2 minutes. Remove from heat and cool slightly. Remove and discard garlic.

3. Drain pasta. Add pasta to brown butter and stir to combine. If spaghetti appears a bit dry, add a little more oil. Add kefalotyri and 1 tablespoon feta and continue to toss until cheeses have blended in with butter. Season with remaining salt and pepper.

4. Serve pasta topped with remaining feta and drizzled with remaining 1 tablespoon oil.

Per Serving: Calories: 367 | Fat: 17g | Protein: 9g | Sodium: 836mg | Fiber: 3g | Carbohydrates: 43g

Makaronia with Tarama

Tarama is fish roe and can be found at Greek or Middle Eastern grocery stores. Makaronia in Greek is like us saying pasta—it is the whole food group; spaghetti is one type of makaronia/pasta.

INGREDIENTS | SERVES 8

1 tablespoon salt

1 pound spaghetti

⅓ cup extra-virgin olive oil

1 cup coarse bread crumbs

¼ cup finely chopped blanched almonds

1 ounce ouzo

4 tablespoons tarama (fish roe)

2 cloves garlic, minced

¼ cup chopped fresh parsley

½ cup chopped fresh scallions, ends trimmed

2 tablespoons grated lemon zest

1 teaspoon dried oregano

1 tablespoon fresh lemon juice

¼–½ teaspoon crushed red pepper

1. Fill a large pot two-thirds with water and place it over medium-high heat. Add salt and bring water to a boil. Add pasta and cook 6–7 minutes or until al dente (follow the package's cooking times).

2. Heat oil in a small skillet over medium heat 30 seconds. Add bread crumbs and almonds and cook, stirring constantly, 2 minutes until lightly browned. Add ouzo, tarama, and garlic and cook another 2 minutes or until ouzo is absorbed.

3. Remove from heat and add parsley, scallions, zest, and oregano. Drain pasta and add to skillet. Toss to combine and to coat pasta.

4. Add lemon juice and crushed red pepper to your taste and toss to combine. Serve immediately.

Per Serving: Calories: 363 | Fat: 12g | Protein: 10g | Sodium: 989mg | Fiber: 3g | Carbohydrates: 53g

Shrimp, Macaroni, and Feta

This dish combines elements of Shrimp Saganaki (see recipe in Chapter 10) with macaroni and cheese. It will be an instant classic in your home.

INGREDIENTS | SERVES 12

1 tablespoon plus ½ teaspoon salt, divided

2½ cups elbow macaroni

2 red chilies, seeded and chopped

3 cloves garlic, (2 whole, 1 minced), divided

¼ cup chopped fresh parsley

1¼ cups sliced fresh basil, divided

½ cup extra-virgin olive oil, divided

½ teaspoon honey

2 tablespoons fresh lemon juice

¼ cup unsalted butter

1 small red onion, peeled and finely chopped

1 cup sliced button mushrooms

1 teaspoon sweet paprika

6 medium ripe plum tomatoes, peeled and puréed

¼ teaspoon ground black pepper

¼ cup dry white wine

1 ounce ouzo

1 cup heavy cream or evaporated milk

1 cup crumbled feta cheese

24 medium shrimp, peeled and deveined

1 cup cubed feta cheese

1 teaspoon dried oregano

1. Fill a large pot two-thirds with water and place it over medium-high heat. Add 1 tablespoon salt and bring water to a boil. Add pasta and cook 6–7 minutes or until al dente (follow the package's cooking times).

2. Preheat broiler. Pulse chilies, whole garlic, parsley, ¼ cup of basil, ¼ cup of oil, honey, lemon juice, and ¼ teaspoon salt in a food processor until ingredients are well incorporated. Set aside.

3. In a large skillet over medium heat, heat remaining oil 30 seconds. Add butter, onions, minced garlic, mushrooms, and paprika. Cook 5 minutes or until onions are soft. Add tomatoes and season with remaining salt and pepper. Simmer 5–7 minutes. Add wine and ouzo and cook until most of the liquid has evaporated.

4. Add cream and crumbled feta and cook 3 minutes or until the sauce thickens. Drain pasta and stir into cream-tomato sauce. Add remaining basil and toss to combine.

5. Pour pasta into a medium baking dish and top with shrimp and cubed feta. Broil 5 minutes or until shrimp turn pink and cheese is melted. Drizzle with reserved parsley-basil sauce and sprinkle with oregano. Let cool 5 minutes before serving.

Per Serving: Calories: 371 | Fat: 26g | Protein: 12g | Sodium: 1,001mg | Fiber: 2g | Carbohydrates: 23g

Tomatoes

It's hard to imagine Mediterranean cuisine without tomatoes. Their bright flavor and rich color make them a staple ingredient in most dishes. The tomato came to Europe via the explorer Hernán Cortés in the 1500s after he discovered the Aztecs eating them in the New World.

Shrimp and Pasta of St. Nicholas

*This recipe can be easily doubled to serve twelve, or increased
even more for larger numbers of hungry guests.*

INGREDIENTS | SERVES 6

1 tablespoon plus ¾ teaspoon
  salt, divided

1 pound linguine

24 medium shrimp, shelled, deveined,
  and shells reserved

¼ teaspoon ground black pepper

⅓ cup extra-virgin olive oil

1 medium onion, peeled and
  finely chopped

6 cloves garlic, minced

¼ cup dry white wine

2 cups puréed canned plum tomatoes

¼ teaspoon crushed red pepper

½ cup chopped fresh parsley

¼ cup chopped fresh basil

1. Fill a large pot two-thirds with water and place it over medium-high heat. Add 1 tablespoon salt and bring water to a boil. Add pasta and cook 6–7 minutes or until al dente (follow the package's cooking times).

2. Wrap reserved shrimp shells in cheesecloth and tie it up tightly. Set aside. Season shrimp with black pepper and ¼ teaspoon salt.

3. Heat oil in a large skillet over medium-high heat 30 seconds. Add shrimp and cook 1 minute on each side or until pink. Remove shrimp from skillet, leaving oil in skillet, and reserve.

4. Reduce heat to medium and add onion, garlic, and shrimp shells. Cook 5–7 minutes or until onions are softened. Add wine and cook 5 minutes.

5. Add tomatoes, increase heat to medium-high, and bring sauce to a boil. Decrease heat to medium and cook 20 minutes or until sauce thickens. Remove shrimp shells and discard.

6. Drain pasta and add it to sauce. Toss to coat pasta with sauce. Remove skillet from heat and add cooked shrimp, crushed red pepper, parsley, remaining salt, and basil. Toss to combine the ingredients and serve immediately.

Per Serving: Calories: 445 | Fat: 14g | Protein: 16g | Sodium: 1,633mg | Fiber: 4g | Carbohydrates: 63g

Spaghetti with Mussels, Parsley, and Lemon

Try using fresh clams or shrimp in place of mussels in this dish.

INGREDIENTS | SERVES 6

¼ cup extra-virgin olive oil

8 garlic cloves, thinly sliced

3 pounds fresh mussels, cleaned and beards removed

¼ cup plus 2 tablespoons chopped parsley, divided

½ cup dry white wine

¼ cup fresh lemon juice

1 pound cooked spaghetti

1½ teaspoons grated lemon zest

½–1 teaspoon crushed red pepper

½ teaspoon salt

1. Heat oil in a large skillet over medium-high heat. Add garlic and cook 1 minute or until light brown. Add mussels and ¼ cup parsley. Cook 2 minutes while stirring. Add wine and cook another 2 minutes. Add lemon juice and cover the skillet. Cook 4–5 minutes. Uncover and discard any unopened mussels.

2. Add spaghetti, lemon zest, crushed red pepper to taste, and salt to the mussels. Toss to combine the ingredients and to coat the pasta. Sprinkle with the remaining parsley and serve immediately.

Per Serving: Calories: 417 | Fat: 15g | Protein: 31g | Sodium: 844mg | Fiber: 2g | Carbohydrates: 34g

Linguine with Tapenade

For a variation, serve this delicious tapenade on its own as you might with any sauce, or use it as a topping on toast.

INGREDIENTS | SERVES 6

1 cup oil-cured pitted olives

2 tablespoons capers, rinsed and drained

1½ tablespoons fresh rosemary leaves

1 clove garlic, smashed

2 anchovy fillets, packed in oil

½ teaspoon sugar

⅔ cup plus 2 tablespoons extra-virgin olive oil, divided

1 pound linguine, cooked

½ cup grated kasseri or sheep's milk cheese

1 tablespoon chopped fresh chives

1. Place olives, capers, rosemary, garlic, anchovies, sugar, and ⅔ cup oil into a food processor. Process until mixture is well incorporated but not smooth. The tapenade should still have texture.

2. Toss pasta with remaining oil and cheese. Arrange pasta on a serving platter and top it with tapenade and chives.

Per Serving: Calories: 648 | Fat: 36g | Protein: 16g | Sodium: 1,578mg | Fiber: 3.5g | Carbohydrates: 58g

Garidomakaronada with Ouzo and Fresh Tomato

Garidomakaronada is a compound word in Greek meaning "pasta and shrimp." The long, thick, hollow shape of bucatini allows this aromatic seafood sauce to get right into the pasta.

INGREDIENTS | SERVES 8

1 tablespoon plus ½ teaspoon salt, divided

1 pound bucatini

16 medium shrimp, shelled and deveined

½ teaspoon ground black pepper, divided

¼ cup extra-virgin olive oil

1 large onion, peeled and finely chopped

3 cloves garlic, smashed

4 large, very ripe tomatoes, peeled and puréed

1½ tablespoons tomato paste

1 ounce ouzo

½ teaspoon crushed red pepper

2 tablespoons chopped fresh parsley

Crushed Red Pepper

Crushed red pepper flakes are made from hot peppers that are dried and crushed. Most crushed red pepper flakes include the seeds, which are the hottest part of the pepper. Depending on the peppers used, some brands are hotter than others. Be careful when you first use them. Only add a little at a time to make sure the dish is not too hot for your taste. You can always add more heat, but you can't take it away.

1. Fill a large pot two-thirds with water and place it over medium-high heat. Add 1 tablespoon salt and bring water to a boil. Add pasta and cook 6–7 minutes or until al dente (follow the package's cooking times).

2. Season shrimp with ¼ teaspoon salt and ¼ teaspoon black pepper. Heat oil in a large skillet over medium-high heat 30 seconds. Add shrimp and cook 1 minute on each side or until pink. Remove shrimp from skillet, leaving the oil in the skillet, and reserve.

3. Reduce heat to medium and add onions and garlic. Cook 5 minutes or until onions soften. Add tomatoes and tomato paste. Increase heat and bring sauce to a boil. Reduce heat to medium-low and cook 15–20 minutes or until thickened. Stir in ouzo and remaining salt and black pepper. Take skillet off the heat.

4. Drain pasta and add it to sauce along with crushed red pepper and cooked shrimp. Toss to coat the pasta.

5. Sprinkle with parsley and serve immediately.

Per Serving: Calories: 309 | Fat: 8g | Protein: 11g | Sodium: 1,083mg | Fiber: 3g | Carbohydrates: 47g

Seven-Ingredient Anchovy Fusilli `SC`

This simple pasta is surprisingly rich and so easy to make. It cooks in about 45 minutes, so plan for the short cooking time in order to keep your pasta from overcooking.

INGREDIENTS | SERVES 8

16 ounces fusilli

4 (15-ounce) cans low-sodium chicken broth

2 (10-ounce) cans anchovies or clams packed in oil, chopped

¼ cup olive oil

1 clove garlic, finely chopped

¼ cup chopped parsley

1 teaspoon salt

1. Place pasta and chicken broth in a 6-quart slow cooker. Cook on high for 30 minutes, check for doneness, and cook an additional 15 minutes if needed.

2. Stir in anchovies, olive oil, and garlic. Sprinkle with parsley and salt. Remove from heat and serve.

Per Serving: Calories: 507 | Fat: 18g | Protein: 33g | Sodium: 1,677mg | Fiber: 2g | Carbohydrates: 51g

Greek-Style Rigatoni

Capers also make a good addition to this dish.

INGREDIENTS | SERVES 4

⅓ cup extra-virgin olive oil

½ pound rigatoni, cooked according to package directions and kept warm

½ pound feta cheese, cubed

¾ cup kalamata olives, pitted and chopped

10 sun-dried tomatoes, drained and sliced

1 tablespoon dried oregano

1 teaspoon ground black pepper

1. Heat oil in large sauté pan over medium heat. Add cooked pasta, feta, olives, and sun-dried tomatoes. Toss mixture to combine and cook 2–3 minutes or until cheese just starts to melt.

2. Season with oregano and pepper. Serve hot.

Per Serving: Calories: 649 | Fat: 31g | Protein: 16g | Sodium: 1,340mg | Fiber: 2.5g | Carbohydrates: 50g

Pasta Salad with Feta, Sun-Dried Tomatoes, and Spinach

Pasta salads are great for backyard entertaining, picnics, or potluck dinners. Use bow-tie pasta because it makes it easy to grab a forkful of all the ingredients with one stab.

INGREDIENTS | SERVES 8

1 tablespoon plus 1 teaspoon salt, divided

1½ cups farfalle (bow-tie pasta)

1 cup chopped baby spinach, rinsed and dried

8 sun-dried tomatoes, sliced

1 cup grated and peeled carrot

2 scallions, ends trimmed, thinly sliced

1 clove garlic, minced

1 medium dill pickle, diced

⅓ cup extra-virgin olive oil

2 tablespoons red wine vinegar

½ cup plain Greek yogurt

½ teaspoon ground black pepper

1 teaspoon chopped fresh oregano

¼ cup chopped fresh basil

1 cup diced feta cheese

¼ cup chopped fresh chives

1. Fill a large pot two-thirds with water and place it over medium-high heat. Add 1 tablespoon salt and bring water to a boil. Add pasta and cook 6–7 minutes or until al dente (follow the package's cooking times). Drain pasta in a colander and cool it under cold running water.

2. In a large bowl, combine spinach, tomatoes, carrot, scallions, garlic, and pickle. Add pasta and toss to combine.

3. In a medium bowl, whisk oil, vinegar, yogurt, remaining salt, and pepper. Add dressing to pasta and toss to combine and coat evenly. Toss in oregano, basil, and feta.

4. Sprinkle salad with chives. Refrigerate or serve at room temperature.

Per Serving: Calories: 235 | Fat: 14g | Protein: 7g | Sodium: 1,472mg | Fiber: 1.5g | Carbohydrates: 21g

Garlic and Artichoke Pasta S C

Artichoke hearts give this sauce a unique and savory flavor that is perfect for pasta or rice.

INGREDIENTS | SERVES 6

2 (14.5-ounce) cans diced tomatoes with basil, oregano, and garlic

2 (14-ounce) cans artichoke hearts, drained and quartered

6 cloves garlic, minced

½ cup heavy cream

3 cups cooked pasta

1. Pour tomatoes, artichokes, and garlic into a 4- to 5-quart slow cooker. Cook on high 3–4 hours or on low 6–8 hours.

2. Twenty minutes prior to serving, stir in cream. Serve over hot pasta.

Per Serving: Calories: 286 | Fat: 8g | Protein: 10g | Sodium: 576mg | Fiber: 8g | Carbohydrates: 40g

Can't Find Seasoned Canned Tomatoes?

If you can't find diced tomatoes with herbs and spices in your grocery store, use regular diced tomatoes and add 2 teaspoons of Italian seasoning to your sauce.

Spanish-Style Saffron Quinoa S C

This fragrant dish goes well with grilled chicken or fish and looks very festive alongside shish kebabs. Use saffron threads instead of powder, if possible.

INGREDIENTS | SERVES 8

Nonstick olive oil cooking spray

2 tablespoons olive oil

1 medium onion, peeled and thinly sliced

4 stalks celery, thinly sliced

3 medium tomatoes, chopped

4 cups water

2 teaspoons salt

¼ teaspoon cayenne pepper

1⅓ cups uncooked quinoa

½ teaspoon saffron threads

1. Spray a 4- to 5-quart slow cooker with cooking spray.

2. Heat oil in a medium skillet over medium heat. Sauté onion and celery until soft, about 5–7 minutes. Transfer to slow cooker.

3. Put tomatoes, water, salt, and cayenne pepper in slow cooker. Cover and cook on low 3–5 hours.

4. Increase heat to high and add quinoa and saffron. Cover slow cooker and allow to cook 1 hour or until quinoa is tender.

Per Serving: Calories: 151 | Fat: 5g | Protein: 5g | Sodium: 613mg | Fiber: 3g | Carbohydrates: 21g

Spanakorizo with Green Olives and Feta

Spanakorizo means "spinach with rice." This makes a great vegetarian meal.

INGREDIENTS | SERVES 8

½ cup extra-virgin olive oil

1 medium onion, peeled and diced

2 cloves garlic, minced

1 cup long-grain rice, rinsed

2 pounds fresh spinach, chopped

1½ cups vegetable stock

½ cup plus 1 tablespoon chopped fresh dill, divided

2 tablespoons fresh lemon juice

1½ teaspoons salt

½ teaspoon ground black pepper

¼ cup crumbled feta cheese

¼ cup chopped pitted green olives

1. Heat oil in a medium heavy bottomed pot over medium heat 30 seconds. Add onions and garlic and cook 5 minutes or until onions are softened.

2. Add rice and stir to coat each grain in oil. Add spinach (in batches) and stir until wilted. Add stock and ¼ cup dill. Cover and cook 20 minutes or until most of the liquid is absorbed.

3. Add lemon juice, ¼ cup dill, salt, and pepper. Fluff rice and transfer to a serving platter. Top with feta, olives, and remaining dill. Serve immediately.

Per Serving: Calories: 262 | Fat: 18g | Protein: 6g | Sodium: 636mg | Fiber: 3g | Carbohydrates: 25g

Baked Rice with Red Peppers

Slide this dish into the oven as you start cooking dinner, and you'll have a hot and savory side dish when you're ready to sit down. You can also switch out the peppers for another vegetable or mushrooms.

INGREDIENTS | SERVES 6

1 cup long-grain rice

½ cup diced red bell pepper

¼ cup extra-virgin olive oil

2½ cups hot vegetable stock

1 teaspoon salt

¼ teaspoon ground black pepper

1. Preheat oven to 400°F. In a medium casserole dish, combine rice, bell peppers, and oil. Toss to coat rice and peppers in oil.

2. Stir in stock and season with salt and black pepper.

3. Bake, uncovered, 40–45 minutes or until liquid is absorbed by rice. Serve warm.

Per Serving: Calories: 212 | Fat: 10g | Protein: 4g | Sodium: 425mg | Fiber: 0.5g | Carbohydrates: 27g

Risotto and Greens S C

This risotto makes a beautiful side dish for meat, chicken, or pork.

INGREDIENTS | SERVES 4

1 tablespoon plus 1 teaspoon olive oil, divided

1 large red onion, peeled and finely diced

½ teaspoon salt

½ teaspoon ground white pepper

1 cup dry white wine, divided

1 cup Arborio rice

2 (14.5-ounce) cans low-sodium chicken broth

2 large leeks (white and pale green parts only), chopped

1 (14.5-ounce) can cannellini beans

½ cup shredded Parmesan cheese

1 cup arugula

1. In a large skillet, heat 1 tablespoon oil over medium heat. Sauté onion until softened, about 5–8 minutes. Season with salt and pepper. Stir in 1 tablespoon wine and deglaze the pan. Add rice and cook 1 minute.

2. Grease a 4- to 5-quart slow cooker with remaining oil. Pour rice mixture into slow cooker. Add remaining wine, broth, leeks, and beans.

3. Cover and cook on high 2 hours. If risotto isn't creamy and cooked through, let it cook another 30 minutes.

4. Add cheese and arugula and stir well. Serve immediately.

Per Serving: Calories: 491 | Fat: 9g | Protein: 15g | Sodium: 632mg | Fiber: 8g | Carbohydrates: 75g

Pilafi

For presentation purposes, a Bundt cake pan or similar style mold can be used for this rice pilaf. When you unmold it on a serving platter, fill the cavity in the center with sautéed mushrooms and onions, or cubed and lightly sautéed vegetables.

INGREDIENTS | SERVES 5

5 cups vegetable stock

2 tablespoons butter

2 tablespoons extra-virgin olive oil

1 bay leaf

1 teaspoon salt

½ teaspoon ground black pepper

2 cups rice

1. In a large saucepan, add stock, butter, oil, bay leaf, salt, and pepper. Bring to a boil over high heat. Add rice, stir well, and return to boiling. Reduce heat to medium-low, cover, and simmer 20 minutes, stirring occasionally. Remove from heat and let stand 5 minutes.

2. Remove bay leaf. Spoon rice into a mold or Bundt cake pan. Let stand 5 minutes before turning pilaf out onto a serving platter.

Per Serving: Calories: 156 | Fat: 8.5g | Protein: 4g | Sodium: 501mg | Fiber: 0g | Carbohydrates: 16g

CHAPTER 7

Vegetable Main Dishes

Grilled Halloumi Sandwiches

Heat the pita bread in a microwave for 30 seconds to puff it up and help make a pocket.

INGREDIENTS | SERVES 4

¼ cup extra-virgin olive oil

½ teaspoon Dijon mustard

1 tablespoon fresh lemon juice

½ teaspoon honey

1 tablespoon chopped fresh mint

⅛ teaspoon dried oregano

½ teaspoon ground black pepper

8 slices (about ¼" thick) halloumi cheese

4 medium pita breads, warmed with the pocket open

½ cup baby spinach

¼ cup sliced red or green bell peppers

¼ cup chopped pitted kalamata olives

½ cup sliced Quick Pickled Red Onions (see sidebar)

1. Into a jar with a lid, put the oil, mustard, lemon juice, honey, mint, oregano, and black pepper. Close the jar and shake vigorously until the ingredients are well incorporated. Reserve.

2. Preheat a gas or charcoal grill to medium-high. Place cheese slices on the grill and cook 1–1½ minutes per side. The cheese should be soft, but still intact.

3. For each sandwich, insert two slices of halloumi into each pita. Stuff pocket with baby spinach, bell peppers, and olives. Top sandwiches with pickled onions and a spoonful of oil-lemon juice dressing.

Per Serving: Calories: 432 | Fat: 29g | Protein: 18g | Sodium: 612mg | Fiber: 3g | Carbohydrates: 25g

Quick Pickled Red Onions

These quick pickled red onions make a great garnish for sandwiches and salads. Combine a thinly sliced medium red onion, 1 teaspoon sugar, ½ teaspoon salt, and 1 tablespoon red wine vinegar. Allow the onions to "pickle" for about 15 minutes and then strain them. Pickled red onions can be refrigerated for 1 week.

Roasted Red Pepper and Feta Sandwiches

This is a lovely vegetarian sandwich.

INGREDIENTS | SERVES 4

4 Roasted Red Peppers (see recipe in Chapter 3)

1 teaspoon extra-virgin olive oil

¼ teaspoon salt

4 sandwich buns, lightly toasted

¾ cup crumbled feta cheese

1. Combine peppers, oil, and salt in a medium bowl. Mix well. Divide peppers over the bottoms of sandwich buns.

2. Top with feta and cap with top sandwich bun. Serve.

Per Serving: Calories: 269 | Fat: 8g | Protein: 12g | Sodium: 728mg | Fiber: 3.5g | Carbohydrates: 38g

Greek Pita

Serve these flavorful sandwiches with a green salad for a hearty lunch or casual dinner.

INGREDIENTS | SERVES 6

6 large loaves pita bread

2 medium cucumbers, peeled and diced

1 large red onion, peeled and thinly sliced

¼ cup chopped oregano

½ cup crumbled feta cheese

1 tablespoon olive oil

½ teaspoon ground black pepper

1. Cut a slit into each pita and stuff with cucumber, onion, oregano, and feta.

2. Drizzle with oil and sprinkle black pepper.

Per Serving: Calories: 161 | Fat: 5g | Protein: 5g | Sodium: 293mg | Fiber: 2g | Carbohydrates: 24g

Tomato-and-Feta Stuffed Peppers

If you're brave, use hot banana peppers. Serve these peppers with crusty bread and ouzo.

1. Preheat oven to 400°F.

2. Fill a medium pot with water and bring it to a boil over high heat. Add 1 teaspoon salt and peppers. Reduce heat to medium-low and simmer 5–6 minutes. Remove peppers with a slotted spoon. Run peppers under cold water until just cool. Pat peppers dry.

3. Place a pepper on your work surface. Leaving the top intact to act as a hinge, slice the pepper open lengthwise and carefully remove seeds. Insert enough feta cheese into the opening of the pepper to line the entire length. Insert strips of tomato along feta. Try and enclose the filling as much as possible. Repeat with the remaining peppers.

4. Place peppers in a small baking dish that will tightly hold peppers. Drizzle tops of peppers with ¼ cup oil and sprinkle with oregano and remaining salt. Cover with foil and bake 20 minutes. Remove foil and bake uncovered another 5 minutes or until most of the liquid has evaporated.

5. Drizzle remaining oil over peppers and serve hot.

Per Serving: Calories: 509 | Fat: 6g | Protein: 14g | Sodium: 1,736mg | Fiber: 6g | Carbohydrates: 20g

Artichokes à la Polita

Recipes with the term polita *refer to dishes from Constantinople/Istanbul.*

INGREDIENTS | SERVES 8

¼ cup extra-virgin olive oil

2 medium onions, sliced

4 medium potatoes, peeled and cut into thirds

3 large carrots, peeled and cut into 2" pieces

1 tablespoon tomato paste

12 medium artichokes, outer layers peeled, trimmed, halved, and chokes removed

2½ teaspoons salt

¾ teaspoon ground black pepper

1 cup peas, frozen (thawed) or fresh

½ cup chopped fresh dill

1 large lemon, cut into wedges

1. Heat oil in a large pot over medium-high heat. Stir in onions, potatoes, and carrots. Reduce heat to medium and cover. Simmer 15–20 minutes.

2. Add tomato paste, artichokes, salt, pepper, and enough water to cover. Bring to a boil, cover pot, and reduce temperature to medium. Cook 10 minutes or until artichokes are tender.

3. Gently stir in peas and dill. Take pot off the heat, and allow peas to cook 5 minutes. Serve hot with lemon wedges.

Per Serving: Calories: 334 | Fat: 7g | Protein: 15g | Sodium: 964mg | Fiber: 21g | Carbohydrates: 58g

Cauliflower Stifado with Kale and Kalamata Olives

This is a vegetarian version of stifado, a Greek dish usually made with beef. Kale is high in beta carotene, vitamin C, and calcium.

INGREDIENTS | SERVES 6

1 medium head cauliflower, leaves removed and trimmed

½ cup extra-virgin olive oil

1 medium onion, peeled and sliced

4 cloves garlic, minced

2 bay leaves

1 large red bell pepper, seeded and chopped

1½ tablespoons tomato paste

3 tablespoons chopped fresh rosemary

1 cup blanched and peeled pearl onions

6 small red potatoes, halved

3–4 cups hot vegetable stock or water

2½ teaspoons salt

¾ teaspoon ground black pepper

4 cups kale, stemmed and chopped

1 cup pitted kalamata olives

1 teaspoon dried oregano

1 tablespoon red wine vinegar

The Origins of Cauliflower

The cauliflower originally came from Cyprus, a large island in the eastern Mediterranean, and was known as Cyprus cabbage.

1. Place cauliflower on a cutting board and cut off the florets (run a small knife down and around the stalk).

2. Heat oil in a large pot over medium-high heat 30 seconds. Add cauliflower florets and cook 5 minutes or until browned. Remove cauliflower with a slotted spoon and set aside.

3. Reduce heat to medium and add onions, garlic, bay leaves, and bell pepper to the pot. Cook 5–6 minutes. Add tomato paste, rosemary, pearl onions, and potatoes. Stir and cook 1 minute.

4. Add enough stock or hot water to cover potatoes. Add salt and pepper. Cover pot and simmer 20 minutes.

5. Uncover pot, and add cauliflower and kale. Cover the pot and simmer another 10 minutes or until kale wilts. Add olives. Simmer uncovered 5 minutes or until sauce is thickened.

6. Add oregano and red wine vinegar. Shake the pot back and forth to mix. (Stirring might break up the cauliflower florets.) Remove bay leaves. Serve hot.

Per Serving: Calories: 445 | Fat: 21g | Protein: 11g | Sodium: 1,879mg | Fiber: 10g | Carbohydrates: 59g

Italian Green Beans with Potatoes

This is a great way to use up leftover baked or boiled potatoes. Switch up the walnuts in this dish with either almonds or hazelnuts.

INGREDIENTS | SERVES 6

1 tablespoon extra-virgin olive oil

1¼ pounds Italian green beans, trimmed

2 cloves garlic, minced

2 large potatoes, peeled, cooked, and diced

½ cup vegetable stock

½ teaspoon dried oregano

¼ cup chopped fresh parsley

1 teaspoon salt

½ teaspoon ground black pepper

¼ cup chopped walnuts, toasted

1. Heat oil in a large skillet over medium heat 30 seconds.

2. Add beans, garlic, potatoes, stock, oregano, parsley, salt, and pepper. Cook 8–10 minutes or until beans are tender.

3. Sprinkle walnuts over beans and serve.

Per Serving: Calories: 176 | Fat: 6g | Protein: 5g | Sodium: 436mg | Fiber: 6g | Carbohydrates: 28g

Grilled Portobello Mushrooms

Serve these giants on rolls with burger accompaniments or as a side dish for grilled steak.

INGREDIENTS | SERVES 6

6 portobello mushrooms

2 tablespoons olive oil

2 cloves garlic, minced

1 teaspoon salt

½ teaspoon ground black pepper

1. Preheat a gas or charcoal grill to medium-high heat.

2. Clean off the mushrooms with damp paper towels or a mushroom brush and scrape out the black membrane on the underside of the cap.

3. Mix oil and garlic together in a shallow dish. Dip each mushroom in the oil and place on a rack to drain. Season with salt and pepper.

4. Grill 5 minutes per side until fork tender. Serve mushrooms whole or sliced.

Per Serving: Calories: 60 | Fat: 5g | Protein: 2g | Sodium: 401mg | Fiber: 1g | Carbohydrates: 4g

Catalan Potatoes

This dish comes from Barcelona, the capital of Catalonia, a province of Spain.

INGREDIENTS | SERVES 6

½ cup extra-virgin olive oil

6 cloves garlic (3 whole and 3 minced)

1 large red onion, peeled and chopped

2 large Idaho or russet potatoes, peeled and sliced into ¼" slices

1 teaspoon salt, divided

½ teaspoon ground black pepper, divided

4 medium plum tomatoes, peeled, seeded, and diced

Cleaning a Cast-Iron Pan

Proper cleaning techniques will keep your cast-iron pan in tiptop shape for a lifetime. Never use soap or steel wool, and never put your cast-iron pan in the dishwasher! Wash your pan while it is still hot or warm with hot water and a sponge or brush. Dry the pan completely. Using a paper towel, lightly coat the inside of the pan with a little vegetable oil before storing it in a dry place.

1. Heat oil in an 8" or 9" cast-iron pan over medium heat 30 seconds. Add the 3 whole garlic cloves. Cook 8 minutes or until brown. Discard garlic cloves.

2. Add onions to the pan and cook 10–12 minutes or until lightly browned. Remove onions with a slotted spoon and reserve.

3. In the pan, layer half the potato slices over oil. Season potatoes with ½ teaspoon salt and ¼ teaspoon pepper. Top potatoes with an even layer of reserved onions, tomatoes, and remaining garlic. Top with remaining potato slices and season with remaining salt and pepper.

4. Cook 15 minutes or until bottom potato layer is browned. Flip potatoes over from the pan onto a wide plate. Using the plate, slide potatoes back into the pan bottom-side up. Press down on potatoes with a spatula.

5. Cook potatoes another 15 minutes or until the bottom layer is brown and potatoes are tender throughout. Slide potatoes from the pan onto a serving platter and serve immediately.

Per Serving: Calories: 264 | Fat: 18g | Protein: 3g | Sodium: 404mg | Fiber: 4g | Carbohydrates: 24g

Ratatouille

There are no limits to the types of vegetables that can be added to ratatouille. Get creative and experiment!

INGREDIENTS | SERVES 6

½ teaspoon olive oil

1 small eggplant, trimmed and chopped

1 small zucchini, trimmed and chopped

1 small yellow squash, trimmed and chopped

½ medium leek, trimmed, cleaned, and chopped

1 medium shallot, peeled and minced

2 cloves garlic, minced

1 medium plum tomato, diced

1 tablespoon chopped thyme

1 cup vegetable broth

¼ cup chopped kalamata olives

1 teaspoon ground black pepper

1. Heat oil in a large saucepan or Dutch oven over medium-high heat. Sauté eggplant, zucchini, yellow squash, leek, shallot, and garlic until slightly softened, about 8 minutes.

2. Add tomato, thyme, and broth. Bring to a boil, then reduce heat to low. Cover and simmer 20 minutes.

3. Add olives and pepper; cook another 5 minutes. Serve hot or at room temperature.

Per Serving: Calories: 46 | Fat: 1g | Protein: 2g | Sodium: 137mg | Fiber: 4g | Carbohydrates: 9g

Pasta with Arugula and Brie

Removing the rind from Brie is an optional step, depending on your personal preference.

INGREDIENTS | SERVES 6

6 cloves Roasted Garlic (see sidebar)

1 teaspoon salt

1¼ pounds pasta

5 ounces baby arugula

6 ounces Brie cheese, roughly chopped

1 teaspoon extra-virgin olive oil

1 teaspoon ground black pepper

Roasted Garlic

You can buy roasted garlic or make your own. To roast garlic, cut off the top of a head of garlic, drizzle it with a little olive oil, wrap the head in foil, and roast at 400°F for about 30 minutes.

1. Remove the roasted garlic from peels.

2. Fill a large pot two-thirds with water and place it over medium-high heat. Add 1 teaspoon salt and bring water to a boil. Add pasta and cook 6–7 minutes or until al dente (follow the package's cooking times). Drain the pasta.

3. Toss all ingredients together in a large bowl until arugula wilts and cheese melts slightly. Serve hot.

Per Serving: Calories: 458 | Fat: 10g | Protein: 19g | Sodium: 189mg | Fiber: 4g | Carbohydrates: 72g

Zucchini Parmesan

Use plain or preseasoned bread crumbs for this recipe. Also, try adding thin-sliced fresh basil or chopped oregano for flair and extra flavor.

INGREDIENTS | SERVES 6

1 tablespoon olive oil

2 large egg whites

1 cup skim milk

½ cup dried bread crumbs

3 medium zucchini, trimmed and cut into
    ½" slices

2 cups jarred marinara sauce

6 ounces part-skim mozzarella
    cheese, shredded

½ teaspoon ground black pepper

Parmesan

Parmesan is best known as a type of cheese, but the term *Parmesan* also loosely refers to a type of cooking—for example, Chicken Parmesan. Any type of Parmesan dish indicates the presence of some type of cheese, but not necessarily Parmesan cheese.

1. Preheat oven to 375°F. Brush a baking sheet with oil.

2. Beat egg whites and milk in a shallow dish. Place bread crumbs in another shallow dish. Dip the zucchini into the egg mixture, then into the bread crumbs. Place on baking sheet and bake 10–15 minutes, until zucchini are just fork tender.

3. Ladle enough sauce into a large casserole or baking dish to cover the bottom. Cover the sauce with a single layer of zucchini. Top with some of the cheese and pepper, then sauce again. Repeat the process until all the ingredients are used up. Bake 5–10 minutes until the cheese melts and begins to brown.

Per Serving: Calories: 251 | Fat: 12g | Protein: 13g | Sodium: 627mg | Fiber: 4g | Carbohydrates: 24g

CHAPTER 8

Beef, Pork, and Lamb

Keftedes MA

You can use a variety of ground meats to make these grilled meat patties. They're also wonderful fried in a skillet: dredge them in a little flour and fry them in extra-virgin olive oil for a delicious treat.

INGREDIENTS | SERVES 6

2 pounds lean ground beef

2 medium onions, grated

2 slices bread, soaked in water, squeezed dry, and crumbled

1 tablespoon minced garlic

2 large eggs, beaten

2 teaspoons dried oregano

2 tablespoons chopped fresh parsley

1 teaspoon chopped fresh mint

⅛ teaspoon ground cumin

2½ teaspoons salt

¾ teaspoon ground black pepper

1. In a large bowl, combine all ingredients and mix well.

2. Use your hands to form sixteen 2½" patties with the meat mixture; place them on a tray. Wrap the tray with plastic wrap and refrigerate for at least 4 hours or overnight.

3. Preheat a gas or charcoal grill to medium-high heat. Bring meat patties to room temperature before grilling. Place patties on the hot grill and cook 3–4 minutes per side. Serve immediately.

Per Serving: Calories: 278 | Fat: 9g | Protein: 35g | Sodium: 1,076mg | Fiber: 1.5g | Carbohydrates: 10g

Greek Oregano

In Greek, *oregano* means "joy of the mountain." Greek oregano has wider and fuzzier leaves than the common variety. When dried, it has an unmistakable and distinct pungent aroma. Whenever possible, use Greek oregano in your dishes.

Steak Sandwiches with Mushrooms and Cheese

Make this sandwich when you have leftover grilled beef.

INGREDIENTS | SERVES 4

2 tablespoons extra-virgin olive oil

1 clove garlic, minced

1 cup sliced cremini mushrooms

½ teaspoon salt

⅛ teaspoon ground black pepper

½ teaspoon fresh thyme leaves

½ teaspoon chopped fresh rosemary

½ cup Melitzanosalata (see recipe in Chapter 3)

4 sandwich buns

1 pound grilled flank steak, thinly sliced

½ cup grated Provolone cheese

1. Preheat oven to 450°F.

2. Heat oil in a medium skillet over medium heat 30 seconds. Add garlic, mushrooms, salt, and pepper. Cook 8–10 minutes until mushrooms are softened. Add thyme and rosemary and remove from heat. Reserve.

3. For each sandwich, spread Melitzanosalata on the bottom bun and top it with flank steak. Top steak with mushroom mixture and cheese.

4. Place sandwiches (without top bun) on a baking sheet and bake 5 minutes or until the cheese is melted.

5. Place top bun on each sandwich and serve warm.

Per Serving: Calories: 458 | Fat: 20g | Protein: 35g | Sodium: 764mg | Fiber: 1.5g | Carbohydrates: 32g

Greek-Style Flank Steak M A

Serve with Greek-Style Chimichurri sauce over this delicious steak (see recipe in Chapter 12).

INGREDIENTS | SERVES 8

¼ cup extra-virgin olive oil

8 cloves garlic, smashed

4 scallions, ends trimmed, chopped

1 tablespoon Dijon mustard

⅓ cup balsamic vinegar

2 bay leaves

2 tablespoons fresh thyme leaves

2 tablespoons fresh rosemary leaves

1 teaspoon dried oregano

1½ teaspoons salt, divided

¾ teaspoon ground black pepper, divided

1 (2-pound) flank steak

3 tablespoons vegetable oil

1. In a food processor, process olive oil, garlic, scallions, mustard, vinegar, bay leaves, thyme, rosemary, oregano, 1 teaspoon salt, and ½ teaspoon pepper until incorporated.

2. Rub steak with marinade and place in a medium baking dish. Cover and refrigerate 3 hours. Return steak to room temperature before grilling. Wipe most of the marinade off steak and season with remaining salt and pepper.

3. Preheat a gas or charcoal grill to medium-high. Brush grill surface to make sure it is thoroughly clean. When grill is ready, dip a clean tea towel in vegetable oil and wipe the grill surface with oil. Place meat on the grill and grill 4 minutes per side.

4. Let steak rest 5 minutes before serving.

Per Serving: Calories: 256 | Fat: 15g | Protein: 25g | Sodium: 530mg | Fiber: 1g | Carbohydrates: 4.5g

Cheese-Stuffed Bifteki 🅼🅰

If you can't find Greek Graviera cheese, use any other firm sheep's milk cheese.

INGREDIENTS | SERVES 8

2 pounds medium ground beef

2 medium onions, grated

3 slices of bread, soaked in water, hand squeezed and crumbled

1 tablespoon minced garlic

1 teaspoon dried oregano

1 teaspoon chopped fresh parsley

¼ teaspoon ground allspice

2 tablespoons salt

1 teaspoon ground black pepper

6 (1") cubes Graviera cheese

3 tablespoons vegetable oil

1. In a large bowl, combine all ingredients except cheese and vegetable oil and mix thoroughly.

2. Using your hands, form 12 (4" × ½") patties with ground beef mixture. Place patties on a tray, cover with plastic wrap, and refrigerate 4 hours or overnight. Allow patties to come to room temperature before grilling.

3. Take a piece of cheese and place it on the middle of a patty. Place another patty on top and press together to form one burger. Using your fingers, pinch the entire perimeter of the burger to seal.

4. Preheat a gas or charcoal grill to medium-high. Brush grill surface to make sure it is thoroughly clean. When grill is ready, dip a clean tea towel in vegetable oil and wipe the grill surface with oil. Place burgers on grill and cook 5 minutes per side.

5. Allow burgers to rest 5 minutes before serving.

Per Serving: Calories: 342 | Fat: 21g | Protein: 28g | Sodium: 2,001mg | Fiber: 1g | Carbohydrates: 10.5g

Braciola S C

Look for steaks that are approximately ⅛" thick, 8"–10" long, and 5" wide to make this Italian dish.

INGREDIENTS | SERVES 8

½ teaspoon olive oil

½ cup diced onions

2 cloves garlic, minced

1 (32-ounce) can diced tomatoes

8 stalks rapini

8 very thin-cut round steaks (about 1¼ pounds total)

4 teaspoons dried bread crumbs

4 teaspoons grated Parmesan cheese

1. Heat oil in a large nonstick skillet over medium-high heat. Sauté onions and garlic until onions are soft, about 5 minutes. Place in a 6-quart oval slow cooker. Add tomatoes and stir to combine.

2. Cut stems off rapini. Place steaks flat on a platter. Sprinkle each steak with ½ teaspoon bread crumbs and ½ teaspoon Parmesan. Place a bunch of rapini leaves on one end of each steak. Roll each steak lengthwise, so that the rapini filling is wrapped tightly. It should look like a spiral.

3. Place in large skillet seam-side down. Cook 1 minute over medium-high heat. Use tongs to carefully flip the steaks and cook the other side 1 minute.

4. Place each roll in a single layer on top of tomato sauce in slow cooker. Cook on low 1–2 hours or until steaks are cooked through.

Per Serving: Calories: 195 | Fat: 6g | Protein: 20g | Sodium: 117mg | Fiber: 5.5g | Carbohydrates: 16g

Ratatouille (Chapter 7)

Tzatziki (Chapter 3)

Basil and Pine Nut Pesto (Chapter 12)

Mussels Marinara (Chapter 10)

Greek Village Salad (Chapter 5)

Pork Souvlaki (Chapter 8)

Classic Minestrone (Chapter 4)

Hummus (Chapter 3)

Greek Roasted Potatoes (Chapter 11)

Gazpacho (Chapter 4)

Windex Cocktail (Chapter 14)

Leek and Potato Soup (Chapter 4)

Fried Calamari (Chapter 3)

Café Frappé (Chapter 14)

Arugula Salad with Figs and Goat Cheese (Chapter 5)

Spaghetti with Tomato and Basil (Chapter 6)

Oysters on the Half Shell (Chapter 10)

Grilled Octopus (Chapter 10)

Phyllo Triangles with Spanokopita Filling (Chapter 3)

Grilled Jumbo Shrimp (Chapter 10)

Strawberry and Feta Salad (Chapter 5)

Roasted Carrots with Honey and Thyme (Chapter 11)

Avgolemono Soup with Chicken and Rice
(Chapter 4)

Berries and Meringue (Chapter 13)

Short Ribs of Beef with Red Wine S C

Use your favorite dry red wine in this succulent beef dish. Serve it on polenta or mashed potatoes to absorb the rich sauce.

INGREDIENTS | SERVES 6

1½ pounds short ribs of beef, excess fat trimmed
1 tablespoon ground cumin
1 teaspoon dried thyme
½ teaspoon onion powder
½ teaspoon garlic powder
1 teaspoon salt
1 teaspoon ground black pepper
1 tablespoon olive oil
2 large red onions, chopped
12 large plum tomatoes, chopped
1 cup dry red wine
4 cups vegetable broth

1. Season ribs with cumin, thyme, onion powder, garlic powder, salt, and pepper.

2. Heat oil over medium-high heat in a Dutch oven, and sear ribs on both sides until browned, about 5 minutes per side. Place ribs in slow cooker.

3. Add onions to Dutch oven and sauté 2 minutes. Add tomatoes and sauté 1 minute more. Add wine and deglaze the pan. Reduce heat to low and let wine reduce by half, about 10 minutes.

4. Add broth and bring to a simmer. Pour wine mixture over ribs. Cover and cook on low 6–8 hours. If you want sauce to thicken up, remove cover from slow cooker and turn on high 15 minutes.

Per Serving: Calories: 325 | Fat: 11g | Protein: 28g | Sodium: 844mg | Fiber: 5.5g | Carbohydrates: 23g

Fasolakia with Veal

This all-in-one meal is great for the summer months when beans, tomatoes, and herbs are in season.

INGREDIENTS | SERVES 8

⅓ cup extra-virgin olive oil

3 medium onions, sliced

5 cloves garlic, sliced

½ cup chopped fresh parsley

¼ cup finely chopped fresh mint

½ cup chopped fresh dill

2 pounds fasolakia (runner beans), trimmed

3 large ripe tomatoes, peeled and grated

1 teaspoon salt

½ teaspoon ground black pepper

2 pounds cooked veal or beef, cut into bite-sized pieces

2 large potatoes, peeled and quartered

2–3 cups hot veal broth

1. Heat oil in a large skillet over medium-high heat 30 seconds. Add onions and cook 5 minutes or until they soften. Add garlic, parsley, mint, dill, beans, and tomatoes. Bring mixture to a boil and then reduce heat to medium-low and cook 30 minutes. Season with salt and pepper.

2. Add veal, potatoes, and enough broth just to cover the ingredients. Cook another 30 minutes or until potatoes are cooked and sauce thickens a little. Serve hot.

Per Serving: Calories: 438 | Fat: 15g | Protein: 16g | Sodium: 447mg | Fiber: 7g | Carbohydrates: 31g

Seared Veal Medallions

Try different varieties of mushrooms and olives for a different flavor.

INGREDIENTS | SERVES 6

2 tablespoons olive oil, divided

1½ pounds veal cutlets

1 teaspoon salt

1½ teaspoons ground black pepper, divided

1 pound mushrooms, sliced

6 cloves garlic, minced

4 cups torn arugula

½ cup dry red wine

½ cup beef broth

¼ cup chopped olives

1. Heat 1 tablespoon oil in a large skillet over medium-high heat. Season cutlets with salt and ½ teaspoon pepper, then sauté 1 minute per side. Remove veal from pan and keep warm.

2. Reduce heat to medium and add remaining oil. Add mushrooms, garlic, and arugula; quickly sauté 2 minutes. Add wine and cook 1 minute, then add broth. Simmer 10 minutes more.

3. Transfer mushroom-arugula mixture to a serving platter. Top with veal cutlets. Sprinkle olives and remaining pepper over the top before serving.

Per Serving: Calories: 212 | Fat: 8g | Protein: 26g | Sodium: 609mg | Fiber: 1g | Carbohydrates: 5g

Meatballs with Mushrooms

*Serve these meatballs with skewers or, for a more substantial dish, provide
rolls and let your guests make little meatball sandwiches.*

INGREDIENTS | SERVES 6

Nonstick olive oil cooking spray
1 pound lean ground beef
1 clove garlic, minced
¼ cup chopped celery
½ cup uncooked rice
½ cup dried bread crumbs
½ teaspoon sage
½ teaspoon salt
½ teaspoon ground white pepper
3 tablespoons vegetable oil, divided
½ pound mushrooms, minced
1 medium onion, peeled and minced
1 tablespoon all-purpose flour
1 cup water
1 cup tomato sauce

Rice and Slow Cooking

When making rice in a slow cooker, use converted rice (not instant) and it will come out light and fluffy. You can also add vegetables and spices to the rice for an easy meal.

1. Spray a 4- to 5-quart slow cooker with cooking spray.

2. In a large bowl, combine ground beef, garlic, celery, rice, bread crumbs, sage, salt, and pepper. Form mixture into ¾" balls.

3. Heat 2 tablespoons oil in a large skillet over medium heat. Brown meatballs on all sides, about 1 minute per side, and drain on a paper-towel-lined plate. Arrange meatballs in slow cooker.

4. Heat remaining oil in a skillet over medium-high heat. Sauté mushrooms and onion until softened, about 5 minutes. Add flour to mushroom mixture and stir to thicken. Add water and tomato sauce and mix until smooth.

5. Pour tomato and mushroom mixture over meatballs.

6. Cover and cook on low 3–4 hours.

Per Serving: Calories: 369 | Fat: 20g | Protein: 20g | Sodium: 533mg | Fiber: 2g | Carbohydrates: 26g

Paprika Meatballs SC

These meatballs can be served with skewers as a finger food or over pasta
as a main dish. They are excellent with fresh angel hair pasta.

INGREDIENTS | SERVES 12

Nonstick olive oil cooking spray
1 pound ground veal
1 pound ground pork
1 clove garlic, minced
¼ pound shredded mozzarella cheese
3 large eggs
1 tablespoon paprika
1 teaspoon salt
1 cup dried bread crumbs
½ cup 2% milk
2 tablespoons vegetable oil
2 large plum tomatoes, diced
1 cup tomato sauce

Pasta and Slow Cooking

Pasta is a great addition to slow-cooked meals, but it shouldn't be added at the beginning of cooking. Add uncooked pasta to the slow cooker about an hour before serving.

1. Spray a 4- to 5-quart slow cooker with cooking spray.

2. Combine veal, pork, garlic, and cheese in a large bowl with eggs, paprika, salt, bread crumbs, and milk; mix well. Form mixture into ¾" balls.

3. Heat oil in a large skillet over medium heat. Brown meatballs on all sides, about 1 minute per side, and drain on a paper-towel-lined plate. Arrange meatballs in slow cooker.

4. Pour tomatoes and tomato sauce over meatballs in slow cooker.

5. Cover and cook on low 3–4 hours.

Per Serving: Calories: 273 | Fat: 17g | Protein: 19g | Sodium: 483mg | Fiber: 1g | Carbohydrates: 10g

Osso Bucco SC

Osso bucco is an extremely inexpensive yet chic dish to make. The slow cooker takes a lot of the work out of making this classic dish.

INGREDIENTS | SERVES 12

1 cup all-purpose flour
1 teaspoon ground black pepper
6 pounds veal shanks (12 shanks)
1 tablespoon olive oil
1 tablespoon butter
2 cups chopped onion
8 cloves garlic, minced
2 anchovies
2 tablespoons minced rosemary
2 tablespoons minced thyme
6 cups beef broth

Soaking and the Slow Cooker

If there is food stuck inside your slow cooker's insert, don't be tempted to soak it in the sink overnight. If your slow cooker insert has an unglazed bottom, it will absorb the water, which may lead to cracking. Instead, place the slow cooker on the counter and use a pitcher to fill the insert with water. Then turn the slow cooker to low and let it cook for a few hours. The heated water will loosen the stuck food and make cleanup easy.

1. In a shallow bowl, mix together flour and pepper. Dredge veal shanks in flour. Set aside.

2. Heat oil in a large nonstick skillet over medium-high heat. Brown veal shanks on all sides, about 5 minutes per side. Drain off all grease. Drain veal on paper-towel-lined plates, and then place shanks in a 6- to 6½-quart slow cooker.

3. Heat butter in a large skillet over medium-high heat. Sauté onion, garlic, and anchovies 3 minutes. Add rosemary, thyme, and broth. Bring to a boil. Boil 5–8 minutes or until mixture starts to reduce. Pour over veal shanks in slow cooker. Cook on low 9 hours.

4. Skim off any fat that has risen to the top. Divide shanks and drizzle each with ¼ cup sauce.

Per Serving: Calories: 334 | Fat: 10g | Protein: 46g | Sodium: 589mg | Fiber: 1g | Carbohydrates: 12g

Slow-Cooked Pork Chops in Wine

Garlic mashed potatoes and some sautéed mushrooms are a great way to round out this dish.

INGREDIENTS | SERVES 4

¼ cup all-purpose flour
1½ teaspoons salt
½ teaspoon ground black pepper
2 teaspoons sweet paprika
4 bone-in pork chops
¼ cup extra-virgin olive oil
½ cup dry white wine
1 cup chicken or vegetable stock
2 bay leaves
8 large green olives, pitted and chopped
1 tablespoon fresh lemon juice
1 tablespoon fresh thyme leaves

1. Combine flour, salt, pepper, and paprika in a medium bowl and stir to combine. Dredge pork chops in flour mixture and set aside.

2. Heat oil in a large skillet over medium-high heat 30 seconds. Add pork chops and brown 2–3 minutes per side. Remove pork chops from skillet and keep warm.

3. Add wine, stock, and bay leaves to the skillet. Stir and cook sauce 2–3 minutes, scraping up brown bits from the bottom of the pan. Return pork chops to the skillet. Cover skillet and reduce heat to medium-low. Cook 30 minutes or until pork is tender and sauce has reduced by half.

4. Add olives, lemon juice, and thyme.

5. Remove bay leaves and serve.

Per Serving: Calories: 392 | Fat: 21g | Protein: 33g | Sodium: 1,133mg | Fiber: 1g | Carbohydrates: 11g

Italian Pork with Cannellini Beans

This incredibly simple one-dish meal is packed with flavor.

INGREDIENTS | SERVES 4

1½ pounds pork loin

1 (28-ounce) can crushed tomatoes

1 medium onion, peeled and minced

2 tablespoons capers

1 head roasted garlic

1 (15-ounce) can cannellini beans, drained and rinsed

2 teaspoons Italian seasoning

1. Place pork loin into a 4- to 5-quart slow cooker.

2. Add tomatoes, onion, and capers. Squeeze roasted garlic out of skins and place garlic in slow cooker. Cook on low 7–8 hours.

3. One hour before serving, add cannellini beans and Italian seasoning.

Per Serving: Calories: 615 | Fat: 7g | Protein: 62g | Sodium: 239mg | Fiber: 23g | Carbohydrates: 77g

Pork Roast with Prunes SC

Pork pairs wonderfully with fruit, and this recipe is no exception. The prunes add richness to the pork. This is a perfect autumn dish.

INGREDIENTS | SERVES 6

1½ pounds lean pork roast, excess fat removed

1 medium onion, peeled and diced

2 cloves garlic, minced

¾ cup pitted prunes

½ cup water

½ teaspoon ground black pepper

¼ teaspoon salt

⅛ teaspoon nutmeg

⅛ teaspoon cinnamon

Place all ingredients into a 4- to 5-quart slow cooker. Cook on low 8 hours.

Per Serving: Calories: 202 | Fat: 4g | Protein: 25g | Sodium: 155mg | Fiber: 2g | Carbohydrates: 15g

Pork Souvlaki MA

Try this marinade with other meats, such as beef shoulder or lamb shoulder.

INGREDIENTS | SERVES 8

1 large onion, peeled and grated

3 cloves garlic, minced

2 teaspoons salt

¾ teaspoon ground black pepper

¼ cup plus 3 tablespoons vegetable oil, divided

4 teaspoons dried oregano, divided

2 pounds boneless pork butt, fat trimmed and cut into 1" cubes

2 large lemons, cut into wedges

Soaking Wooden Skewers

When using wooden skewers for grilling, always soak them in water for 2 hours before spearing the food. Soaking the skewers prevents them from burning when placed on the grill.

1. In a large bowl, whisk onion, garlic, salt, pepper, ¼ cup oil, and 2 teaspoons oregano. Add pork and toss to coat. Refrigerate pork at least 5 hours or overnight. Bring pork to room temperature before grilling.

2. Put meat onto wooden or metal skewers. Add 4 pieces of pork per skewer.

3. Preheat a gas or charcoal grill to medium-high. Brush grill surface to make sure it is thoroughly clean. When grill is ready, dip a clean tea towel in the remaining oil and wipe the grill surface with oil. Put pork on the grill and cook 3–4 minutes per side or until the pork is cooked through.

4. Sprinkle pork with the remaining 2 teaspoons oregano and serve it with lemon wedges.

Per Serving: Calories: 220 | Fat: 11g | Protein: 26g | Sodium: 646mg | Fiber: 1g | Carbohydrates: 5g

Caper Pork SC

Here is your opportunity to use capers in your cooking. The capers in this recipe give the pork a refreshing zing.

INGREDIENTS | SERVES 8

Nonstick olive oil spray

2 tablespoons olive oil

2 pounds pork loin, cut into serving-sized pieces

1 medium onion, peeled and sliced

4 stalks celery, sliced

2 medium carrots, peeled and sliced

3 cloves garlic, minced

1 cup tomato sauce

6 black olives, pitted and quartered

¼ cup dry white wine

1 tablespoon capers

The Right Olives

Just say no to pimiento-stuffed green olives. Many grocery stores now have olive bars with a wide variety of olives. Try the giant black olives and the small wrinkled ones. You might discover varieties of olives that you didn't even know existed. Once you taste them, chances are you'll forsake the pimiento-stuffed versions in jars and use those other varieties in your cooking instead.

1. Spray a 4- to 5-quart slow cooker with cooking spray.

2. Heat oil in a large skillet over medium-high heat. Sauté pork until lightly browned, about 5 minutes per side. Remove pork from pan and place in prepared slow cooker, leaving meat juices in the pan.

3. In the same skillet, sauté onion, celery, carrots, and garlic over high heat 5 minutes. Transfer vegetable mixture to slow cooker. Pour tomato sauce over vegetables and pork. Cover and cook on low 6–8 hours.

4. Half an hour before serving, add olives, wine, and capers to slow cooker.

Per Serving: Calories: 234 | Fat: 11g | Protein: 25g | Sodium: 284mg | Fiber: 1.5g | Carbohydrates: 5.5g

Fennel Chops   SC

These chops are very flavorful. To complement them, all you need is a
simple side of white rice or some fresh homemade bread.

INGREDIENTS | SERVES 6

Nonstick olive oil cooking spray
2 cloves garlic
½ teaspoon salt
6 (6-ounce) pork chops
2 tablespoons olive oil
1 tablespoon fennel seed
1 cup white wine

1. Spray a 4- to 5-quart slow cooker with cooking spray. Crush garlic and salt into a paste; rub paste over chops.

2. Heat oil in a large skillet over medium-high heat. Sauté chops until lightly browned, about 5 minutes per side. Put chops, pan drippings, fennel seed, and white wine into slow cooker.

3. Cover and cook on low 3–4 hours.

Per Serving: Calories: 293 | Fat: 11g | Protein: 36g | Sodium: 298mg | Fiber: 0.5g | Carbohydrates: 2g

Pork Chops in Wine

Though boneless center-cut pork chops can be used in this recipe, it is recommended
that you use chops with the bone in for optimum flavor and tenderness.

INGREDIENTS | SERVES 4

½ cup extra-virgin olive oil, divided
4 thick-cut pork chops
1 cup white wine
½ cup hot water
1 tablespoon dried oregano
1 teaspoon salt
½ teaspoon ground black pepper

1. Heat 2 tablespoons oil in a large skillet over medium-high heat. Brown pork chops 3 minutes per side.

2. Pour remaining oil in a large frying pan with deep sides over medium-high heat. Cook pork chops 3–4 minutes per side. Add wine and bring to a boil. Reduce heat to medium and simmer 10 minutes, turning chops once.

3. Add hot water to pan and increase heat to medium-high. Bring to a boil and cook until sauce is thickened, about 5 minutes. Sprinkle with oregano, salt, and pepper and serve immediately.

Per Serving: Calories: 403 | Fat: 37g | Protein: 16g | Sodium: 27mg | Fiber: 0g | Carbohydrates: 1g

Sautéed Pork Medallions and Potatoes

Use a variety of your favorite olives to add your own distinctive touch to this recipe.

INGREDIENTS | SERVES 6

1½ tablespoons olive oil

1½ pounds pork tenderloin, sliced into thin medallions

2 tablespoons chopped oregano, divided

4 cloves garlic, minced

2 pounds russet potatoes, thinly sliced

½ teaspoon ground black pepper

2 tablespoons minced black olives

1. Heat oil in a large skillet over medium heat. Add pork, 1 tablespoon oregano, and garlic. Top with potatoes, pepper, and remaining oregano.

2. Reduce heat to medium-low, cover, and cook approximately 20 minutes.

3. Flip potatoes and pork and cook, uncovered, 10 more minutes. Invert onto a serving platter. Top with olives before serving.

Per Serving: Calories: 198 | Fat: 5g | Protein: 11g | Sodium: 52mg | Fiber: 3g | Carbohydrates: 29g

Lamb with Garlic, Lemon, and Rosemary 🆂🄲

You can use the spice rub in this recipe as a marinade by applying it to the leg of lamb several hours (or up to one full day) before cooking. The red wine in this dish can be replaced with chicken or beef stock.

INGREDIENTS | SERVES 4

4 cloves garlic, crushed

1 tablespoon chopped rosemary

1 tablespoon olive oil

½ teaspoon salt

1 teaspoon ground black pepper

1 (3-pound) leg of lamb

Nonstick olive oil cooking spray

1 large lemon, cut into ¼" slices

½ cup red wine

1. In a small bowl, mix together garlic, rosemary, olive oil, salt, and pepper. Rub this mixture onto lamb.

2. Spray a 4- to 5-quart slow cooker with cooking spray. Place a few lemon slices in the bottom of slow cooker. Place spice-rubbed lamb on top of lemon slices.

3. Add remaining lemon slices on top of lamb. Pour wine around lamb.

4. Cook on low 8–10 hours or on high 4–6 hours.

Per Serving: Calories: 733 | Fat: 48g | Protein: 62g | Sodium: 487mg | Fiber: 0g | Carbohydrates: 1.5g

Zucchini and Sausage Casserole S C

Serve this casserole on a bed of mixed greens with a fruit salad on the side.

INGREDIENTS | SERVES 6

1 pound mild pork sausage, casings removed

Nonstick olive oil cooking spray

1¼ cups grated Parmesan cheese

½ teaspoon salt

½ teaspoon ground black pepper

2 teaspoons Greek seasoning or 1 teaspoon dried mint, ½ teaspoon dried oregano, and ½ teaspoon basil

2 large eggs, beaten

1 cup whole milk

3 medium zucchini, trimmed and sliced into ½" rounds

1 small onion, peeled and sliced

1. In a large skillet, brown sausage over medium heat about 10 minutes until no longer pink. Drain fat from skillet and set sausage aside.

2. Grease a 4- to 5-quart slow cooker with cooking spray. In a large bowl, whisk together cheese, salt, pepper, and Greek seasoning.

3. In another bowl, whisk together eggs and milk.

4. Place ⅓ of zucchini over the bottom of the slow cooker. Add ⅓ of onion over the zucchini. Add ⅓ of cooked sausage over the onion. Add ⅓ of milk-egg mixture over the sausage. Lastly add ⅓ of cheese mixture over everything. Repeat layers two more times, ending with cheese mixture.

5. Cover, vent lid with a chopstick, and cook on low 6 hours or on high 3 hours. Cut into squares to serve.

Per Serving: Calories: 255 | Fat: 12g | Protein: 29g | Sodium: 600mg | Fiber: 1g | Carbohydrates: 7g

Greek-Style Meatballs and Artichokes

Mediterranean flavors abound in this dish. Serve it with an orzo pilaf.

INGREDIENTS | SERVES 10

2 thin slices white sandwich bread
½ cup 1% milk
2¾ pounds lean ground pork
2 cloves garlic, minced
1 large egg
½ teaspoon grated lemon zest
¼ teaspoon ground black pepper
16 ounces frozen artichoke hearts, defrosted
3 tablespoons lemon juice
2 cups low-sodium chicken broth
¾ cup frozen chopped spinach, defrosted
⅓ cup sliced Greek olives
1 tablespoon minced oregano

1. Preheat oven to 350°F.

2. Place bread and milk in a shallow saucepan. Cook over low heat until milk is absorbed, about 1 minute. Transfer to a large bowl and add pork, garlic, egg, zest, and pepper. Mix until all ingredients are evenly distributed. Roll into 1" balls.

3. Line two baking sheets with parchment paper. Place meatballs in a single layer on baking sheets. Bake 15 minutes and then drain on paper-towel-lined plates.

4. Add meatballs to a 6- to 6½-quart slow cooker. Add remaining ingredients.

5. Cook on low 6–8 hours.

Per Serving: Calories: 399 | Fat: 28g | Protein: 2g | Sodium: 496mg | Fiber: 2.5g | Carbohydrates: 10g

Spetsofai

This is a one-pan dish of spicy sausages, onions, peppers, and tomatoes. Pick your favorite sausage and enjoy this spetsofai with crusty bread and a dry red wine.

INGREDIENTS | SERVES 8

¼ cup extra-virgin olive oil, divided

4 (5") fresh pork sausages

4 medium hot banana peppers, cored and skins pierced

2 large red or yellow bell peppers, seeded and sliced

2 medium onions, sliced

4 cloves garlic, minced

2 large ripe tomatoes, peeled and grated

½ teaspoon salt

½ teaspoon ground black pepper

2 teaspoons dry oregano

1. Heat 2 tablespoons oil in a large skillet over medium-high heat 30 seconds. Add sausages and brown 2–3 minutes on each side. Remove sausages from the skillet and reserve.

2. Add banana peppers and fry on all sides until they are just brown, about 1–1½ minutes per side. Remove banana peppers and set aside. Slice peppers.

3. Add bell peppers, onions, garlic, and tomatoes. Bring mixture to a boil and then reduce heat to medium-low. Season with salt and black pepper. Return sausages and banana peppers to the skillet. Cover and cook 15–20 minutes or until sauce thickens.

4. Uncover skillet and add oregano. Drizzle remaining oil over sausage mixture. Serve hot.

Per Serving: Calories: 156 | Fat: 12g | Protein: 4.5g | Sodium: 265mg | Fiber: 3g | Carbohydrates: 10g

Lemon Verbena Rack of Lamb MA

Lamb works wonderfully with lemon verbena, but you can always use lemon thyme in a pinch. Roasted potatoes are a wonderful side for this easy rack of lamb dish.

INGREDIENTS | SERVES 4

2 (2-pound) racks lamb, silver skin removed and tied

¼ cup extra-virgin olive oil

2 cloves garlic, crushed

1 tablespoon Dijon mustard

1 teaspoon sweet paprika

1 tablespoon honey

2 teaspoons grated lemon zest

2 tablespoons chopped fresh parsley

2 tablespoons lemon verbena leaves

2 teaspoons fresh thyme leaves

3 teaspoons salt

1 teaspoon ground black pepper

Ask the Butcher

Ask your butcher to trim the rack of lamb and remove its silver skin. He or she will then tie the lamb into a crown rack, which will save you some preparation time.

1. Place lamb in a medium baking dish. In a food processor, pulse oil, garlic, mustard, paprika, honey, zest, parsley, lemon verbena, and thyme until well incorporated. Pour marinade over lamb and rub it all over to coat. Cover and marinate 1 hour at room temperature. Season lamb with salt and pepper.

2. Preheat broiler. Place lamb on a baking tray lined with parchment paper and roast under the broiler 5 minutes.

3. Set oven temperature to 450°F and roast lamb 25 minutes, or until internal temperature reads 135°F. If you prefer the meat well done, roast lamb a few more minutes.

4. Tent lamb with foil and let it rest 5 minutes before serving.

Per Serving: Calories: 348 | Fat: 18g | Protein: 20g | Sodium: 1,983mg | Fiber: 1g | Carbohydrates: 6g

Tangy Maple-Mustard Lamb   MA

Serve this lamb with a side of grilled vegetables and roasted potatoes or rice pilaf.

INGREDIENTS | SERVES 6

3 pounds lamb chops
¼ cup extra-virgin olive oil
2 tablespoons chopped fresh rosemary
2 cloves garlic, minced
1 teaspoon ground black pepper
1 tablespoon Dijon mustard
¼ cup maple syrup
1 teaspoon orange zest
2 teaspoons salt
3 tablespoons vegetable oil
1 large lemon, cut into wedges

1. Put lamb chops in a medium baking dish.

2. In a medium bowl, whisk oil, rosemary, garlic, pepper, mustard, maple syrup, and orange zest. Reserve ⅓ cup and set aside. Pour remaining marinade over lamb and rub it all over to coat. Cover and marinate 1 hour at room temperature or refrigerate overnight. Remove lamb from marinade and discard marinade. Bring lamb to room temperature if it was refrigerated. Season with salt.

3. Preheat a gas or charcoal grill to medium-high. Brush grill surface to make sure it is thoroughly clean. When grill is ready, dip a clean tea towel in vegetable oil and wipe the grill's surface with oil. Place lamb on the grill, and grill it 3–4 minutes per side for medium rare or 4 minutes per side for medium. Brush reserved marinade on the lamb chops and let them rest 5 minutes.

4. Serve lamb with lemon wedges.

Per Serving: Calories: 542 | Fat: 25g | Protein: 45g | Sodium: 999mg | Fiber: 1g | Carbohydrates: 11g

Grilled Lamb Chops MA

Serve these chops with Politiki Cabbage Salad (see recipe in Chapter 5).

INGREDIENTS | SERVES 4

½ cup extra-virgin olive oil

3 cloves garlic, minced

1 teaspoon Dijon mustard

2 tablespoons chopped fresh parsley

1 tablespoon fresh thyme leaves

1 tablespoon fresh lemon juice

2 teaspoons ground black pepper

2½ teaspoons salt

2 teaspoons dried oregano, divided

2½ pounds lamb chops

3 tablespoons vegetable oil

1 large lemon, cut into wedges

1. In a small bowl, thoroughly whisk olive oil, garlic, mustard, parsley, thyme, lemon juice, pepper, salt, and 1 teaspoon oregano. Reserve one third of the marinade.

2. Place lamb in a medium baking dish and top with remaining marinade. Rub lamb to coat it in the marinade. Cover and refrigerate 2 hours. Return lamb to room temperature before grilling.

3. Preheat a gas or charcoal grill to medium-high heat. Brush grill surface to make sure it is clean. When grill is ready, dip a clean tea towel in the vegetable oil and wipe the grill surface with the oil. Place lamb on the grill and cook 3–4 minutes per side for medium-rare and 4 minutes per side for medium. Brush reserved marinade on lamb and let the chops rest 5 minutes.

4. Sprinkle chops with the remaining oregano and serve with lemon wedges.

Per Serving: Calories: 793 | Fat: 46g | Protein: 57g | Sodium: 1,719mg | Fiber: 1g | Carbohydrates: 4g

Ginger Tomato Lamb SC

You can substitute beef or pork for lamb in this recipe if you wish. Serve with triangles of fresh pita bread.

INGREDIENTS | SERVES 6

Nonstick olive oil cooking spray
2 tablespoons butter
2 pounds lamb, cubed
1 medium onion, peeled and chopped
1 clove garlic, minced
3 tablespoons all-purpose flour
1½ tablespoons curry powder
2 large tomatoes, chopped
1" piece gingerroot, peeled and grated
1 teaspoon salt
¼ cup water

1. Spray a 4- to 5-quart slow cooker with cooking spray.

2. Heat butter in a large skillet over medium heat. Sauté lamb until slightly browned, about 8 minutes. Transfer meat to slow cooker; set aside pan with juices.

3. Add onion and garlic to pan used for lamb and sauté over medium heat until onion is tender, about 10 minutes. Stir in flour and curry powder. Continue cooking until thickened, about 5 minutes. Add onion mixture to slow cooker.

4. Add tomatoes, ginger, salt, and water to slow cooker.

5. Cover and cook on low 4–5 hours.

Per Serving: Calories: 317 | Fat: 17g | Protein: 30g | Sodium: 532mg | Fiber: 2g | Carbohydrates: 8g

Poultry

Chicken Souvlaki MA

*These chicken skewers are traditionally served with lightly grilled
pita bread and Tzatziki (see recipe in Chapter 3).*

(see recipe in Chapter 3)

INGREDIENTS | SERVES 6

2 pounds boneless, skinless chicken
thighs, cut into 1" cubes

⅓ cup extra-virgin olive oil

2 medium onions, grated

4 cloves garlic, minced

2 tablespoons grated lemon zest

1 teaspoon dried oregano

1 teaspoon chopped fresh
rosemary leaves

2 teaspoons salt

1 teaspoon ground black pepper

2 tablespoons fresh lemon juice

1. In a large bowl, combine chicken, oil, onions, garlic, lemon zest, oregano, rosemary, salt, and pepper. Toss to coat. Cover bowl with plastic wrap and refrigerate 8 hours or overnight. Take chicken out of the refrigerator 30 minutes before skewering.

2. Preheat a gas or charcoal grill to medium-high. Put chicken onto wooden or metal skewers; each skewer should hold 4 pieces.

3. Place skewers on grill and grill 3–4 minutes per side or until chicken is no longer pink inside.

4. Drizzle lemon juice over skewers and serve.

Per Serving: Calories: 306 | Fat: 18g | Protein: 30g | Sodium: 918mg | Fiber: 1g | Carbohydrates: 5g

Grape-Leaf Chicken Stuffed with Feta

These moist chicken breasts can be served with a side of couscous.

INGREDIENTS | SERVES 4

½ cup crumbled feta cheese

2 scallions, ends trimmed, finely chopped

4 sun-dried tomatoes, finely chopped

1 tablespoon chopped fresh lemon verbena or lemon thyme

¾ teaspoon ground black pepper

4 boneless, skinless chicken breasts

1½ teaspoons salt

8–12 large jarred grape leaves, rinsed and stems removed

¼ cup extra-virgin olive oil

Grape Leaves

Tender grape leaves, when wrapped around chicken breasts, act like a second skin and keep the chicken moist.

1. Preheat oven to 375°F. Line a baking sheet with parchment paper.

2. In a medium bowl, combine feta, scallions, tomatoes, lemon verbena, and pepper. Mash with a fork and set aside.

3. Using a sharp knife, cut a slit 3" long in the middle of the thickest part of a chicken breast. The slit should penetrate two-thirds of the way into the chicken breast to create a pocket. Stuff one-fourth of the feta filling into the pocket. Secure opening with toothpicks. Repeat with remaining chicken breasts. Season chicken with salt.

4. Place 2 or 3 grape leaves on a work surface and place a chicken breast on top. Wrap leaves around chicken and set seam-side down on the baking sheet. Brush wrapped chicken on both sides with oil. Repeat with remaining chicken.

5. Bake 20–25 minutes. Let chicken rest 5 minutes before slicing each breast and serving.

Per Serving: Calories: 446 | Fat: 24g | Protein: 53g | Sodium: 1,410mg | Fiber: 1g | Carbohydrates: 2g

Skillet Chicken Parmesan

This crowd-pleasing weeknight meal is easy to prepare in one skillet. Serve it with a green salad.

INGREDIENTS | SERVES 4

⅔ cup cornmeal

⅓ cup all-purpose flour

1 teaspoon dried oregano

1 teaspoon finely chopped fresh basil

1 teaspoon finely chopped
fresh rosemary

4 (6-ounce) boneless, skinless chicken
breasts or thighs

5 tablespoons extra-virgin olive
oil, divided

1 teaspoon salt, divided

½ teaspoon ground black
pepper, divided

1 medium onion, peeled and diced

6 cloves garlic, minced

3 cups canned whole tomatoes,
hand crushed

¼ cup dry white wine

1 cup roughly chopped fresh basil

2 cups grated mozzarella cheese

1. In a large bowl, combine cornmeal, flour, oregano, finely chopped basil, and rosemary. Set aside.

2. Using a heavy pot or kitchen mallet, pound chicken to ½" thickness. Cut chicken pieces in half. Brush pieces with 2 tablespoons oil and season with ½ teaspoon salt and ¼ teaspoon pepper. Dredge chicken in reserved cornmeal-flour mixture.

3. Heat 2 tablespoons oil in a large skillet over medium-high heat 30 seconds. Add chicken (in batches) and fry 2–3 minutes per side or until browned. Place chicken on a tray lined with paper towels to soak up excess oil. Discard oil used for frying and wipe skillet clean.

4. Heat remaining oil in skillet over medium heat 30 seconds. Add onions and garlic and cook 5–6 minutes. Add tomatoes and wine. Increase heat to medium-high and bring sauce to a boil then reduce heat to medium-low. Season with remaining salt and pepper. Nestle chicken into the sauce. Cover the skillet and cook 30 minutes or until sauce has thickened and chicken is tender.

5. Stir in roughly chopped basil and top sauce with cheese. Cover skillet and let cheese melt 2 minutes. Serve warm.

Per Serving: Calories: 773 | Fat: 36g | Protein: 67g | Sodium: 1,477mg | Fiber: 4g | Carbohydrates: 40g

Chianti Chicken

If you can't find lemon verbena, use lemon thyme or a combination of lemon zest and regular thyme. Serve this dish with some couscous and mushrooms.

INGREDIENTS | SERVES 4

3 cloves garlic, minced

2 tablespoons finely chopped lemon verbena or lemon thyme

2 tablespoons finely chopped fresh parsley

2¼ teaspoons salt, divided

5 tablespoons extra-virgin olive oil, divided

4 bone-in chicken quarters (legs and thighs)

¾ teaspoon ground black pepper

2 tablespoons unsalted butter, divided

2 cups red grapes (in clusters)

1 medium red onion, peeled and sliced

1 cup Chianti red wine

1 cup chicken or vegetable stock

Chianti

Chianti is a wine-growing region in Tuscany (near Florence) Italy. Its gentle rolling hills contain a mix of olive groves and vineyards.

1. Preheat oven to 400°F.

2. In a small bowl, whisk garlic, lemon verbena, parsley, ¼ teaspoon salt, and 2 tablespoons oil.

3. Season chicken with remaining salt and pepper. Place your finger under the skin of a chicken thigh and loosen it by moving your finger back and forth to create a pocket. Spread ¼ of garlic-herb mixture into pocket. Repeat the process with remaining chicken quarters.

4. Heat remaining oil and 1 tablespoon butter in a large oven-safe pot over medium-high heat 30 seconds. Add chicken quarters and brown 3–4 minutes per side.

5. Top chicken with grapes. Transfer pot to oven and roast the chicken 20–30 minutes or until internal temperature reaches 180°F. Remove chicken and grapes from the pot and keep them warm. Remove excess fat from the pot.

6. Return pot to the stovetop over medium heat, add onions, and cook 3–4 minutes. Add wine and stock and increase heat to medium-high. Bring mixture to a boil, then reduce heat to medium-low. Cook sauce until it thickens, about 30 minutes. Remove from heat and stir in remaining butter.

7. To serve, put some of the sauce on a plate and top with chicken and grapes. Serve with extra sauce on the side.

Per Serving: Calories: 612 | Fat: 30g | Protein: 47g | Sodium: 1,612mg | Fiber: 1g | Carbohydrates: 21g

Chicken Breasts with Spinach and Feta

Spinach and feta is a classic Greek combination that pairs well with chicken, wine, and cream.

INGREDIENTS | SERVES 4

½ cup frozen spinach, thawed, excess water squeezed out

4 tablespoons chopped fresh chives

4 tablespoons chopped fresh dill

½ cup crumbled feta cheese

⅓ cup ricotta cheese

4 (6-ounce) boneless, skinless chicken breasts

1½ teaspoons salt

½ teaspoon ground black pepper

½ teaspoon sweet paprika

2 tablespoons extra-virgin olive oil

2 tablespoons unsalted butter

½ cup dry white wine

2 tablespoons minced red onions

1 clove garlic, smashed

2 tablespoons all-purpose flour

1 cup chicken stock

⅓ cup heavy cream

1. In a medium bowl, combine spinach, chives, dill, feta, and ricotta. Set aside.

2. Using a sharp knife, cut a 3" slit into the middle of the thickest part of a chicken breast. The slit should penetrate two-thirds of the way into the chicken breast to create a pocket. Stuff one-fourth of the spinach-cheese filling into the pocket. Secure opening with toothpicks. Repeat with remaining chicken, then season with salt, pepper, and paprika.

3. Heat oil and butter in a large skillet over medium-high heat 30 seconds. Brown chicken 3–4 minutes per side. Set chicken aside and keep warm. Add wine to skillet and deglaze the pan. Cook 2 minutes or until most of the wine has evaporated. Reduce heat to medium and stir in onions, garlic, and flour. Cook 2 minutes.

4. Add stock, increase heat to medium-high, and bring sauce to a boil. Reduce heat to medium and return chicken to skillet. Cover skillet and cook 25 minutes. Remove chicken again and keep warm. Add cream and cook until sauce thickens.

5. Slice chicken and place on four plates. Pour sauce over chicken and serve extra sauce on the side.

Per Serving: Calories: 629 | Fat: 34g | Protein: 59g | Sodium: 1,497mg | Fiber: 1g | Carbohydrates: 11g

Pomegranate-Glazed Chicken

Make sure you use pure pomegranate juice in this recipe. Mastiha can be found at Greek or Middle Eastern grocery stores.

INGREDIENTS | SERVES 4

4 (6-ounce) bone-in skinless chicken breasts, rinsed and dried

1 teaspoon salt

½ teaspoon ground black pepper

2 cups pomegranate juice

⅛ teaspoon ground mastiha

2 teaspoons grated orange zest

3 cloves garlic, smashed

1 teaspoon dried rosemary

Fresh Pomegranate Juice

You can make your own pomegranate juice. Slice three or four pomegranates in half. With the seed side over a bowl, tap each pomegranate bottom with a wooden spoon to release the seeds. You'll need to tap several times to release all the seeds. Remove any white pith from the bowl. Put the seeds in a food processor and process for 5 minutes. Strain the juice with a fine-mesh sieve to remove the pits. Refrigerate the juice.

1. Preheat oven to 375°F.

2. Season chicken with salt and pepper and place on a baking sheet lined with parchment paper. Bake chicken 25–30 minutes or until the internal temperature reaches 180°F.

3. In a small pan over medium-high heat, combine pomegranate juice, mastiha, orange zest, garlic, and rosemary. Bring mixture to a boil, reduce heat to medium-low, and cook until sauce reduces to ¼ cup and has a syrup-like consistency. Remove garlic and take sauce off the heat.

4. Brush chicken with reserved sauce before serving.

Per Serving: Calories: 145 | Fat: 2g | Protein: 15g | Sodium: 672mg | Fiber: 1g | Carbohydrates: 16g

Rosemary Chicken with Potatoes S C

This simple rustic dish will make you feel like you're dining in a bistro in Paris.

INGREDIENTS | SERVES 6

1 tablespoon olive oil

2 pounds boneless, skinless chicken thighs

½ teaspoon salt

½ teaspoon ground black pepper

6 small red potatoes, halved

1 leek (white and pale green parts only), sliced into 1" pieces

6 sprigs rosemary, divided

1 garlic clove, minced

½ cup low-sodium chicken broth

¼ cup capers

1. Heat olive oil in a large skillet over medium heat until hot but not smoking. Add chicken and season with salt and pepper. Cook 5 minutes on one side and flip. Cook an additional 5 minutes.

2. Place potatoes and leek in a 4- to 5-quart slow cooker. Top with 5 rosemary sprigs and garlic.

3. Place chicken thighs on rosemary. Pour broth over chicken and potatoes.

4. Cover and cook on high 3–4 hours or until juices run clear from chicken. Sprinkle with capers just before serving and garnish with remaining rosemary.

Per Serving: Calories: 336 | Fat: 9g | Protein: 33g | Sodium: 595mg | Fiber: 3g | Carbohydrates: 30g

Lemony Roast Chicken S C

Come home from a day of work or play to an incredibly moist roast chicken!

INGREDIENTS | SERVES 6

1 (3½- to 4-pound) frying chicken

1 teaspoon salt ·

1 teaspoon ground black pepper

1 clove garlic, crushed

3 tablespoons olive oil

2 large lemons, quartered

½ cup low-sodium chicken broth

1. Rinse chicken inside and out and pat dry. Rub with salt, pepper, and garlic. Brush with olive oil.

2. Place lemon quarters in the bottom of a 4- to 5-quart slow cooker. Top with chicken. Pour broth over chicken.

3. Cover and cook on high 1 hour. Reduce heat to low and cook 5–6 hours.

4. Insert a meat thermometer into the thickest part of a thigh. Chicken is done when it registers 165°F.

Per Serving: Calories: 608 | Fat: 20g | Protein: 96g | Sodium: 825mg | Fiber: 1g | Carbohydrates: 3g

Tuscan Chicken and White Beans SC

Hearty white beans with warm Tuscan spices and tomatoes make this super-easy slow-cooked chicken special enough for company! Serve this dish over rice or pasta if you like.

INGREDIENTS | SERVES 4

3 large (6-ounce) boneless, skinless chicken breasts, cut into large chunks

1 (15.5-ounce) can white beans, drained and rinsed

1 (14.5-ounce) can diced tomatoes with juice

1 (4-ounce) can mushrooms, drained

¼ cup halved Spanish olives stuffed with pimientos

2 teaspoons onion powder

1 teaspoon garlic powder

1 teaspoon basil

1 teaspoon oregano

1 teaspoon ground black pepper

½ teaspoon salt

2 teaspoons olive oil

1. Place chicken breasts in a greased 4- to 5-quart slow cooker.

2. Add beans, tomatoes (including juice), mushrooms, and olives. Add onion powder, garlic powder, basil, oregano, pepper, and salt.

3. Mix all ingredients together in slow cooker. Drizzle olive oil over chicken and vegetables.

4. Cook on high 3½–4 hours or on low 6 hours.

Per Serving: Calories: 304 | Fat: 7.5g | Protein: 35g | Sodium: 1,109mg | Fiber: 8g | Carbohydrates: 23g

White Beans

White beans, which are also called navy beans, Boston beans, or Yankee beans, are small, lightly colored beans that are very mild in taste and work well in a variety of recipes. If you don't have white beans available, cannellini beans or northern beans, which are slightly larger, are excellent substitutes.

Chicken in Lemon Sauce S C

This is a lovely one-pot meal. By completing a simple step at the end of the cooking time, you have meat, potatoes, vegetables, and sauce all ready to serve and eat.

INGREDIENTS | SERVES 4

1 (16-ounce) bag frozen cut green beans, thawed

1 small onion, peeled and cut into thin wedges

4 (4-ounce) boneless, skinless chicken breast halves

4 medium potatoes, peeled and cut into quarters

2 cloves garlic, minced

¼ teaspoon ground black pepper

1 cup low-sodium chicken broth

4 ounces cream cheese, cut into cubes

1 teaspoon grated lemon zest

1. Place green beans and onion in a 4- to 5-quart slow cooker. Arrange chicken and potatoes over vegetables. Sprinkle with garlic and pepper. Pour broth over all. Cover and cook on low 5 or more hours or until chicken is cooked through and moist.

2. Evenly divide chicken, potatoes, and vegetables between 4 serving plates; cover to keep warm.

3. To make sauce, add cream cheese and lemon zest to broth in the slow cooker. Stir until cheese melts into sauce. Pour sauce over the chicken, potatoes, and vegetables.

Per Serving: Calories: 439 | Fat: 14g | Protein: 32g | Sodium: 502mg | Fiber: 8g | Carbohydrates: 47g

Spicy Olive Chicken   SC

As the chicken cooks, a delicious sauce is created underneath the roasted chicken. The olives and capers add a briny flavor to the sauce.

INGREDIENTS | SERVES 8

1 (3-pound) whole chicken, cut into 8 pieces

1 teaspoon salt

½ teaspoon ground black pepper

4 tablespoons unsalted butter

⅔ cup chopped sweet onion

2 tablespoons capers, drained and rinsed

24 green olives, pitted

½ cup low-sodium chicken broth

½ cup dry white wine

1 teaspoon Dijon mustard

½ teaspoon hot sauce

2 cups cooked white rice

¼ cup chopped parsley

1. Sprinkle chicken pieces with salt and pepper and brown them in butter in a large skillet over medium-high heat about 3 minutes per side. Remove chicken from skillet and place in a greased 4- to 5-quart slow cooker.

2. Sauté onion in the same skillet for 3–5 minutes. Add onion to slow cooker, along with capers and olives.

3. In a small bowl, whisk together broth, wine, and mustard. Pour over chicken in slow cooker. Add hot sauce. Cover and cook on high 3–3½ hours or on low 5½–6 hours.

4. When ready to serve, place chicken over rice. Ladle sauce and olives over each serving. Garnish with parsley.

Per Serving: Calories: 351 | Fat: 13g | Protein: 37g | Sodium: 686mg | Fiber: 1g | Carbohydrates: 17g

Capers

Capers are flavorful unopened buds from the *Capparis spinosa* bush. They can be packed in salt or brine. Try to find the smallest—they seem to have more flavor than the big ones do. Capers are great on their own or incorporated into sauces. They are also good in salads and as a garnish on many dishes that would otherwise be dull.

Chicken with Figs SC

This recipe was inspired by the traditional Moroccan tagine, a type of savory slow-cooked stew. Try it with whole-grain couscous or quinoa.

INGREDIENTS | SERVES 8

½ pound boneless, skinless chicken thighs, cubed

¾ pound boneless, skinless chicken breasts, cubed

¾ cup dried figs

1 medium sweet potato, peeled and diced

1 medium onion, peeled and chopped

3 cloves garlic, minced

2 teaspoons cumin

1 teaspoon coriander

½ teaspoon cayenne pepper

½ teaspoon ground ginger

½ teaspoon turmeric

½ teaspoon ground orange peel

½ teaspoon ground black pepper

2¾ cups low-sodium chicken broth

¼ cup orange juice

1. Quickly sauté chicken in a dry nonstick skillet over medium-high heat until it starts to turn white, about 3 minutes. Drain off excess grease.

2. Place chicken and remaining ingredients into a 4- to 5-quart slow cooker. Stir. Cook for 6 hours on low. Stir before serving.

Per Serving: Calories: 179 | Fat: 4g | Protein: 17g | Sodium: 445mg | Fiber: 2g | Carbohydrates: 19g

Balsamic Chicken and Spinach   S C

Balsamic vinegar is delicious in any dish, but is especially well-paired with chicken. Serve this tangy and nutritious dish with rice pilaf.

INGREDIENTS | SERVES 4

¾ pound boneless, skinless chicken breasts, cut into strips

¼ cup balsamic vinegar

4 cloves garlic, minced

1 tablespoon minced oregano

1 tablespoon minced parsley

½ teaspoon ground black pepper

5 ounces baby spinach

1. Place chicken, vinegar, garlic, and spices into a 4- to 5-quart slow cooker. Stir. Cover and cook on low 6 hours.

2. Add baby spinach and cover again. Cook until spinach is wilted, about 15 minutes. Stir before serving.

Per Serving: Calories: 123 | Fat: 2g | Protein: 19g | Sodium: 129mg | Fiber: 1g | Carbohydrates: 5g

Five-Ingredient Greek Chicken   S C

If you've got these five things in your kitchen, you've got a gorgeously slow-cooked meal waiting to feed you and your family. This is the perfect meal to serve with crusty French bread on a cold, rainy night.

INGREDIENTS | SERVES 6

6 (5-ounce) bone-in chicken thighs, skinned

½ cup kalamata olives

1 (6.5-ounce) jar artichoke hearts in olive oil, undrained

1 pint cherry tomatoes

¼ cup chopped parsley

1. Place chicken, olives, artichokes and artichoke oil, and cherry tomatoes in a 4- to 5-quart slow cooker.

2. Cover and cook on low 4–6 hours. Serve in large bowls garnished with parsley.

Per Serving: Calories: 231 | Fat: 5g | Protein: 29g | Sodium: 153mg | Fiber: 2.5g | Carbohydrates: 8g

Sage-Ricotta Chicken Breasts

If you have difficulty spreading the cheese mixture under the skin, you can lift the chicken skin completely off, spoon on the cheese mixture, and replace the skin.

INGREDIENTS | SERVES 6

½ cup part-skim ricotta cheese

6 fresh sage leaves, sliced

1 large egg white

6 chicken breast halves with bone and skin on

¼ cup chopped niçoise olives

½ teaspoon ground black pepper

1. Preheat oven to 375°F.

2. In a small bowl, mix together ricotta, sage, and egg white.

3. Using your finger, make an opening in the skin of each breast and loosen the skin away from the breast.

4. Transfer ricotta mixture to a small zip-top plastic bag and snip off one corner. Squeeze ricotta mixture under chicken skin through the opening you made. Place chicken on a rack in a large baking dish. Roast 30–45 minutes until the internal temperature of the chicken reaches 165°F and the outside is browned.

5. Transfer chicken to a serving platter. Top with olives and sprinkle with pepper.

Per Serving: Calories: 238 | Fat: 11g | Protein: 32g | Sodium: 582mg | Fiber: 0g | Carbohydrates: 1g

Stuffed Grilled Chicken Breasts

Make sure to pin the open end of the breasts closed tightly so the stuffing does not drip out into your grill and cause flare-ups.

INGREDIENTS | SERVES 6

1 cup crumbled feta cheese

½ cup finely minced sun-dried tomatoes

1 teaspoon dried oregano

6 (6-ounce) boneless, skinless chicken breasts

2 tablespoons extra-virgin olive oil

1½ teaspoons salt

1 teaspoon ground black pepper

1. Preheat a gas or charcoal grill to medium-high heat.

2. In a small bowl, combine feta, sun-dried tomatoes, and oregano; mix thoroughly.

3. Using a sharp knife, cut a slit 3" long in the middle of the thickest part of a chicken breast. The slit should penetrate two-thirds of the way into the chicken breast to create a pocket. Stuff one-sixth of the filling into the pocket. Repeat with remaining chicken breasts. Use poultry pins or toothpicks to close openings.

4. Heat oil in a large skillet over medium-high heat. Brown chicken breasts in batches, 2–3 minutes per side. Sprinkle breasts with salt and pepper.

5. Grill chicken until cooked through, approximately 8 minutes per side. Serve immediately.

Per Serving: Calories: 267 | Fat: 11g | Protein: 39g | Sodium: 372mg | Fiber: 0.5g | Carbohydrates: 3.5g

Chicken Livers in Red Wine

For a nice (and sweet!) variation on this recipe, try using a fortified wine.
Serve these decadent morsels over a bed of mashed potatoes.

INGREDIENTS | SERVES 8

1 cup chicken broth
½ cup butter
1 small onion, peeled and diced
1 pound chicken livers
1 tablespoon all-purpose flour
½ cup red wine
1 teaspoon salt
½ teaspoon ground black pepper
2 tablespoons fresh parsley,
  finely chopped

1. Bring broth to boil in small saucepan over high heat. Reduce heat and keep warm over low heat.

2. Melt butter in a medium skillet over medium-high heat. Add onion and sauté 3 minutes. Add chicken livers and cook 3–5 minutes, stirring constantly to avoid browning.

3. Sprinkle flour over livers in skillet and continue to stir well to form a sauce. Stir constantly to avoid clumping.

4. Slowly add hot broth to pan with livers, stirring constantly. Turn heat to high and slowly add wine. Reduce heat to low and simmer 5–10 minutes to thicken sauce.

5. Sprinkle with salt, pepper, and parsley. Serve hot.

Per Serving: Calories: 224 | Fat: 19g | Protein: 8g | Sodium: 405mg | Fiber: 0g | Carbohydrates: 5g

Turkey Breast Piccata

Try this lighter version of the Italian classic that traditionally uses veal or chicken.

INGREDIENTS | SERVES 6

¼ cup all-purpose flour
1½ pounds turkey cutlets
¼ cup extra-virgin olive oil
¼ cup dry white wine
3 tablespoons fresh lemon juice
½ cup turkey or chicken stock
½ tablespoon capers
¼ cup chopped fresh parsley

1. Pour flour into a shallow dish. Dredge cutlets in flour.

2. Heat oil in a large skillet over medium-high heat 30 seconds. Add turkey cutlets and brown 2 minutes on each side.

3. Add wine and lemon juice and let the liquid reduce by half. Add stock and cook 5–6 minutes or until the sauce thickens.

4. To serve, sprinkle cutlets with capers and parsley and drizzle sauce over the cutlets.

Per Serving: Calories: 240 | Fat: 10g | Protein: 29g | Sodium: 108mg | Fiber: 0g | Carbohydrates: 6g

Grilled Duck Breast with Fruit Salsa

Duck breast has the best flavor when cooked rare to medium-rare. For this recipe, try using Moulard duck breast.

INGREDIENTS | SERVES 6

1 medium plum, pitted and diced
1 medium peach, pitted and diced
1 medium nectarine, pitted and diced
1 medium red onion, peeled and diced
3 sprigs mint, minced
½ teaspoon ground black pepper
1 tablespoon olive oil
1 teaspoon chili powder
1½ pounds boneless duck breast

1. Preheat a gas or charcoal grill to medium-high heat.

2. Toss together plum, peach, nectarine, onion, mint, and pepper in a medium bowl.

3. In a shallow dish, mix oil and chili powder together. Dip duck breast in oil mixture. Place duck on grill and cook about 8–10 minutes per side.

4. Slice duck diagonally and serve with spoonful of salsa.

Per Serving: Calories: 285 | Fat: 15g | Protein: 29g | Sodium: 96mg | Fiber: 1.5g | Carbohydrates: 9g

CHAPTER 10

Fish and Seafood

Grilled Whole Fish

One of the finest dining experiences in the Mediterranean region is eating a whole grilled fish as you sit by the sea. As any good fishmonger will tell you, the best fish is the freshest fish.

INGREDIENTS | SERVES 4

4 (½-pound) whole fish (sea bream, sea bass, or red snapper), cleaned, gutted, and scaled

½ cup extra-virgin olive oil

4 teaspoons salt

1½ teaspoons ground black pepper

1 large lemon, thinly sliced

2 tablespoons chopped fresh oregano

2 tablespoons fresh thyme leaves

2 tablespoons chopped fresh rosemary

2 tablespoons chopped fresh tarragon

3 tablespoons vegetable oil

½ cup Ladolemono (see recipe in Chapter 12)

1. Rinse fish and pat dry with a paper towel. Rub fish on both sides with olive oil, then sprinkle both sides and the cavity with salt and pepper. Refrigerate fish 30 minutes and then return them to room temperature.

2. Fill the cavity of each fish with equal amounts of lemon slices and herbs.

3. Preheat a gas or charcoal grill to medium-high. Brush grill surface to make sure it is thoroughly clean. When grill is ready, dip a clean tea towel in vegetable oil and wipe the grill surface with oil.

4. Place fish on the grill and grill 5–6 minutes per side.

5. Serve fish with Ladolemono sauce. Serve immediately.

Per Serving: Calories: 351 | Fat: 23g | Protein: 1g | Sodium: 2,362g | Fiber: 3g | Carbohydrates: 5g

How to Pick the Freshest Fish

Fresh fish should smell only of the sea. The eyes should be bright and shiny, not sunken. Open the gills with your finger; they should be bright red. Finally, press your finger into the body; the flesh should be firm and the scales should be firmly attached to the body.

Olive Oil–Poached Cod

Poaching cod in olive oil produces a succulent, delicate fish that will wow your family or guests. Serve this poached fish on a bed of Spanakorizo with Green Olives and Feta (See recipe in Chapter 6).

INGREDIENTS | SERVES 4

4 (6-ounce) fresh cod fillets,
  skins removed

2½–3 cups extra-virgin olive oil

1 teaspoon salt

2 tablespoons fresh lemon juice

1 tablespoon grated lemon zest

Poaching

Poaching is a gentle cooking method for fish, meat, chicken, and eggs. The item is submerged in a liquid (oil, broth, or water) and cooked at a low temperature. This method helps keep food moist while giving it the flavor of the cooking liquid.

1. Rinse fillets and pat dry with a paper towel.

2. Choose a pot that will just fit the fillets and fill it with oil. Bring oil to a temperature of 210°F. Adjust heat to keep the temperature at 210°F while poaching fish.

3. Carefully place fillets in the oil and poach 6 minutes or until fish is opaque in color. Carefully remove fish from the oil and place on a plate. Sprinkle fish with salt.

4. Spoon some of the warm oil over fish and then drizzle it with lemon juice. Sprinkle lemon zest over fish and serve immediately.

Per Serving: Calories: 498 | Fat: 41g | Protein: 30g | Sodium: 685mg | Fiber: 0g | Carbohydrates: 1g

Pistachio-Crusted Halibut

This elegant dish is easy enough to make for a weekday meal, but you might want to save it for company. All you need is a food processor and an oven. Serve this fish with rice pilaf or roasted potatoes.

INGREDIENTS | SERVES 4

½ cup roughly chopped shelled unsalted pistachios

2 teaspoons grated lemon zest

1 teaspoon grated lime zest

2 teaspoons grated orange zest

4 teaspoons chopped fresh parsley

1 cup bread crumbs

¼ cup extra-virgin olive oil

4 (6-ounce) halibut fillets, skins removed

1½ teaspoons salt

½ teaspoon ground black pepper

4 teaspoons Dijon mustard

Pistachios

Pistachios are grown all over Italy, Greece, and Turkey. These Mediterranean favorites are high in fiber and rich in B vitamins.

1. Preheat oven to 400°F. Line a baking sheet with parchment paper.

2. Pulse pistachios, zests, parsley, and bread crumbs in a food processor to combine the ingredients. With the processor running, add oil until well incorporated.

3. Rinse fish and pat dry with a paper towel. Season fish with salt and pepper.

4. Brush the tops of fish with mustard. Divide pistachio mixture evenly and place some on the top of each fish. Press down on mixture to help the crust adhere.

5. Carefully place crusted fish on the baking sheet. Bake 20 minutes or until crust is golden brown.

6. Let cool 5 minutes, and serve immediately.

Per Serving: Calories: 504 | Fat: 26g | Protein: 42g | Sodium: 1,233mg | Fiber: 3g | Carbohydrates: 25g

Spinach-Stuffed Sole

This is an impressive dish that is easy to make. Choose any flat fish fillet as a substitute for sole. Serve these fillets on a bed of braised lentils.

INGREDIENTS | SERVES 4

¼ cup + 2 tablespoons extra-virgin olive oil, divided

4 scallions, ends trimmed, sliced

1 pound package frozen spinach, thawed and drained

3 tablespoons chopped fennel fronds or tarragon

1 teaspoon salt, divided

½ teaspoon ground black pepper, divided

4 (6-ounce) sole fillets, skins removed

2 tablespoons plus 1½ teaspoons grated lemon zest, divided

1 teaspoon sweet paprika

1. Preheat oven to 400°F. Line a baking sheet with parchment paper.

2. Heat 2 tablespoons oil in a medium skillet over medium heat 30 seconds. Add scallions and cook 3–4 minutes. Remove scallions from skillet and place in a medium bowl. Cool to room temperature.

3. Add spinach and fennel to scallions and mix well. Season with ½ teaspoon salt and ¼ teaspoon pepper.

4. Rinse fish fillets and pat dry with a paper towel. Rub fish with 2 tablespoons oil and sprinkle with 2 tablespoons lemon zest. Season fillets with remaining salt and pepper and sprinkle with paprika.

5. Divide spinach filling among fillets. Roll up each fillet, starting from the widest end. Use two toothpicks to secure each fillet. Place rolled fillets on the baking sheet and drizzle 2 tablespoons oil over them.

6. Bake 15–20 minutes. Remove toothpicks and sprinkle fillets with remaining lemon zest. Serve immediately.

Per Serving: Calories: 313 | Fat: 16g | Protein: 36g | Sodium: 811mg | Fiber: 4g | Carbohydrates: 7g

Bianko from Corfu

This dish comes from the Ionian island of Corfu. Although the island is Greek, its dishes have an Italian flair.

INGREDIENTS | SERVES 4

3 tablespoons extra-virgin olive oil, divided

2 large onions, sliced

6 cloves garlic, minced

2 medium carrots, peeled and sliced

1 cup chopped celery

1½ teaspoons salt

1 teaspoon ground black pepper

4 large potatoes, peeled and cut into ½" slices

4 whitefish fillets (cod or grouper), skinned

4 tablespoons fresh lemon juice

¼ cup chopped fresh parsley

Whitefish

Whitefish have a light, white, flaky flesh. Low in fat, whitefish is a healthy meal option. Halibut, cod, sea bass, pollock, tilapia, and hake are all considered whitefish.

1. Heat 1 tablespoon oil in a large heavy-bottomed pot over medium heat 30 seconds. Add onions, garlic, carrots, and celery. Cook 5–7 minutes or until onions soften. Season with salt and pepper.

2. Add potatoes and just enough hot water to cover. Increase heat to medium-high and bring to a boil. Reduce heat to medium-low, cover the pot, leaving the lid slightly ajar, and cook 12 minutes.

3. Place fillets over the potatoes and top with remaining oil. Cover and cook another 12–15 minutes or until fish is opaque and flaky.

4. Uncover pot and add lemon juice. Don't stir it; shake the pot back and forth to allow liquid to penetrate the layers.

5. Place fish and potatoes on a large platter and top with parsley. Serve immediately.

Per Serving: Calories: 670 | Fat: 22g | Protein: 46g | Sodium: 1,063mg | Fiber: 12g | Carbohydrates: 72g

Grilled Salmon with Lemon and Lime

With a clean grill top and a little patience, anyone can grill fish without it sticking. Serve this salmon with Tzatziki (see recipe in Chapter 3).

INGREDIENTS | SERVES 4

4 (6-ounce) salmon fillets, skins on
1 tablespoon extra-virgin olive oil
1 tablespoon grated lemon zest
1½ teaspoons grated lime zest
1½ teaspoons salt
½ teaspoon ground black pepper
3 tablespoons vegetable oil
1 large lemon, cut into wedges

Salmon

Salmon is one of the most healthful fish and one of the tastiest. It helps with heart health, is high in protein, and is rich in omega-3 fatty acids.

1. Preheat a gas or charcoal grill to medium-high. Brush grill surface to make sure it is thoroughly clean.

2. Rinse fillets and pat dry with a paper towel. Rub fillets with olive oil on both sides. Sprinkle both sides with lemon zest, lime zest, salt, and pepper.

3. When grill is ready, dip a clean tea towel in vegetable oil and wipe the grill surface with oil.

4. Place salmon on the grill, skin-side down, and grill 6–7 minutes. Flip salmon over and grill another 2–3 minutes.

5. Serve salmon with lemon wedges.

Per Serving: Calories: 401 | Fat: 26g | Protein: 39g | Sodium: 1,489mg | Fiber: 0g | Carbohydrates: 0g

Beer-Battered Fish MA

Every country in the Mediterranean has its own version of a beer-battered fish. Greeks use cod, but you can try whatever is fresh at your fishmonger or supermarket. Serve this fish with a garlicky Almond-Potato Skordalia (see recipe in Chapter 12).

INGREDIENTS | SERVES 4

¾ cup all-purpose flour

¾ cup cornstarch

1 teaspoon baking powder

1¼ teaspoons salt, divided

1–1½ cups cold dark beer

4 (6-ounce) haddock or cod fillets, skins removed and cut into 3 or 4 pieces each

Sunflower oil for frying

1. In a large bowl, combine flour, cornstarch, baking powder, and ½ teaspoon salt. Slowly stir in beer to reach the consistency of a thin pancake batter (you might not need all the beer). Refrigerate batter 1 hour.

2. Rinse fish and pat dry with a paper towel. Season with ½ teaspoon salt.

3. Fill a deep frying pan with 3 inches oil. Over medium-high heat, bring oil temperature to 365°F. Adjust heat to keep the temperature at 365°F while frying. Fry fish in batches 3–4 minutes or until just golden. Transfer fish to a tray lined with paper towels to soak up excess oil.

4. Season fish with remaining salt and serve immediately.

Per Serving: Calories: 472 | Fat: 15g | Protein: 35g | Sodium: 979mg | Fiber: 1g | Carbohydrates: 43g

Cod with Raisins

In ancient Greece, raisins were often used as a seasoning in savory dishes. They add a sweet taste to this unusual meal.

INGREDIENTS | SERVES 4

3 tablespoons extra-virgin olive oil

2 medium onions, chopped

1 tablespoon tomato paste diluted in ¾ cup water

¾ cup raisins

1 cup water

1½ pounds fresh or frozen cod

1. Heat oil in a large saucepan over medium heat. Add onions and sauté 5 minutes, stirring constantly. Add tomato paste and simmer 10 minutes. Stir in raisins and continue to cook 3 more minutes.

2. Add water and increase heat to high. Bring to a boil, then reduce heat to medium-low and simmer 30 minutes until raisins are plump. Add cod and simmer 15 minutes until sauce is thickened. Serve immediately.

Per Serving: Calories: 328 | Fat: 12g | Protein: 30g | Sodium: 147mg | Fiber: 2g | Carbohydrates: 29g

Baked Sea Bream with Feta and Tomato

If you have trouble finding sea bream, it may be the name— this fish is also sometimes referred to as porgy.

INGREDIENTS | SERVES 4

½ cup extra-virgin olive oil

6 ripe tomatoes, peeled and minced

1 teaspoon dried marjoram

1 teaspoon salt

½ teaspoon ground black pepper

½ cup water

4 small whole sea bream, cleaned

½ cup fresh parsley, finely chopped

½ pound feta cheese, crumbled

1. Preheat oven to 400°F.

2. In a small saucepan, heat olive oil over medium-high heat. Add tomatoes, marjoram, salt, pepper, and water and bring to boil. Reduce heat to medium-low and simmer 15 minutes.

3. Place fish side by side in a large baking dish and top with tomato mixture. Sprinkle with parsley. Bake 30 minutes.

4. Remove baking dish from oven and sprinkle feta over fish. Return to oven to bake another 5–7 minutes, until cheese starts to melt. Remove and serve immediately.

Per Serving: Calories: 508 | Fat: 32g | Protein: 27g | Sodium: 711mg | Fiber: 1.5g | Carbohydrates: 7.5g

Aegean Baked Sole

Turbot, halibut, or flounder can be used as substitutes for the sole in this recipe.

INGREDIENTS | SERVES 4

2 medium lemons, divided

8 (6-ounce) sole fillets

1 teaspoon salt

½ teaspoon ground black pepper

4 tablespoons extra-virgin olive oil, divided

1 teaspoon dried oregano

¼ cup capers

4 tablespoons chopped fresh dill

2 tablespoons chopped scallions

1. Preheat oven to 250°F.

2. Slice 1 lemon into thin slices, then cut slices in half. Set aside. Salt and pepper sole fillets.

3. Pour 2 tablespoons oil into a medium baking dish. Layer fish and lemon slices alternately.

4. Sprinkle oregano, capers, dill, and scallions over fish and lemon slices. Drizzle remaining olive oil and squeeze juice of remaining lemon over dish.

5. Cover and bake 30 minutes.

Per Serving: Calories: 236 | Fat: 3g | Protein: 47g | Sodium: 455mg | Fiber: 3g | Carbohydrates: 6.5g

Tomato-Poached Fish

Due to the heat of the summer months in Mediterranean countries, poached dishes like this are common, as you do not have to use an oven that will add to the heat in the kitchen.

INGREDIENTS | SERVES 4

3 tablespoons extra-virgin olive oil

4 cloves garlic, minced

1 pound ripe tomatoes, peeled and minced

8 fresh mint leaves, finely chopped

1 teaspoon salt

½ teaspoon ground black pepper

1 tablespoon dried oregano

½ cup water

2 pounds white fish fillets

½ cup chopped parsley

1. Heat oil in a large skillet over medium-high heat. Sauté garlic 1 minute. Add tomatoes, mint, salt, pepper, and oregano and bring to boil. Reduce heat to medium-low and simmer 10 minutes until thickened.

2. Add water and continue to simmer another 3–4 minutes.

3. Add fish to skillet and simmer 15 minutes. Do not stir; simply shake pan gently from time to time to avoid sticking.

4. Garnish with chopped parsley before serving.

Per Serving: Calories: 261 | Fat: 12g | Protein: 33g | Sodium: 122mg | Fiber: 1g | Carbohydrates: 5.2g

Lime-Poached Flounder

Lime brings out the delicate flavor of the fish and complements the zip of the cilantro.

INGREDIENTS | SERVES 6

1 medium leek, trimmed, cleaned, and sliced

½ bunch cilantro, leaves separated from stems

1½ pounds flounder fillets

1¾ cups fish stock or fat-free chicken broth

2 tablespoons lime juice

½ teaspoon grated lime zest

½ teaspoon salt

½ teaspoon ground black pepper

2 medium yellow onions, grated

2 large carrots, peeled and grated

2 medium stalks celery, grated

2 tablespoons extra-virgin olive oil

1. Place leek slices and cilantro stems in a large skillet, then lay the flounder on top.

2. Add stock, lime juice, zest, salt, and pepper. Bring to a slow boil over medium-high heat. Reduce heat to medium-low, cover, and cook 7–10 minutes until flounder is thoroughly cooked. Remove from heat. Strain off and discard the liquid.

3. To serve, lay grated onions, carrots, and celery in separate strips on a serving platter. Top with fish, drizzle with olive oil, and sprinkle with cilantro leaves.

Per Serving: Calories: 191 | Fat: 6g | Protein: 24g | Sodium: 441mg | Fiber: 3g | Carbohydrates: 8g

Using Frozen Fish

Don't fret if you don't have fresh fish available in your area. Using a quality fish frozen at sea is perfectly fine. In fact, sometimes the frozen fish is fresher than the fresh!

Oven-Poached Bass with Kalamata Chutney

Kalamata olives have a very distinctive flavor and add a touch of saltiness to this dish.

INGREDIENTS | SERVES 6

1 medium shallot, peeled and chopped

1 stalk celery, chopped

½ teaspoon ground black pepper

1½ pounds bass fillet

½ cup dry white wine

1 cup fish stock or clam juice

¼ cup chopped kalamata olives

2 cloves garlic, minced

¼ teaspoon grated lemon zest

1. Preheat oven to 400°F.

2. Place shallot and celery in the bottom of a large baking dish; sprinkle with pepper. Place fish on top and add wine and stock. Cover and bake 15–20 minutes.

3. While fish cooks, prepare the chutney by mixing olives, garlic, and lemon zest in a small bowl.

4. Remove fish from the cooking liquid and serve with a spoonful of chutney.

Per Serving: Calories: 165 | Fat: 4g | Protein: 22g | Sodium: 147mg | Fiber: 0g | Carbohydrates: 4g

Salmon with Anchovy-Caper Vinaigrette

If you see multicolored heirloom tomatoes in your market, try them in this dish.

INGREDIENTS | SERVES 6

1 tablespoon olive oil
6 (5-ounce) salmon fillets
6 anchovy fillets
1 large beefsteak tomato, thinly sliced
½ cup plain Greek yogurt
¼ cup capers
3 tablespoons finely chopped chives

1. Preheat oven to 375°F.

2. Pour oil into a large roasting pan, then place salmon in the pan. Place anchovies on top and roast 10 minutes.

3. Remove from oven. Slice salmon and place on plates.

4. Top salmon with tomato slices. Dollop yogurt on tomato slices, then sprinkle with capers and chives.

Per Serving: Calories: 366 | Fat: 18g | Protein: 47g | Sodium: 2,335mg | Fiber: 1g | Carbohydrates: 2g

Lemon Sole with Capers

If you are searching for something to serve with this dish, consider crème fraîche; it makes for a very nice accompaniment.

INGREDIENTS | SERVES 6

1½ pounds sole
½ teaspoon ground black pepper
1 teaspoon grated lemon zest
3 cloves garlic, minced
1 tablespoon olive oil
1 tablespoon chopped dill
½ teaspoon capers

1. Preheat broiler.

2. Place the sole on a broiler pan or baking sheet. Top with pepper, zest, and garlic, and drizzle with oil. Place under broiler 3 minutes, then turn carefully and broil 1 minute longer.

3. Remove from broiler and top with dill and capers.

Per Serving: Calories: 125 | Fat: 4g | Protein: 21g | Sodium: 98mg | Fiber: 0g | Carbohydrates: 1g

Haddock with Rosemary   MA

Marinating the fish in milk lightens its flavor and adds a touch of sweetness.

INGREDIENTS | SERVES 6

1 cup skim milk

½ teaspoon ground black pepper

2 tablespoons chopped rosemary, divided

1½ pounds haddock fillet

2 tablespoons extra-virgin olive oil, divided

1. Mix together milk, pepper, and 1 tablespoon rosemary in a shallow dish. Place haddock fillet in milk mixture and marinate 8 hours in the refrigerator.

2. Preheat oven to 375°F. Grease a medium baking dish with 1 tablespoon oil.

3. Gently remove fish from marinade, drain thoroughly, and place in prepared baking dish. Cover and bake 15–20 minutes until fish is flaky.

4. Remove fish from oven and let it rest 5 minutes. Cut into 6 portions. Drizzle with remaining oil and sprinkle with remaining rosemary.

Per Serving: Calories: 158 | Fat: 6g | Protein: 23g | Sodium: 95mg | Fiber: 1g | Carbohydrates: 3g

Parchment Salmon

Try this method with any type of fish. If you would like to use bluefish, increase the onions and decrease the butter since bluefish is already oily.

INGREDIENTS | SERVES 4

¼ cup butter, softened
½ pound mushrooms, chopped
1 tablespoon minced shallot
½ cup chopped scallions
2 teaspoons chopped marjoram
1½ pounds salmon fillet
¼ cup dry white wine

1. Combine butter, mushrooms, shallot, scallions, and marjoram in a small bowl.

2. Preheat oven to 400°F.

3. Cut salmon into 4 portions and place each on a folded sheet of parchment paper. Top each with 1 tablespoon butter mixture. Sprinkle with 1 tablespoon wine. For each packet, fold parchment paper over the top and continuing to fold until well sealed. Place packets on a baking sheet.

4. Roast 7–10 minutes, until paper is slightly brown. Slit open paper and serve immediately.

Per Serving: Calories: 370 | Fat: 22g | Protein: 35g | Sodium: 81mg | Fiber: 1g | Carbohydrates: 3g

Grilled Grouper Steaks MA

Grouper has a firm meat that doesn't dry out easily and holds up well on the grill. Serve this fish with a heaping spoonful of Mediterranean Saltsa (see recipe in Chapter 12) and roasted potatoes.

INGREDIENTS | SERVES 4

¼ cup extra-virgin olive oil
1 tablespoon grated lemon zest
½ cup dry white wine
½ teaspoon chopped fresh rosemary
4 (½-pound) grouper steaks, rinsed and dried
3 tablespoons vegetable oil
1½ teaspoons salt

1. In a medium baking dish, whisk olive oil, zest, wine, and rosemary. Add fish and toss to combine. Cover with plastic and refrigerate 1 hour. Allow fish to return to room temperature 30 minutes before grilling.

2. Preheat a gas or charcoal grill to medium-high. Dip a clean tea towel in vegetable oil and wipe the grill surface with oil.

3. Season fish on both sides with salt. Place fish on grill and grill 5–6 minutes per side.

Per Serving: Calories: 441 | Fat: 26g | Protein: 43g | Sodium: 955mg | Fiber: 1g | Carbohydrates: 1g

Red Snapper with Peppers and Vinegar

*The tartness of the vinegar and the sweetness of the peppers
perfectly complement the unique flavor of red snapper.*

INGREDIENTS | SERVES 6

¼ cup all-purpose flour

1 tablespoon curry powder

½ teaspoon ground black pepper

1½ pounds red snapper

1 tablespoon olive oil

1 medium red bell pepper, seeded and thinly sliced

1 medium green bell pepper, seeded and thinly sliced

1 tablespoon cider vinegar

¼ cup chopped cilantro leaves

1. Mix together the flour, curry powder, and black pepper in a shallow dish. Dredge fish in flour mixture.

2. Heat oil in a large skillet over medium-high heat. Cook fish 5 minutes per side.

3. Add bell peppers and vinegar, reduce heat to medium-low, and simmer 5 minutes more until fish flakes easily with a fork. Sprinkle with cilantro before serving.

Per Serving: Calories: 166 | Fat: 4g | Protein: 24g | Sodium: 74mg | Fiber: 1g | Carbohydrates: 7g

Curry Powder

Since curry powder is a blend of several spices and herbs, the flavor varies quite a bit. Use your favorite Caribbean or Indian curry powder, or venture to make your own mixture.

Grilled Tuna

Kalamata olives can be used in place of the anchovies if you like.

INGREDIENTS | SERVES 6

¼ cup apple juice

¼ cup dry red wine

1 tablespoon olive oil

½ tablespoon honey

¼ cup minced serrano chili pepper

Zest of 1 large lemon

1½ pounds fresh tuna

2 medium anchovies, chopped

1 teaspoon ground black pepper

1. In a large baking dish, mix together juice, wine, oil, honey, serrano pepper, and lemon zest. Add tuna and turn to coat. Marinate 30 minutes at room temperature.

2. Preheat a gas or charcoal grill to medium-high heat.

3. Remove tuna from marinade and place on grill. Reserve marinade. Grill tuna 2–4 minutes per side.

4. While tuna cooks, place reserved marinade in a small saucepan over medium heat and cook 5 minutes or until liquid is slightly thickened.

5. Place tuna on a serving platter and drizzle with marinade syrup, then sprinkle with anchovies and black pepper.

Per Serving: Calories: 237 | Fat: 9g | Protein: 31g | Sodium: 596mg | Fiber: 0g | Carbohydrates: 5g

Baked Tuna

Archaeologists have discovered evidence of extensive tuna fishing operations in Argolis, Greece, as early as 6000 B.C.

INGREDIENTS | SERVES 4

¼ cup extra-virgin olive oil, divided
1 large yellow onion, peeled and sliced
1 large green bell pepper, seeded and diced
2 cloves garlic, minced
3 tablespoons chopped parsley, divided
1 teaspoon dried marjoram (or ½ teaspoon dried oregano)
1 teaspoon salt
½ teaspoon ground black pepper
2 cups peeled minced tomatoes
½ cup water
4 (8-ounce) center-cut tuna fillets

1. Preheat oven to 400°F.

2. In a large skillet, heat 2 tablespoons olive oil over medium-high heat. Sauté onion and bell pepper until soft, about 6–8 minutes.

3. Add garlic, 2 tablespoons parsley, marjoram, salt, and black pepper. Stir and cook 2 minutes.

4. Add tomatoes and water and bring to boil. Reduce heat to medium-low and simmer 15–20 minutes.

5. Place tuna steaks in a large baking dish and top with remaining olive oil, making sure to coat the tuna with the oil. Pour prepared sauce over top. Bake uncovered 45 minutes.

6. Serve immediately, spooning some sauce over each portion and garnishing with remaining parsley.

Per Serving: Calories: 301 | Fat: 8.5g | Protein: 41g | Sodium: 353mg | Fiber: 2g | Carbohydrates: 11g

Tuna Panini MA

Here's a perfect make-ahead sandwich for a picnic or a trip to the beach.

INGREDIENTS | SERVES 6

1 medium apple, peeled, cored, and diced

¼ teaspoon lemon juice

1 cup water

1 pound cooked or canned tuna, drained and flaked

1 large hard-cooked egg, peeled and diced

1 medium red onion, peeled and diced

¼ cup chopped walnuts

2 tablespoons extra-virgin olive oil

1 tablespoon balsamic vinegar

1 teaspoon salt

½ teaspoon ground black pepper

1 loaf Italian bread

6 large Boston lettuce leaves

1. Combine apple, lemon juice, and water in a medium bowl; let sit 5 minutes. Drain and set aside.

2. In a medium bowl, mix together tuna, egg, onion, apple, nuts, oil, vinegar, salt, and pepper.

3. Cut bread in half lengthwise, then layer lettuce and tuna mixture on bottom half. Replace the top half and wrap tightly with plastic wrap. Refrigerate 1 hour.

4. Slice into 6 equal portions and serve.

Per Serving: Calories: 298 | Fat: 13g | Protein: 22g | Sodium: 618mg | Fiber: 2g | Carbohydrates: 21g

Grilled Jumbo Shrimp

Jumbo shrimp are plump, juicy, and perfect for grilling. Serve the grilled shrimp with rice pilaf or couscous.

INGREDIENTS | SERVES 4

¼ cup extra-virgin olive oil
¾ teaspoon salt
¼ teaspoon ground black pepper
½ teaspoon sweet paprika
12 large jumbo shrimp
½ cup butter
2 tablespoons fresh lemon juice
1 clove garlic, minced
⅛ teaspoon crushed red pepper
1 teaspoon minced fresh ginger
1 tablespoon chopped fresh parsley
1 tablespoon chopped fresh chives
3 tablespoons vegetable oil

1. Preheat a gas or charcoal grill to medium-high. Brush grill surface to make sure it is thoroughly clean.

2. In a medium bowl, whisk together olive oil, salt, black pepper, and paprika. Add shrimp and marinate 10 minutes.

3. In a small pot over medium heat, cook butter, lemon juice, garlic, crushed red pepper, and ginger until butter melts. Add parsley and chives. Keep sauce warm.

4. When grill is ready, dip a clean tea towel in the vegetable oil and wipe grill surface with oil. Place shrimp on grill and grill 2 minutes per side or until they turn pink.

5. Drizzle shrimp with butter sauce and serve remaining sauce on the side.

Per Serving: Calories: 470 | Fat: 39g | Protein: 28g | Sodium: 647mg | Fiber: 0.3g | Carbohydrates: 2g

Shrimp Saganaki

Saganaki refers to the two-handled cooking vessel traditionally used to serve this appetizer. You'll need lots of crusty bread for this dish.

INGREDIENTS | SERVES 4

¼ cup extra-virgin olive oil
½ cup sliced mushrooms
¼ cup finely chopped red onion
¼ cup diced green bell peppers
¼ cup diced red bell peppers
1 medium tomato, diced
½ cup crumbled feta cheese
1 teaspoon dried oregano
¼ teaspoon crushed red pepper
1 ounce ouzo
⅓ teaspoon salt
8 large head-on shrimp, deveined
¼ cup grated mozzarella

Shrimp Shells

Don't throw out your shrimp shells! Store shells in the freezer and then use them to create delicious seafood stock.

1. Preheat broiler.

2. Add oil to a medium skillet over medium-high heat and heat 30 seconds. Add mushrooms and sauté 2–3 minutes or until browned. Add onions, bell peppers, and tomatoes. Reduce heat to medium and simmer 5–7 minutes.

3. Remove the skillet from heat and stir in feta, oregano, crushed red pepper, ouzo, and salt.

4. Pour sauce into a medium baking dish. Add shrimp, nestling them slightly into the sauce. Top with mozzarella.

5. Broil about 5–6 minutes or until shrimp are pink and cheese is golden brown.

Per Serving: Calories: 123 | Fat: 6.5g | Protein: 8g | Sodium: 453mg | Fiber: 1g | Carbohydrates: 4g

Scallops Saganaki

If you want to tone down the heat in this dish, use just half a chili pepper.
Be sure to have plenty of crusty bread to soak up the sauce.

INGREDIENTS | SERVES 4

16 medium scallops, rinsed and patted dry
1 teaspoon salt
½ teaspoon ground black pepper
½ cup extra-virgin olive oil
⅓ cup dry white wine
2 ounces ouzo
2 tablespoons fresh lemon juice
6 cloves garlic, thinly sliced
1 small red chili pepper, stemmed and thinly sliced
½ teaspoon sweet paprika
1 small leek, trimmed, cleaned, and cut into matchsticks
⅔ cup bread crumbs
2 tablespoons chopped fresh parsley
1 large lemon, cut into wedges

1. Preheat oven to 450°F.

2. Season both sides of scallops with salt and black pepper. Place scallops in a medium baking dish (or divide them among four small baking dishes or ramekins). Set aside.

3. In a medium bowl, whisk oil, wine, ouzo, lemon juice, garlic, chili, and paprika. Pour sauce over scallops. Top with leeks and then bread crumbs.

4. Bake scallops on a middle rack 8–10 minutes.

5. Set oven to broil and bake another 2–3 minutes or until bread crumbs are golden.

6. Let scallops cool 5 minutes and top with parsley. Serve scallops with lemon wedges.

Per Serving: Calories: 353 | Fat: 18g | Protein: 6g | Sodium: 757mg | Fiber: 1g | Carbohydrates: 16g

Grilled Lobster

This grilled lobster is tender, juicy, and smoky. Always make sure you use live, whole lobsters the day you buy them.

INGREDIENTS | SERVES 4

- 4 (1¼ pound) live lobsters, split lengthwise
- ¼ cup plus ⅔ cup extra-virgin olive oil, divided
- 1½ teaspoons salt, divided
- ½ teaspoon ground black pepper
- ¾ teaspoon sweet paprika
- 1 clove garlic, peeled and minced
- 2 tablespoons fresh lemon juice
- 1½ tablespoons Dijon mustard
- 1 scallion, ends trimmed, finely chopped
- 1 tablespoon chopped parsley
- 1 tablespoon dried oregano
- 3 tablespoons vegetable oil

Splitting a Lobster

Purchase a live lobster the day you're going to eat it. Keep it in the refrigerator until you're ready. To numb the lobster, place it in the freezer for 20 minutes before killing it. Grip the lobster by the back of the body and stick a chef's knife into the area where the head and body meet. Press the knife down, cutting the lobster (lengthwise) in half.

1. Preheat a gas or charcoal grill to medium-high. Brush the flesh side of lobster with ¼ cup olive oil and season with 1 teaspoon salt, pepper, and paprika. Break off claws and reserve.

2. In a medium bowl, whisk remaining oil, garlic, lemon juice, mustard, scallion, parsley, oregano, and remaining salt. Set sauce aside.

3. When grill is hot, dip a clean tea towel in vegetable oil and wipe the grill surface with oil.

4. Place lobster claws on grill first. A minute later, place lobster bodies on grill, flesh-side down. Grill 3–4 minutes and then flip the bodies and claws. Grill another 2–3 minutes or until the shells have turned red and the meat is cooked.

5. Drizzle half of the sauce over the lobsters and serve the remaining sauce on the side.

Per Serving: Calories: 550 | Fat: 50g | Protein: 21g | Sodium: 1,244mg | Fiber: 1g | Carbohydrates: 2g

Grilled Octopus   MA

Braising octopus in its own liquid is the best and easiest way to tenderize it.

INGREDIENTS | SERVES 4

1 medium octopus, cleaned and ink
sac removed

⅓ cup red wine

2 tablespoons balsamic or red wine
vinegar, divided

1¼ teaspoons dried oregano, divided

¼ cup extra-virgin olive oil, divided

1 teaspoon salt

½ teaspoon ground black pepper

1 large lemon, cut into wedges

1. Add octopus to a large pot over medium-high heat. Cover the pot and cook octopus about 5–8 minutes. Uncover and check to see that octopus has released liquid. The octopus should be almost submerged in its own liquid. Cover and reduce heat to medium-low and cook about 45 minutes.

2. Take the pot off the heat and add wine, 1 tablespoon vinegar, and ½ teaspoon oregano. Let octopus cool completely. (You can do this step the day before; just keep the octopus refrigerated in its braising liquid until you need it.)

3. When you're ready to grill, take octopus out of the braising liquid and cut it into pieces; separate the tentacles and cut up the head. Discard braising liquid.

4. In a large bowl, combine octopus pieces, 2 tablespoons oil, remaining vinegar, ½ teaspoon oregano, salt, and pepper.

5. Preheat a gas or charcoal grill to medium-high heat. Place octopus on the grill and cook 2 minutes per side. Drizzle with remaining oil and sprinkle remaining oregano over octopus. Serve warm or room temperature with lemon wedges.

Per Serving: Calories: 213 | Fat: 14g | Protein: 13g | Sodium: 445mg | Fiber: 0g | Carbohydrates: 4g

Grilled Sardines

Serve these delicious sardines with some boiled greens, such as kale or spinach.

INGREDIENTS | SERVES 8

2 pounds fresh sardines, heads removed, cleaned, gutted, and scaled

½ cup extra-virgin olive oil, divided

2 teaspoons salt

¾ teaspoon ground black pepper

3 tablespoons vegetable oil

3 tablespoons fresh lemon juice

1½ teaspoons dried oregano

Sardines

If you were to visit any Mediterranean country, you'd notice the locals eating these small fish in restaurants. This little powerhouse fish is high in calcium, rich in B and D vitamins, and high in omega-3 fatty acids.

1. Preheat a gas or charcoal grill to medium-high. Brush grill surface to make sure it is thoroughly clean. Rinse sardines and pat dry with a paper towel.

2. Rub sardines on both sides with ¼ cup olive oil. Sprinkle both sides with salt and pepper.

3. When grill is ready, dip a clean tea towel in vegetable oil and wipe the grill surface with oil.

4. Place sardines on the grill and grill 2–3 minutes on each side.

5. Drizzle sardines with remaining olive oil and lemon juice. Sprinkle with oregano and serve.

Per Serving: Calories: 343 | Fat: 29g | Protein: 20g | Sodium: 692mg | Fiber: 0g | Carbohydrates: 0.5g

Oysters on the Half Shell

Serve these oysters with hot sauce or with Mediterranean Mignonette Sauce (see recipe in Chapter 12).

INGREDIENTS | SERVES 4

16 live fresh oysters

4 cups crushed ice

1 large lemon, cut into wedges

1. Place an oyster on a steady work surface with the hinged end facing up. Using a tea towel to help you hold the oyster, grip it with one hand. With the other hand, carefully stick a knife or oyster shucker into the hinge. Dig the knife into the hinge, wiggling the knife until the shell begins to open.

2. Slide the knife across the top shell to disconnect the muscle from the shell.

3. Discard the top shell. Slip the knife underneath the oyster and disconnect it from the bottom shell. Remove any pieces of dirt or broken shell.

4. Repeat this process with remaining oysters.

5. Serve oysters (in their bottom shells) on a bed of crushed ice with lemon wedges.

Per Serving: Calories: 46 | Fat: 1g | Protein: 4g | Sodium: 119mg | Fiber: 0.8g | Carbohydrates: 5g

Grilled Calamari

Serve this delicious and tender calamari dish with a green salad and some cold white wine. It's a wonderful summer meal.

INGREDIENTS | SERVES 4

4 (5" long) squid, cleaned
¼ cup extra-virgin olive oil
1 clove garlic, minced
1 teaspoon salt
½ teaspoon ground black pepper
3 tablespoons vegetable oil
2 tablespoons fresh lemon juice
½ teaspoon dried oregano

1. Preheat a gas or charcoal grill to medium-high heat.

2. In a medium bowl, combine squid, olive oil, garlic, salt, and pepper.

3. Dip a clean tea towel in vegetable oil and wipe the grill surface with oil. Place squid on the grill and cook 2–3 minutes per side.

4. Drizzle lemon juice on squid, sprinkle with oregano, and serve warm.

Per Serving: Calories: 226 | Fat: 15g | Protein: 18g | Sodium: 641mg | Fiber: 0g | Carbohydrates: 4g

Broiled Oysters

As with all shellfish, it is vital to keep oysters chilled. Do not open the shells until right before cooking.

INGREDIENTS | SERVES 6

36 oysters
2 tablespoons extra-virgin olive oil
½ teaspoon ground black pepper
1 teaspoon grated lemon zest
¼ cup minced parsley
½ teaspoon salt

1. Preheat broiler.

2. Shuck/open oyster shells (see opening instructions in Oysters on the Half Shell recipe in this chapter). Place on broiler pan or baking sheet in their bottom shell, discarding top shell. Drizzle each oyster with oil. Sprinkle with pepper and lemon zest.

3. Place under broiler until oysters are fully cooked, approximately 2–3 minutes. Top with parsley and salt and serve warm.

Per Serving: Calories: 98 | Fat: 7g | Protein: 6g | Sodium: 375mg | Fiber: 0g | Carbohydrates: 4g

Mussels Saganaki

This mussel dish is a specialty of Thessaloniki, Greece, where much of the local cuisine is spicy. Use sweet peppers if you wish to tone down the heat.

INGREDIENTS | SERVES 2

2 tablespoons extra-virgin olive oil

1 medium hot banana pepper, seeded and thinly sliced

2 medium tomatoes, chopped

½ teaspoon salt

1 pound fresh mussels, scrubbed and beards removed

⅓ cup crumbled feta cheese

2 teaspoons dried oregano

1. In a medium pot over medium heat, add oil and heat 30 seconds. Add pepper slices, tomatoes, and salt and cook 2–3 minutes.

2. Add mussels and cover. Increase heat to medium-high and steam mussels 5–6 minutes. Discard any mussels that haven't opened.

3. Add feta and oregano and shake the pan to combine them into the sauce. Serve hot.

Per Serving: Calories: 415 | Fat: 24g | Protein: 32g | Sodium: 1,518mg | Fiber: 3g | Carbohydrates: 18g

Mussels Marinara

Serve these mussels on a bed of pasta and have lots of bread on hand to soak up the sauce.

INGREDIENTS | SERVES 6

1 tablespoon olive oil

2 small shallots, peeled and minced

3 cloves garlic, minced

6 medium plum tomatoes, roughly chopped

1½ dozen mussels

1 cup dry red wine

½ cup fish stock or clam juice

¼ teaspoon crushed red pepper

1 teaspoon dried oregano

1. Heat oil in a large saucepan over medium heat. Add shallots, garlic, and tomatoes and sauté 5 minutes.

2. Add mussels, wine, stock, crushed red pepper, and oregano. Cook, stirring occasionally, until the mussels open, about 3–5 minutes.

Per Serving: Calories: 97 | Fat: 3g | Protein: 3g | Sodium: 52mg | Fiber: 2g | Carbohydrates: 9g

Slow Cooker Paella SC

Using a slow cooker to make paella really helps to develop the deep and delicious flavors of this popular Spanish dish.

INGREDIENTS | SERVES 6

1½ cups long grain rice

1 (14.5-ounce) can chopped tomatoes

2¼ cups low-sodium chicken broth

½ teaspoon crushed saffron threads or ½ teaspoon turmeric

½ teaspoon hot smoked paprika

1 tablespoon olive oil

½ pound Andouille sausage, halved and sliced

1 medium red onion, peeled and finely diced

6 (3-ounce) boneless, skinless chicken thighs

1 cup frozen baby peas, thawed

6 large deveined, shelled, and cooked shrimp, frozen

Slow Cooking with Shrimp

When slow cooking with shrimp, resist the temptation to put the shrimp in at the beginning of the recipe. While it takes longer to overcook foods in the slow cooker, delicate shrimp can go from tender to rubbery very quickly. For most recipes, 20 minutes on high is sufficient cooking time for shrimp.

1. In a 4- to 5-quart slow cooker, mix together rice, tomatoes, broth, saffron, and paprika.

2. In a large skillet or Dutch oven, heat oil over medium heat until hot but not smoking. Add sausage and onion and cook until sausage is brown and onion is softened. Remove sausage and onion with a slotted spoon. Add sausage and onion to slow cooker and stir well.

3. In the same skillet or Dutch oven, brown chicken thighs in reserved oil over medium-high heat until golden brown, about 10 minutes.

4. Place chicken on top of rice mixture. Cover and cook on low 5–6 hours.

5. Add thawed peas to mixture and stir well. Top with shrimp and cook an additional 30 minutes, or until shrimp and peas are cooked through.

Per Serving: Calories: 448 | Fat: 16g | Protein: 28g | Sodium: 421mg | Fiber: 3g | Carbohydrates: 45g

Cioppino   S C

This hearty and delicious seafood stew is best served with crusty sourdough bread to sop up all the juices.

INGREDIENTS | SERVES 8

1 medium onion, peeled and chopped

2 stalks celery, diced

6 cloves garlic, minced

1 (28-ounce) can diced tomatoes

8 ounces clam juice

¾ cup fish stock

1 (6-ounce) can tomato paste

1 teaspoon crushed red pepper

2 tablespoons minced oregano

2 tablespoons minced parsley

1 teaspoon red wine vinegar

10 ounces catfish nuggets

10 ounces large shrimp, peeled and deveined

6 ounces diced cooked clams

6 ounces lump crabmeat

¾ cup diced cooked lobster meat

¼ cup diced green onion

1. Place onion, celery, garlic, tomatoes, clam juice, stock, tomato paste, crushed red pepper, oregano, parsley, and vinegar in a 4- to 5-quart slow cooker. Stir vigorously. Cook on low 8 hours.

2. Add remaining ingredients and cook on high 30 minutes. Stir prior to serving.

Per Serving: Calories: 150 | Fat: 2g | Protein: 21g | Sodium: 434mg | Fiber: 2.5g | Carbohydrates: 11g

Better Butter

Set out some delicious herbed or spiced butter next to the bread, potatoes, or vegetables on your table. Blend 2 tablespoons of fresh tarragon, dill weed, dried rosemary, or 2 teaspoons of fresh minced garlic or crushed peppercorns into ¼ pound of softened butter.

CHAPTER 11

Sides

Amaranth Greens

The beautiful red, purple, and green leaves will brighten any dinner table.
If you can't find amaranth greens, use dandelion greens.

INGREDIENTS | SERVES 4

3 cups roughly chopped
   amaranth greens
3 teaspoons salt, divided
2 tablespoons extra-virgin olive oil
1 tablespoon lemon juice

Amaranth Greens

Amaranth greens, which grow wild in the Mediterranean region, are loaded with iron and are good for your blood. Look for amaranth at Asian markets. Young amaranth greens can be eaten raw, but mature greens need to be cooked because they are bitter.

1. Fill a large pot two-thirds with water and set it over medium-high heat. Bring water to a boil, and add amaranth and 2 teaspoons salt. Lower heat to medium and cook 10–12 minutes or until amaranth stems are fork-tender. Drain amaranth and discard the cooking water.

2. In a medium bowl, combine amaranth, oil, and lemon juice. Season greens with remaining salt and serve warm.

Per Serving: Calories: 65 | Fat: 7g | Protein: 0g | Sodium: 1,777mg | Fiber: 0g | Carbohydrates: 1g

Dandelion Greens

Be sure to wash dandelion greens well and cut away all of the root stalk when cleaning. The root stock is very tough and doesn't become tender when cooked. These greens are perfect as a side for grilled fish, or on their own with some crusty bread, kalamata olives, and feta.

INGREDIENTS | SERVES 6

4 pounds dandelion greens,
  stalks removed
½ cup extra-virgin olive oil
½ cup fresh lemon juice
1 teaspoon salt
½ teaspoon ground black pepper

1. Bring a large pot of water to a rolling boil over high heat. Add dandelion greens and cook until greens are tender, about 8–10 minutes. Remove and drain well. Place greens in a large serving bowl.

2. Combine oil, lemon juice, salt, and pepper in a small bowl and whisk to combine. Pour dressing over greens. Serve hot or at room temperature.

Per Serving: Calories: 300 | Fat: 20g | Protein: 8g | Sodium: 231mg | Fiber: 11g | Carbohydrates: 30g

Braised Escarole

Add grated Parmesan or Romano cheese to enhance the flavor of the escarole.

INGREDIENTS | SERVES 6

1 tablespoon olive oil

3 large heads escarole, torn into bite-sized pieces

2 large leeks, trimmed, cleaned, and sliced

8 cloves garlic, minced

1 cup canned cannellini beans, drained and rinsed

½ cup dry white wine

2 cups chicken broth

½ teaspoon ground black pepper

1. Heat the oil in a large Dutch oven over medium heat. Add escarole, leeks, and garlic; sauté 1 minute. Add beans and wine. Stir and cook 1 minute.

2. Add broth, cover, and simmer approximately 20 minutes. Remove from heat. Season with pepper and serve.

Per Serving: Calories: 181 | Fat: 4g | Protein: 9g | Sodium: 357mg | Fiber: 7g | Carbohydrates: 36g

Dutch Oven

If you don't have a Dutch oven, don't disregard this recipe. Any deep pan with a heavy bottom and tight-fitting lid can be substituted for a Dutch oven.

Braised Radicchio

Adding dried fruit, like raisins or dried apricots, will offset the bitterness of the greens.

INGREDIENTS | SERVES 6

1 tablespoon olive oil

6 medium heads radicchio, cut in half

2 large leeks, trimmed, cleaned, and cut into ½" strips

3 cloves garlic, minced

¼ cup dry red wine

1 cup orange juice

1 cup vegetable broth

½ teaspoon ground black pepper

1 teaspoon salt

1. Preheat oven to 375°F.

2. Heat the oil in a heavy-bottomed roasting pan over medium heat on stovetop. Add radicchio, leeks, and garlic; toss about 2 minutes.

3. Add wine and cook 5 minutes or until reduced by half. Add orange juice and broth. Remove roasting pan from stovetop, cover, and bake 25–30 minutes.

4. Remove from oven and arrange in a shallow bowl. Sprinkle with pepper and salt and serve.

Per Serving: Calories: 109 | Fat: 3g | Protein: 6g | Sodium: 626mg | Fiber: 5g | Carbohydrates: 16g

Arakas Latheros

This vegetarian dish of green peas, tomatoes, and mint, like many others in Greek cuisine, is called ladera, *which means "in oil."*

INGREDIENTS | SERVES 4

3 tablespoons extra-virgin olive oil, divided
1 tablespoon unsalted butter
4 scallions, ends trimmed, thinly sliced
18 ounces fresh peas
2 medium tomatoes, grated into a purée
3 tablespoons chopped fresh dill
1 teaspoon salt
½ teaspoon ground black pepper
1 cup hot water
1 tablespoon chopped fresh mint

1. Heat 2 tablespoons oil in a medium skillet over medium heat 30 seconds. Add butter and scallions. Cook 2 minutes until scallions are softened.

2. Add peas and cook another 2 minutes.

3. Add tomatoes, dill, salt, pepper, and hot water. Cover and cook 30 minutes or until all liquid is absorbed and only the oil remains.

4. Serve warm topped with mint and remaining oil.

Per Serving: Calories: 232 | Fat: 13g | Protein: 8g | Sodium: 503mg | Fiber: 7.5g | Carbohydrates: 21g

Roasted Carrots with Honey and Thyme

The honey brings out the sweetness of the carrots.

INGREDIENTS | SERVES 4

8 medium carrots, peeled
⅓ cup extra-virgin olive oil
1 teaspoon grated orange zest
1 tablespoon honey
2 tablespoons dry white wine
1 teaspoon salt
½ teaspoon ground black pepper
2 teaspoons fresh thyme leaves

1. Preheat oven to 400°F.

2. In a large bowl, combine carrots, oil, zest, honey, wine, salt, pepper, and thyme. Stir to coat. Empty the contents of the bowl evenly onto a baking tray.

3. Bake 25–30 minutes or until tender. Serve immediately or at room temperature.

Per Serving: Calories: 232 | Fat: 18g | Protein: 1g | Sodium: 574mg | Fiber: 3.5g | Carbohydrates: 16g

Steamed Cauliflower

You can use broccoli instead of the cauliflower, or try both for a colorful side dish.

INGREDIENTS | SERVES 6

1 head cauliflower, leaves removed, trimmed, and cut into florets
2 tablespoons extra-virgin olive oil
1 tablespoon fresh lemon juice
1 teaspoon salt
¼ cup chopped fresh chives

1. Pour water into a large pot with a steaming basket until water barely touches the basket. Bring water to a boil over medium-high heat, add cauliflower, and cover the pot. Steam cauliflower 15 minutes until cooked but not mushy.

2. In a large bowl, whisk oil, lemon juice, salt, and chives. Toss cauliflower in the dressing and serve.

Per Serving: Calories: 65 | Fat: 5g | Protein: 2g | Sodium: 422mg | Fiber: 2g | Carbohydrates: 5g

Preparing a Cauliflower

To prepare a cauliflower, first remove the leaves and trim away any brown spots. On the underside of the cauliflower, turn a small knife downward and around the stalk to release the florets.

Grilled Asparagus with Roasted Peppers and Feta

Keep an eye on the asparagus while grilling because they burn easily.

INGREDIENTS | SERVES 4

½ pound asparagus, trimmed

4 tablespoons extra-virgin olive oil, divided

½ teaspoon salt

¼ teaspoon ground black pepper

3 tablespoons vegetable oil

1 Roasted Red Pepper (see recipe in Chapter 3), chopped

½ cup crumbled feta cheese

1. In a large bowl, combine asparagus, 2 tablespoons olive oil, salt, and black pepper. Toss to coat asparagus.

2. Preheat a gas or charcoal grill to medium-high. When grill is ready, dip a clean tea towel in vegetable oil and wipe the grill's surface with oil.

3. Grill asparagus 2 minutes per side. Arrange on a platter and top with roasted pepper. Sprinkle cheese on top and drizzle with remaining olive oil.

Per Serving: Calories: 186 | Fat: 16g | Protein: 4g | Sodium: 406mg | Fiber: 2g | Carbohydrates: 4g

Sautéed Mushrooms with Brandy and Cream

Evaporated milk can be used as a lighter alternative to heavy cream in this dish. Try Metaxa brandy from Greece . . . it has a touch of honey!

INGREDIENTS | SERVES 4

1 tablespoon unsalted butter

1 tablespoon extra-virgin olive oil

1 pound cremini mushrooms, cleaned and halved

1 medium shallot, peeled and finely chopped

1 clove garlic, minced

1 teaspoon fresh thyme leaves

2 tablespoons chopped fresh parsley, divided

½ teaspoon salt

¼ teaspoon ground black pepper

1 ounce brandy

2 tablespoons heavy cream

1. Heat butter and oil in a large skillet over medium-high heat 30 seconds. Add mushrooms, shallots, and garlic. Stirring frequently, sauté mushrooms 5–6 minutes.

2. Reduce heat to medium and add thyme, 1 tablespoon parsley, salt, and pepper. Cover skillet and cook 3 minutes. Remove lid and continue cooking until most of the liquid has evaporated.

3. Add brandy and cook 2 minutes. Stir in cream and let sauce thicken 1 minute.

4. Sprinkle with remaining parsley and serve.

Per Serving: Calories: 126 | Fat: 9g | Protein: 4g | Sodium: 298mg | Fiber: 1.5g | Carbohydrates: 4g

Spend a Little More

Cremini mushrooms are a little more expensive than regular button mushrooms, but they are so worth the price. Cremini mushrooms are darker and have a firmer texture than button mushrooms. And cremini mushrooms taste richer and nuttier as well.

Lemon Garlic Green Beans SC

Lemon zest and sliced garlic add a fresh and bright flavor to these slow-cooked green beans.

INGREDIENTS | SERVES 4

Nonstick olive oil cooking spray

1½ pounds green beans, trimmed

3 tablespoons olive oil

3 large shallots, peeled and cut into thin wedges

6 cloves garlic, sliced

1 tablespoon grated lemon zest

½ teaspoon salt

½ teaspoon ground black pepper

½ cup water

1. Spray a 4- to 5-quart slow cooker with cooking spray. Place green beans in slow cooker. Add remaining ingredients over beans.

2. Cook on high 4–6 hours or on low 8–10 hours.

Per Serving: Calories: 167 | Fat: 10g | Protein: 4g | Sodium: 308mg | Fiber: 4.5g | Carbohydrates: 17g

Grilled Fennel

Fennel is a good source of vitamin A—add some to your next salad or soup.

INGREDIENTS | SERVES 6

3 large fennel bulbs, trimmed and cut lengthwise into 1½" slices

1 tablespoon olive oil

1 teaspoon salt

1 teaspoon ground black pepper

1. Preheat a gas or charcoal grill to medium-high heat.

2. Brush fennel with oil and season with salt and pepper. Grill fennel 4 minutes per side.

Per Serving: Calories: 57 | Fat: 2g | Protein: 1g | Sodium: 454mg | Fiber: 4g | Carbohydrates: 8g

Fennel Tops

Don't throw out the tops! Fennel tops can be used in stocks, but don't forget about their distinctive licorice flavor. Take that flavor into consideration when adding them to a stock.

Slow-Cooked White Beans MA SC

These beans are perfect for potlucks and parties! You can complete some parts of this recipe in advance, and save the final assembly until just before you lay out the food and start eating.

INGREDIENTS | SERVES 10

2 pounds dried white beans
Nonstick olive oil cooking spray
1 ham bone
2 cups water
1 bouquet garni
1 teaspoon salt
3 tablespoons butter
3 medium onions, peeled and diced
1 clove garlic, sliced
¼ cup chopped parsley
1 cup tomato sauce
½ teaspoon ground black pepper

1. In a large bowl, cover beans with cold water. Soak beans overnight, then drain.

2. Spray a 4- to 5-quart slow cooker with nonstick olive oil spray. Combine beans, ham bone, 2 cups water, bouquet garni, and salt in slow cooker.

3. Cover and cook on low 5–7 hours. Remove bone and bouquet garni; drain.

4. Heat butter in a large skillet over medium heat until butter is melted. Sauté onions and garlic until soft, about 5 minutes.

5. Add onion mixture, parsley, tomato sauce, and black pepper to beans in slow cooker. Cover and cook another hour.

Per Serving: Calories: 353 | Fat: 4g | Protein: 20g | Sodium: 382mg | Fiber: 18g | Carbohydrates: 61g

Cannellini Beans with Pancetta, Rosemary, and Thyme MA SC

These beans are so creamy and decadent, they'll be requested over and over again.

INGREDIENTS | SERVES 10

2 pounds dried cannellini beans
2 cups low-sodium chicken broth
½ teaspoon salt
½ teaspoon ground white pepper
1 tablespoon chopped rosemary
1 tablespoon chopped thyme
4 slices pancetta, chopped

1. Soak beans in cold water overnight. Drain and rinse.

2. Place beans, broth, salt, pepper, rosemary, and thyme in a 4- to 5-quart slow cooker. Cover and cook on low 6–8 hours.

3. Place pancetta in a medium skillet and cook over low heat, stirring occasionally. When meat is golden brown, after about 5–8 minutes, drain on paper towels.

4. Serve beans topped with crispy pancetta.

Per Serving: Calories: 364 | Fat: 5g | Protein: 21g | Sodium: 419mg | Fiber: 17g | Carbohydrates: 59g

Sherry and Balsamic Eggplant with Tomatoes and Goat Cheese S C

Combining sherry and balsamic vinegars creates a beautiful depth of flavor in this elegant eggplant dish.

INGREDIENTS | SERVES 4

1 large eggplant, cut into 1" pieces
3 large tomatoes, chopped
2 tablespoons olive oil
1 tablespoon balsamic vinegar
1 tablespoon sherry vinegar
½ teaspoon salt
½ teaspoon ground black pepper
1 tablespoon chopped basil
1 tablespoon chopped oregano
2 tablespoons crumbled goat cheese

1. Place eggplant, tomatoes, oil, and vinegars in a 4- to 5-quart slow cooker. Season with salt and pepper and stir well.

2. Cover and cook on high 3 hours.

3. Sprinkle basil, oregano, and goat cheese over eggplant and tomatoes before serving.

Per Serving: Calories: 185 | Fat: 12g | Protein: 7g | Sodium: 354mg | Fiber: 6g | Carbohydrates: 14g

Vegetable and Chickpea Stew with Lemon Couscous

This delectable side dish marries perfectly with chicken. It could also be a meal itself!

INGREDIENTS | SERVES 4

1 cup cooked chickpeas

2 large carrots, peeled and cut into 1" pieces

1 large onion, peeled and chopped

1 (14.5-ounce) can diced tomatoes

¼ cup low-sodium chicken broth

1 teaspoon cumin

1 teaspoon turmeric

1 teaspoon hot smoked paprika

2 cups boiling water

2 teaspoons lemon juice

1 cup couscous

¼ cup chopped parsley

1. Place chickpeas, carrots, onion, and tomatoes in a 4- to 5-quart slow cooker. Add broth, cumin, turmeric, and paprika. Stir well. Cover and cook on high 3½ hours.

2. Combine boiling water, lemon juice, and couscous in a medium bowl. Cover tightly and let cook 5 minutes. Stir into slow cooker.

3. Garnish with parsley before serving.

Per Serving: Calories: 287 | Fat: 2g | Protein: 11g | Sodium: 249mg | Fiber: 8g | Carbohydrates: 57g

Broccoli Raab with Bread Crumbs

Use a baking dish that doubles as a serving dish. This leaves the layered look of the finished recipe undisturbed.

INGREDIENTS | SERVES 6

2 tablespoons olive oil, divided
1½ pounds broccoli raab
1¼ cups bread crumbs
1 teaspoon ground black pepper
¼ cup grated Romano cheese

1. Preheat oven to 375°F. Grease a 13" × 9" baking dish with ¼ tablespoon of the oil.

2. Fill a large bowl with ice water. Bring 1 quart of water to a boil in a large stockpot. Blanch the broccoli raab in boiling water 2 minutes, then immediately drain in a colander and shock in ice-water bath. Drain thoroughly.

3. In a small bowl, mix remaining oil with bread crumbs.

4. Place the broccoli raab in a baking dish and crumble bread crumb mixture over the top. Sprinkle with pepper and cheese.

5. Place dish in oven for 5–10 minutes to heat through, then serve.

Per Serving: Calories: 204 | Fat: 9g | Protein: 9g | Sodium: 314mg | Fiber: 4g | Carbohydrates: 24g

Sautéed Artichoke Hearts

Fresh baby artichokes cut in half work well for this recipe.

INGREDIENTS | SERVES 6

½ cup all-purpose flour

½ cup skim milk

3 cups artichoke hearts, cut in half

1 tablespoon chopped marjoram

2 tablespoons chopped rosemary

2 tablespoons olive oil

1. Place flour in a shallow dish and milk in another shallow dish. Dip artichoke hearts in flour, then in milk, then in flour again. Place coated artichoke hearts on a rack. Sprinkle with marjoram and rosemary.

2. Heat the oil in a large skillet over medium heat. Sauté artichokes on all sides until golden brown, about 10 minutes. Drain on rack covered with paper towels before serving.

Per Serving: Calories: 143 | Fat: 5g | Protein: 6g | Sodium: 115mg | Fiber: 7g | Carbohydrates: 22g

Sautéed Mushrooms

A good assortment of mushrooms to try in this recipe include button, oyster, enoki, shiitake, and portobello.

INGREDIENTS | SERVES 6

1 tablespoon olive oil
1½ pounds assorted mushrooms, sliced
1 medium shallot, peeled and diced
4 cloves garlic, minced
¼ cup dry white wine
1 teaspoon ground black pepper
1 teaspoon tarragon leaves

1. Heat oil in a large skillet over medium heat, then add mushrooms, shallots, and garlic. Sauté approximately 10 minutes.

2. Add wine to pan and cook 10 minutes more, until reduced by half. Remove from heat and sprinkle with pepper and tarragon.

Per Serving: Calories: 368 | Fat: 3g | Protein: 11g | Sodium: 16mg | Fiber: 13g | Carbohydrates: 87g

Broiled Eggplant

If you use small Chinese eggplants, cut them in half rather than into slices.

INGREDIENTS | SERVES 6

4 small eggplants, sliced lengthwise into ⅛" pieces

4 cloves garlic, minced

1 tablespoon olive oil

2 teaspoons salt, divided

½ teaspoon ground black pepper

Broiler Pans

If you plan to do a lot of broiling, purchasing a broiler pan will be a good investment. Broiler pans work well because the vents and grooves allow the grease to drain off of whatever foods are being cooked.

1. Preheat broiler.

2. Toss all ingredients, except 1 teaspoon salt, together in a large bowl. Place eggplant slices on a broiler pan or baking sheet.

3. Broil 5 minutes per side until golden brown outside and soft inside. Season with remaining salt.

Per Serving: Calories: 111 | Fat: 3g | Protein: 4g | Sodium: 401mg | Fiber: 13g | Carbohydrates: 22g

Citrus-Steamed Carrots

Figs and carrots go together surprisingly well. The citrus and capers provide a tart contrast to the sweetness.

INGREDIENTS | SERVES 6

1 cup orange juice
2 tablespoons lemon juice
2 tablespoons lime juice
1 pound carrots, peeled and julienned
3 large figs, cut into wedges
1 tablespoon extra-virgin olive oil
1 tablespoon capers

1. In a large saucepan, combine orange, lemon, and lime juices over medium-high heat. Add carrots, cover, and steam until al dente, about 6 minutes. Remove from heat and cool.

2. Transfer carrots to a serving platter and arrange figs around carrots. Sprinkle olive oil and capers on top and serve.

Per Serving: Calories: 100 | Fat: 3g | Protein: 1g | Sodium: 95mg | Fiber: 3g | Carbohydrates: 19g

Bulgur-Stuffed Zucchini

The bulgur, tomatoes, parsley, mint, and lemon in the stuffing are reminiscent of a Middle Eastern tabouli.

INGREDIENTS | SERVES 6

3 small zucchini

2 teaspoons extra-virgin olive oil

1 medium shallot, peeled and diced

3 cloves garlic, minced

1 cup bulgur wheat

2 medium leeks, trimmed, cleaned, and thinly sliced

½ cup dry white wine

3 cups vegetable broth

1 medium tomato, chopped

1 teaspoon grated lemon zest

½ cup chopped mint

¼ cup chopped parsley

1. Preheat oven to 375°F.

2. Cut zucchini in half lengthwise and use a spoon to hollow out each half. Place halves in a microwave-safe dish, cut-side down. Pour in just enough water to cover the bottom of the dish. Microwave 1–2 minutes on high. Set aside to cool slightly.

3. Heat oil in a medium stockpot over medium heat. Add shallot, garlic, and bulgur. Cook, stirring constantly until slightly brown, about 5 minutes. Add leeks and cook 3 minutes more. Pour in wine and let reduce about 1 minute.

4. Add broth and simmer 15 minutes, until bulgur is thoroughly cooked. Remove from heat and stir in tomato, lemon zest, mint, and parsley.

5. Spoon bulgur mixture into the zucchini halves and place on a baking sheet. Bake until zucchini is reheated, about 5–8 minutes.

Per Serving: Calories: 141 | Fat: 2g | Protein: 6g | Sodium: 411mg | Fiber: 6g | Carbohydrates: 23g

Shaved Fennel with Orange Sections and Hazelnuts

Tangelos, mandarin, or any easily sectioned citrus work wonderfully with this recipe.

INGREDIENTS | SERVES 6

6 large oranges

3 medium fennel bulbs, thinly shaved with mandoline

1 tablespoon chopped hazelnuts

3 tablespoons fresh orange juice

2 tablespoons extra-virgin olive oil

1 tablespoon fresh orange zest

1. Remove the peel and pith from the oranges. With a small paring knife, remove each section of the oranges.

2. Form a mound of fennel on a serving platter and arrange orange sections on top. Sprinkle with nuts, then drizzle with orange juice and oil. Finish with a sprinkle of zest.

Per Serving: Calories: 176 | Fat: 6g | Protein: 3g | Sodium: 61mg | Fiber: 8g | Carbohydrates: 32g

Greek Roasted Potatoes

Lemony roasted potatoes are a must for any Greek feast and are often paired with roast lamb, beef, or chicken.

INGREDIENTS | SERVES 12

8 large Yukon gold or russet potatoes, peeled and sliced lengthwise into wedges

½ cup extra-virgin olive oil

2 tablespoons fresh lemon juice

½ teaspoon ground black pepper

1½ teaspoons salt

1 teaspoon dried oregano

½ cup hot water

1. Preheat oven to 425°F.

2. In a large bowl, combine potatoes, oil, lemon juice, pepper, salt, oregano, and water. Stir to coat.

3. Empty the bowl into a deep roasting pan. Bake 20 minutes. Stir potatoes and bake another 20 minutes or until fork-tender.

Per Serving: Calories: 245 | Fat: 9g | Protein: 4g | Sodium: 310mg | Fiber: 5g | Carbohydrates: 34g

Crispy Roasted Potatoes

These potatoes are crispy outside and fluffy inside. Serve them with a Sunday roast of lamb or pork.

INGREDIENTS | SERVES 12

12 medium Yukon gold potatoes, peeled
3½ teaspoons salt, divided
½ cup extra-virgin olive oil
4 cloves garlic, minced

1. In a large pot over medium-high heat, put potatoes, 1 teaspoon salt, and just enough water to cover potatoes by 1 inch. Bring to a boil and reduce heat to medium. Cook 10 minutes.

2. Preheat oven to 425°F.

3. In a medium roasting pan, combine oil and garlic.

4. Drain potatoes and add them to the pan. Sprinkle potatoes with remaining salt and toss gently to coat potatoes in oil and garlic.

5. Roast 20 minutes. Remove pan from oven. Using a potato masher, gently flatten potatoes until they are about 1 inch thick. Spoon some oil from the pan over potatoes and roast another 10 minutes or until golden.

6. Serve immediately.

Per Serving: Calories: 218 | Fat: 8g | Protein: 3.5g | Sodium: 600mg | Fiber: 5g | Carbohydrates: 31g

Feta Fries

Making the perfect fries involves great ingredients and proper techniques. Potatoes fried in olive oil are an amazing treat. Try them once and you won't want fries any other way.

INGREDIENTS | SERVES 6

3 cups olive oil

4 large Yukon gold potatoes, peeled and cut into strips

2 teaspoons salt

½ cup Feta-Yogurt Sauce (see recipe in Chapter 12)

Frying with Olive Oil

Olive oil has a smoke point of 410°F, well above the 365°F–375°F range that is ideal for frying. So don't shy away from frying with delicious olive oil.

1. Heat oil in a medium deep pot over medium-high heat until the temperature reaches 275°F. Adjust heat to keep temperature at 275°F while frying.

2. Add potatoes and fry 8 minutes or until fork-tender. Remove potatoes with a slotted spoon and allow to cool at least 10 minutes.

3. Reheat oil to 375°F. Adjust heat to keep temperature at 375°F while frying. Add cooked potatoes and fry until golden and crispy.

4. Place fries on a tray lined with paper towels to soak up excess oil and season with salt.

5. Serve fries hot with Feta-Yogurt Sauce either spooned over them or on the side for dipping.

Per Serving: Calories: 408 | Fat: 27g | Protein: 4g | Sodium: 749mg | Fiber: 6g | Carbohydrates: 38g

Lemony Sweet Potatoes with Pomegranate Seeds

Not only is this dish visually stunning; it's healthful and simple to make.

INGREDIENTS | SERVES 4

1 teaspoon plus 1 tablespoon olive oil, divided

2 large sweet potatoes, peeled and diced into ½" cubes

1½ tablespoons packed light brown sugar

½ teaspoon nutmeg

½ teaspoon cinnamon

1 tablespoon lemon juice

½ cup pomegranate seeds

1 teaspoon sea salt

1. Grease a 4- to 5-quart slow cooker with 1 teaspoon oil. Place sweet potato cubes in slow cooker.

2. In a small bowl, mix remaining oil with brown sugar, nutmeg, and cinnamon. Add to slow cooker and mix well. Cover and cook on low 6–8 hours.

3. Stir in lemon juice and pomegranate seeds. Crush sea salt with a mortar and pestle and sprinkle over potatoes. Serve immediately.

Per Serving: Calories: 136 | Fat: 5g | Protein: 1.5g | Sodium: 628mg | Fiber: 3g | Carbohydrates: 22g

Removing Pomegranate Seeds Without Staining

Pomegranate seeds are wonderful, but they can stain a wooden chopping board. To avoid that, cut the top off of the pomegranate, quickly cut it into quarters, and drop them into a large bowl filled with water. Work the seeds out in the water, drain, and discard skins.

Sauerkraut Rice

This side dish is savory and a little tangy, with just a hint of smoky flavor from the paprika. It's perfect when paired with roast pork.

INGREDIENTS | SERVES 6

3 cups water

1½ cups long-grain rice, rinsed

2½ teaspoons salt, divided

¼ cup unsalted butter

1 small onion, peeled and chopped

1 (32-ounce) jar sauerkraut or choucroute, rinsed and drained

1½ teaspoons sweet paprika

½ teaspoon smoked paprika

¾ teaspoon ground black pepper

1. Bring water to a boil in a medium pot over medium-high heat. Add rice and 2 teaspoons salt to the boiling water, reduce heat to medium, and cook 20–25 minutes.

2. Melt butter in a medium skillet over medium heat and add onions. Cook 4–5 minutes until onions soften. Add sauerkraut, sweet paprika, and smoked paprika and cook another 2 minutes. Stir in rice and cook another 2 minutes.

3. Season with remaining salt and pepper. Serve warm.

Per Serving: Calories: 271 | Fat: 8g | Protein: 5g | Sodium: 1,373mg | Fiber: 5g | Carbohydrates: 44g

Saffron Couscous

This bright yellow dish is a delicious side for fish or seafood. Add some chopped grilled vegetables to the couscous and you have a fantastic vegetarian main dish.

INGREDIENTS | SERVES 6

2¼ cups water

½ teaspoon salt

⅛ teaspoon saffron threads

2 tablespoons unsalted butter, divided

1½ cups couscous, uncooked

Saffron

Saffron is a spice derived from the dried stigmas of crocus plants. The crocus must be picked by hand so that the delicate stigmas are kept intact. Because of this, saffron is the most expensive spice in the world. Thankfully, a little goes a long way to add rich flavor and bright color to a dish.

1. In a medium pot over medium-high heat, combine water, salt, saffron, and 1 tablespoon butter. Bring mixture to a boil and remove it from heat. Stir in couscous and cover the pot. Let couscous stand 5 minutes or until all liquid has been absorbed.

2. Fluff couscous with a fork and stir in remaining butter. Serve hot or at room temperature.

Per Serving: Calories: 196 | Fat: 4g | Protein: 5.5g | Sodium: 194mg | Fiber: 2g | Carbohydrates: 33g

Herb and Lemon Couscous

Change up the herbs and use whatever you have on hand. Serve this side with fish or chicken.

INGREDIENTS | SERVES 6

2¼ cups water

½ teaspoon salt

2 teaspoons grated lemon zest

1 tablespoon fresh lemon juice

2 tablespoons extra-virgin olive oil, divided

1½ cups couscous, uncooked

1 tablespoon finely chopped fresh parsley

1 tablespoon finely chopped fresh chives

1 tablespoon finely chopped fresh mint

1. In a medium pot over medium-high heat, combine water, salt, lemon zest, lemon juice, and 1 tablespoon oil. Bring mixture to a boil and remove from heat. Stir in couscous. Cover and let stand 5 minutes or until couscous has absorbed the liquid.

2. Fluff couscous with a fork. Stir in parsley, chives, mint, and remaining oil. Serve couscous hot or at room temperature.

Per Serving: Calories: 204 | Fat: 4g | Protein: 5.5g | Sodium: 204mg | Fiber: 2.5g | Carbohydrates: 33g

Katsamaki

Most people are familiar with Italian polenta; this is the Greek version.

INGREDIENTS | SERVES 6

2½ cups chicken or vegetable stock

1 cup cornmeal

¼ cup grated kefalotyri or other sharp
  goat's milk cheese

½ teaspoon ground black pepper

1. Heat stock in a medium pot over medium-high heat until almost boiling.

2. Slowly whisk in a steady stream of cornmeal. Continue to whisk to remove any lumps until you get a smooth porridge-like consistency. Remove pot from heat.

3. Stir in cheese and pepper. Serve immediately.

Per Serving: Calories: 120 | Fat: 2.5g | Protein: 5g | Sodium: 60mg | Fiber: 1g | Carbohydrates: 19g

Garlic Bread

This recipe will have your guests asking for more, so make a lot!

INGREDIENTS | SERVES 8

½ cup extra-virgin olive oil
2 cloves garlic, minced
1 sun-dried tomato, minced
¼ cup chopped fresh chives
2 tablespoons chopped fresh parsley
1 teaspoon dried rosemary
1 teaspoon dried oregano
1 teaspoon salt
¼ teaspoon crushed red pepper
1 (20") baguette

1. Preheat oven to 300°F.

2. In a small bowl, whisk oil, garlic, tomato, chives, parsley, rosemary, oregano, salt, and crushed red pepper until ingredients are well incorporated.

3. Slice baguette lengthwise, but leave the back seam intact. Spread garlic mixture evenly inside both the top and bottom of the baguette. Fold bread closed.

4. Wrap bread in aluminum foil and bake 15–20 minutes.

5. Unwrap garlic bread and serve it warm.

Per Serving: Calories: 470 | Fat: 16g | Protein: 14g | Sodium: 1,081mg | Fiber: 3g | Carbohydrates: 68g

CHAPTER 12

Sauces and Accompaniments

Fresh Tomato Sauce

Fresh tomato sauce can be made in minutes. Use it to top pasta, polenta, or grilled chicken.

INGREDIENTS | MAKES 1 GALLON

1 tablespoon olive oil

2 large yellow onions, peeled and diced

1 medium shallot, peeled and minced

8 cloves garlic, minced

20 medium plum tomatoes, chopped

½ cup dry red wine

10 large basil leaves, chopped

2 tablespoons chopped oregano leaves

¼ cup chopped parsley

½ teaspoon ground black pepper

1. Heat oil in a large stockpot over medium heat. Add onions, shallots, and garlic. Sauté lightly approximately 2–3 minutes then add tomatoes. Cook, stirring frequently, approximately 3 minutes.

2. Add wine and cook approximately 10 minutes more.

3. Stir in basil, oregano, parsley, and pepper before serving.

Per Serving (½ cup): Calories: 30 | Fat: 1g | Protein: 1g | Sodium: 6mg | Fiber: 1g | Carbohydrates: 5g

Wine in Cooking

Don't use cooking wines—they have a high salt content and don't taste very good! Use a full-bodied red wine that you would drink with dinner. You don't have to spend a lot—ordinary table wines are usually more than sufficient for cooking purposes.

Red Pepper Coulis

Coulis can be made using any fruit or vegetable. To add variety, experiment with the addition of herbs and spices. Use this sauce with fried cheese, grilled/roasted lamb, beef, or chicken.

INGREDIENTS | MAKES 2 CUPS

6 Roasted Red Peppers (see recipe in Chapter 3), diced

1 teaspoon olive oil

1½ teaspoons salt

½ teaspoon ground black pepper

Place roasted peppers and oil in a food processor and purée until smooth. Season with salt and black pepper.

Per Serving (2 tablespoons): Calories: 18 | Fat: 1g | Protein: 1g | Sodium: 445mg | Fiber: 1g | Carbohydrates: 3g

Ladolemono

Ladolemono is a compound word in Greek that means "oil-lemon." This basic recipe is great on grilled meats like steak, souvlaki, and fish. Try adding different herbs to this versatile sauce.

INGREDIENTS | MAKES ½ CUP

3 tablespoons fresh lemon juice

½ cup extra-virgin olive oil

1 teaspoon salt

2 teaspoons dried oregano

Whisk all ingredients in a small bowl until well combined. Serve at room temperature.

Per Serving (2 tablespoons): Calories: 120 | Fat: 13g | Protein: 0g | Sodium: 286mg | Fiber: 0g | Carbohydrates: 0.5g

Romesco Sauce

This sauce from Spain is delicious served on grilled or toasted bread, spread on chicken or fish, or offered with grilled vegetables.

INGREDIENTS | MAKES 2 CUPS

1 small Roasted Red Pepper (see recipe in Chapter 3)

1 small chili pepper, stemmed

¼ cup chopped roasted almonds

3 cloves garlic, smashed

1 slice stale white bread

3 ripe plum tomatoes, peeled, seeded, and roughly chopped

1 tablespoon balsamic vinegar

½ teaspoon salt

¼ teaspoon ground black pepper

⅔ cup extra-virgin olive oil

1. Combine all ingredients except oil in a food processor. Process until puréed into a paste.

2. With the processor running, slowly add oil until it is well incorporated. Serve at room temperature.

Per Serving (¼ cup): Calories: 199 | Fat: 14g | Protein: 1.5g | Sodium: 145mg | Fiber: 1g | Carbohydrates: 5g

Feta-Yogurt Sauce

Try this sauce on stuffed zucchini blossoms, a salad, fries, or nachos.

INGREDIENTS | MAKES 2 CUPS

½ cup crumbled feta cheese
½ cup plain yogurt
1 clove garlic, minced
½ cup warm vegetable stock
¼ cup chopped fresh chives

1. Combine feta, yogurt, and garlic in a medium bowl and mash with a fork.

2. Add stock and stir until well combined. Stir in chives. Serve at room temperature or warm over low heat 8–10 minutes.

Per Serving (¼ cup): Calories: 37 | Fat: 2.5g | Protein: 2g | Sodium: 116mg | Fiber: 0g | Carbohydrates: 1.5g

Tartar Sauce

This tartar sauce is a little more healthful than a traditional recipe because the amount of mayonnaise is reduced and Greek yogurt is added. Serve this sauce with fried fish or other seafood.

INGREDIENTS | MAKES 1 CUP

¼ cup mayonnaise
3 tablespoons plain Greek yogurt
¼ cup finely chopped red onion
2 tablespoons minced dill pickles
2 tablespoons chopped chives
2 tablespoons chopped fresh parsley
2 tablespoons chopped fresh dill
2 tablespoons capers, drained and finely chopped
2 tablespoons lemon juice
¼ teaspoon ground black pepper

Combine all ingredients in a small bowl. Refrigerate or serve at room temperature.

Per Serving (2 tablespoons): Calories: 59 | Fat: 5g | Protein: 0.5g | Sodium: 118mg | Fiber: 0g | Carbohydrates: 2g

Greek-Style Chimichurri

Chimichurri is a specialty of Argentina and is often served with grilled meats. This Greek-style recipe highlights Greek oregano. You may use fresh or dried oregano in this sauce.

INGREDIENTS | MAKES 2 CUPS

1 cup fresh parsley leaves

2 tablespoons Greek oregano

4 scallions, ends trimmed, chopped

3 cloves garlic, smashed

½ large carrot, peeled and grated

½ cup extra-virgin olive oil

2 tablespoons red wine vinegar

½ teaspoon salt

¼ teaspoon ground black pepper

Combine all ingredients in a food processor and process until smooth. Serve at room temperature.

Per Serving (¼ cup): Calories: 126 | Fat: 12g | Protein: 0.5g | Sodium: 146mg | Fiber: 1g | Carbohydrates: 2g

Shortcut Sour Cherry Spoon Sweet

This is a shortcut recipe for making a sour cherry sauce. It's ideal for topping a cheesecake, serving on top of plain Greek yogurt, or spiking a sauce for pork or game meat.

INGREDIENTS | MAKES 2½ CUPS

1½ cups jarred sour cherries, plus 1 cup of the liquid

1 cup sugar

1 teaspoon vanilla extract

1. Bring cherries, cherry liquid, and sugar to a boil in a medium pot over medium-high heat. Reduce heat to medium-low, and cook 15–20 minutes to break down the cherries a little and to thicken the sauce to a consistency like syrup.

2. Remove from heat and add vanilla. Cool. Serve at room temperature.

Per Serving (¼ cup): Calories: 93 | Fat: 0g | Protein: 0g | Sodium: 0mg | Fiber: 0.5g | Carbohydrates: 23g

Almond-Potato Skordalia

Skordalia is a garlicky Greek condiment that is often paired with fried salted cod. It also goes well with roasted beets.

INGREDIENTS | MAKES 2 CUPS

2 large Yukon gold potatoes, unpeeled
1 teaspoon salt, divided
5 cloves garlic, peeled and minced
½ cup chopped blanched almonds
2 tablespoons red wine vinegar
⅓ cup olive oil

1. Place potatoes, ½ teaspoon salt, and enough water to cover potatoes by 1 inch in a medium pot over high heat. Cover pot, and bring to a boil. Reduce heat to medium and simmer 15 minutes or until potatoes are fork-tender. Drain potatoes and set aside to cool.

2. As soon as potatoes are cool enough to handle, remove skins with the back of a knife. Cut potatoes into quarters and set aside.

3. Put garlic, almonds, remaining salt, and vinegar in a large mortar. Using the pestle, mash ingredients into a paste. Add potatoes to the mortar and mash into garlic mixture. Stir oil into the potato mash in small increments.

4. Serve at room temperature.

Per Serving (¼ cup): Calories: 101 | Fat: 3g | Protein: 3g | Sodium: 298mg | Fiber: 3g | Carbohydrates: 16g

Fig-Ouzo Sauce

This sauce makes a wonderful topping for ice cream. You can also use it to top Greek yogurt, soft cheeses, or grilled halloumi.

INGREDIENTS | MAKES 2 CUPS

1 cup boiling water
15 dried figs, halved
¼ cup honey
¼ cup ouzo

1. Combine hot water and figs in a medium bowl. Cover bowl and allow figs to steep 10 minutes.

2. Put figs and soaking water into a food processor and process until puréed.

3. Transfer half the fig mixture to a small saucepan over medium heat. Add honey, and cook 5 minutes. Stir in remaining fig mixture and cook 5 more minutes.

4. Stir in ouzo, increase heat to medium-high, and cook 2–3 minutes.

5. Allow to cool to room temperature before using.

Per Serving (¼ cup): Calories: 87 | Fat: 0g | Protein: 0.5g | Sodium: 3mg | Fiber: 1.5g | Carbohydrates: 18g

Basil and Pine Nut Pesto

Enjoy this sauce simply tossed in spaghetti or paired with a simply cooked chicken breast or fish fillet.

INGREDIENTS | MAKES 1 CUP

½ cup pine nuts

8 cloves garlic, smashed

1 cup basil leaves

¼ cup extra-virgin olive oil

¼ cup grated Parmesan or
Romano cheese

½ teaspoon salt

¼ teaspoon ground black pepper

1. Pulse pine nuts and garlic in a food processor until nuts are finely chopped and garlic is minced. Add basil and pulse until mixture becomes a paste.

2. With processor running, slowly add oil until mixture is smooth. Empty sauce into a bowl and add cheese, salt, and pepper.

3. Serve at room temperature.

Per Serving (2 tablespoons): Calories: 123 | Fat: 11g | Protein: 2.5g | Sodium: 209mg | Fiber: 1g | Carbohydrates: 2.5g

The Old-Fashioned Way

Although it is easier to use a food processor or blender to prepare this pesto sauce, you can also make this pesto the old-fashioned way: using a mortar and pestle. The perfect texture that is achieved using this method cannot be duplicated with a food processor.

Parsley and Walnut Pesto

Try this variation of a classic pesto sauce on any pasta for a delicious meal. Serve the sauce warm or at room temperature.

INGREDIENTS | MAKES 1 CUP

½ cup walnuts

8 cloves garlic, smashed

1 cup parsley leaves

¼ cup extra-virgin olive oil

¼ cup grated Parmesan or
　Romano cheese

½ teaspoon salt

¼ teaspoon ground black pepper

A New Twist on an Old Recipe

Most people are familiar with traditional pesto, which is made with basil and pine nuts, but this variation with parsley and walnuts is very popular.

1. Pulse walnuts and garlic in a food processor until nuts are finely chopped and garlic is minced. Add parsley and pulse until mixture becomes a paste.

2. With processor running, slowly add oil until the mixture is smooth. Empty sauce into a small bowl and add cheese, salt, and pepper.

3. Serve at room temperature.

Per Serving (2 tablespoons): Calories: 128 | Fat: 12g | Protein: 2.5g | Sodium: 194mg | Fiber: 1g | Carbohydrates: 2.5g

Almond and Arugula Pesto

Arugula spices up any dish with its peppery taste. It is complemented by any nut or fruit.

INGREDIENTS | MAKES 1 CUP

¼ cup almonds

6 cloves garlic

3 cups roughly chopped arugula

⅓ cup olive oil

1 teaspoon salt

½ teaspoon ground black pepper

1. Pulse almonds in a food processor until finely chopped. Add garlic and pulse until a paste is formed. Add arugula and pulse 1 minute.

2. While the blender is running, drizzle in oil until the mixture is smooth. Add salt and pepper.

Per Serving (2 tablespoons): Calories: 102 | Fat: 11g | Protein: 1g | Sodium: 297mg | Fiber: 1g | Carbohydrates: 2g

Creamy Lemon Sauce

This sauce is creamy without the use of eggs or cream, and is an ideal sauce for vegans or people who are lactose-intolerant. Try this sauce on baked or poached fish.

INGREDIENTS | MAKES 2 CUPS

1½ cups vegetable stock

1 medium white onion, peeled and chopped

1 (½") lemon slice

½ cup extra-virgin olive oil

2 tablespoons Arborio rice

¼ teaspoon salt

⅛ teaspoon ground black pepper

½ teaspoon fresh lemon juice

1. In a small pan over medium-high heat, boil stock, onions, lemon slice, and oil. Reduce heat to medium-low.

2. Add rice, cover, and cook 15 minutes, stirring occasionally. Remove pot from heat and remove and discard lemon slice. Let sauce cool 5 minutes.

3. Using an immersion blender or a regular blender, purée sauce until smooth. Season with salt and pepper. Stir in lemon juice. Serve warm.

Per Serving (¼ cup): Calories: 145 | Fat: 13g | Protein: 1.5g | Sodium: 88mg | Fiber: 0.5g | Carbohydrates: 5g

Paprika Sauce

This sauce is great with Keftedes (see recipe in Chapter 8) and over French fries as an alternative to ketchup.

INGREDIENTS | MAKES 2½ CUPS

1 tablespoon unsalted butter

2 tablespoons all-purpose flour

1 cup warm whole milk

¼ cup finely diced onion

1 teaspoon sweet paprika

½ cup grated Graviera or Gruyère cheese

⅓ cup plain Greek yogurt

½ teaspoon salt

¼ teaspoon ground black pepper

¼ cup chopped fresh chives

⅛ teaspoon crushed red pepper

1. Melt butter in a medium pot over medium heat. Stir in flour and keep stirring 2 minutes.

2. Whisk in milk, onions, and paprika. Once milk has thickened, add cheese and cook until cheese melts into the sauce. If sauce is too thick, add a little more milk.

3. Take sauce off the heat and stir in yogurt then salt and black pepper.

4. Stir in chives and crushed red pepper. Serve warm or at room temperature.

Per Serving (2 tablespoons): Calories: 30 | Fat: 2g | Protein: 1.5g | Sodium: 75mg | Fiber: 0g | Carbohydrates: 1.5g

Mediterranean Mignonette Sauce

Serve with fresh shucked Oysters on the Half Shell (see recipe in Chapter 10).

INGREDIENTS | MAKES 1 CUP

⅔ cup sparkling rosé wine

2 tablespoons red wine vinegar

½ teaspoon ground pepper

2 tablespoons finely diced red onions or shallots

1 tablespoon finely diced radishes

1. Bring wine and vinegar to a boil in a small pot over medium heat. Reduce heat to medium-low, and cook until liquid is reduced by half.

2. Remove pot from the heat, and add pepper, onions, and radishes.

3. Let sauce cool to room temperature before serving.

Per Serving (1 tablespoon): Calories: 9 | Fat: 0g | Protein: 0g | Sodium: 1mg | Fiber: 0g | Carbohydrates: 0.5g

Rosemary-Mushroom Sauce S C

Try this sauce with egg noodles. Add 8 ounces of dried egg noodles to the slow cooker at the end of the cooking time and cook on high for 15 minutes or until the noodles are tender.

INGREDIENTS | SERVES 4

1 teaspoon butter

1 large onion, peeled and thinly sliced

8 ounces sliced mushrooms

1 tablespoon crushed rosemary

3 cups low-sodium chicken broth

Save Time!

Buy sliced mushrooms instead of slicing them yourself. Most stores carry several varieties in the produce section. Cremini and button are popular small mushrooms. Portobello mushrooms are large and meaty enough to use as a meat substitute.

1. Melt butter in a nonstick skillet over medium heat. Add onion and mushrooms and sauté until onion is soft, about 5 minutes.

2. Place onion mixture in a 4- to 5-quart slow cooker. Add rosemary and broth. Stir. Cook on low 6–8 hours or on high 3 hours.

Per Serving: Calories: 67 | Fat: 3g | Protein: 5g | Sodium: 599mg | Fiber: 1.5g | Carbohydrates: 14g

Artichoke Sauce   SC

Cooking artichokes slowly gives them a velvety texture. Try this sauce to top roast or grilled chicken or even baked fish.

INGREDIENTS | SERVES 4

1 teaspoon olive oil

8 ounces frozen artichoke hearts, defrosted

3 cloves garlic, minced

1 medium onion, peeled and minced

2 tablespoons capote capers

1 (28-ounce) can crushed tomatoes

Cleaning Slow Cookers

Do not use abrasive tools or cleansers on a slow cooker insert. They may scratch the surface, allowing bacteria and food to be absorbed. Use a soft sponge and baking soda for stubborn stains.

1. Heat oil in a large nonstick skillet over medium heat. Sauté artichokes, garlic, and onion until onion is translucent and most of the liquid has evaporated, about 8 minutes. Put mixture in a 4- to 5-quart slow cooker. Stir in capers and tomatoes.

2. Cook on high 4 hours or on low 8 hours.

Per Serving: Calories: 85 | Fat: 2g | Protein: 4g | Sodium: 300mg | Fiber: 5.5g | Carbohydrates: 16g

Fennel and Caper Sauce S C

Try this sauce over boneless pork chops or boneless, skinless chicken breasts or egg noodles.

INGREDIENTS | SERVES 4

2 fennel bulbs with stalks

2 tablespoons nonpareil capers

½ cup low-sodium chicken broth

2 shallots, peeled and thinly sliced

2 cups diced tomatoes

¼ teaspoon salt

½ teaspoon ground black pepper

⅓ cup minced parsley

1. Cut off fennel stalks and discard or freeze for another use. Reserve 2 tablespoons fennel fronds. Thinly slice fennel bulbs.

2. Place fennel, capers, broth, shallots, tomatoes, salt, and pepper in a 4- to 5-quart slow cooker. Cook on low 2 hours, and then add parsley. Cook an additional 15–30 minutes on high. Garnish with reserved fronds.

Per Serving: Calories: 76 | Fat: 0.5g | Protein: 4g | Sodium: 444mg | Fiber: 5g | Carbohydrates: 15g

Lemon Mustard Sauce

This sauce goes well with grilled fish. It can also serve as a dressing for green salads.

INGREDIENTS | MAKES 2/3 CUP

¼ cup fresh lemon juice
2 cloves garlic, pressed
1 tablespoon grated lemon zest
1 tablespoon prepared mustard
¼ cup extra-virgin olive oil
1 teaspoon thyme honey
1 teaspoon salt
½ teaspoon ground black pepper

Combine all ingredients in a small bowl and whisk until smooth. Serve immediately.

Per Serving (1 tablespoon): Calories: 54 | Fat: 5.4g | Protein: 0g | Sodium: 2mg | Fiber: 0g | Carbohydrates: 1.4g

Garlic and Herb Oil

You can omit garlic and substitute dried chili, or use any fresh herb in place of the tarragon. Use this oil to finish grilled meats, fish, or even vegetables.

INGREDIENTS | MAKES 2 CUPS

1 pint olive oil
5 cloves garlic
2 sprigs fresh tarragon

Place all ingredients in a glass jar. Cover and store up to 1 month in the refrigerator.

Per Serving (1 tablespoon): Calories: 120 | Fat: 14g | Protein: 0g | Sodium: 0mg | Fiber: 0g | Carbohydrates: 0g

Mediterranean Saltsa

Use this fresh sauce as a topping for grilled salmon or any other grilled fish.

INGREDIENTS | MAKES 2 CUPS

16 kalamata olives, pitted and sliced

2 tablespoons capers

¼ cup finely sliced scallions

½ cup diced red bell peppers

½ cup chopped tomato

1 clove garlic, minced

¼ cup chopped parsley

⅓ cup extra-virgin olive oil

1 teaspoon lemon juice

Gently mix all ingredients in a small bowl. Refrigerate or serve at room temperature.

Per Serving (¼ cup): Calories: 103 | Fat: 9g | Protein: 0.5g | Sodium: 68mg | Fiber: 0.5g | Carbohydrates: 6g

CHAPTER 13

Sweets and Desserts

Greek Mess

If you can't find Greek almond cookies, use the classic Italian amaretti.
Mastiha can be found at Greek or Middle Eastern grocery stores.

INGREDIENTS | SERVES 10

2 cups whipping cream

1 teaspoon ground mastiha

1 cup confectioners' sugar, divided

2 pints raspberries or other seasonal berry, divided

12 greek almond cookies, crumbled, divided

½ cup chopped almonds

4 tablespoons chopped mint leaves

1. In a medium bowl, beat whipping cream until soft peaks form. Add mastiha and ½ cup sugar. Continue whipping mixture until stiff peaks form. Keep mixture cool.

2. In another medium bowl, combine ⅔ of the berries and remaining sugar. Stir until sugar is melted. Coarsely mash berries into the consistency of a chunky jam.

3. Gently fold berry mixture into whipped cream mixture. Fold half the crumbled cookies into the berry–whipped cream mixture.

4. Divide the mixture into individual serving bowls or glasses, and top with remaining crumbled cookies, remaining berries, almonds, and mint.

5. Serve immediately or cover and refrigerate up to 1 day.

Per Serving: Calories: 289 | Fat: 18g | Protein: 4g | Sodium: 38mg | Fiber: 4g | Carbohydrates: 28g

Lemon Halva

Semolina flour looks like Cream of Wheat and comes in fine, medium, and coarse textures. Look for it at Greek and Middle Eastern grocers.

INGREDIENTS | SERVES 10

4 cups water

2 cups sugar

8 (2") strips lemon peel, pith removed

⅛ teaspoon ground cinnamon

1 cup plus 1 tablespoon unsalted butter, divided

2 cups coarse semolina

½ cup plus 2 tablespoons chopped blanched almonds, divided

½ cup plus 2 tablespoons pine nuts, divided

½ teaspoon vanilla

2 tablespoons grated lemon zest

2 tablespoons lemon juice

Halva

Halva originated in the Arab world but is a popular Mediterranean dessert. It is a molded and firm dessert that is like a pudding but could be confused as a cake.

1. Put water, sugar, and lemon peels in a medium pot over medium-high heat. Bring to a boil, then reduce heat to medium-low and cook 5 minutes. Add cinnamon. Cool to room temperature. Remove and discard lemon peels. Set syrup aside.

2. Melt 1 cup butter in a large pot over medium heat. Stir in semolina with a wooden spoon and continue stirring 5–6 minutes until semolina is lightly toasted. Add ½ cup almonds and ½ cup pine nuts and stir 2 more minutes.

3. To the pot, add syrup and vanilla and reduce heat to medium-low. Keep stirring 2–3 minutes or until semolina absorbs the liquid and starts to come away from the sides of the pan. Take the pot off the heat. Add lemon zest and juice. Place a tea towel over the pan, then cover the pan with a lid to prevent a crust from forming. Cool 10 minutes.

4. Grease a Bundt pan with remaining butter. Spoon halva into the pan and smooth out the top. Let halva cool completely. Unmold onto a serving platter.

5. Top halva with remaining almonds and pine nuts. Serve at room temperature or cold.

Per Serving: Calories: 483 | Fat: 22g | Protein: 6g | Sodium: 9mg | Fiber: 2.4g | Carbohydrates: 62g

Tiramisu MA

Tiramisu means "pick me up" in Italian, referring to the caffeine kick from the coffee in the dessert.

INGREDIENTS | SERVES 10

3 large eggs, separated
⅛ teaspoon nutmeg
¼ cup sugar, divided
1 cup mascarpone cheese
½ cup strong black coffee, freshly made
6 tablespoons marsala or coffee liqueur
16 ladyfinger cookies, divided
2 tablespoons cocoa powder

1. In a medium bowl, whisk egg yolks, nutmeg, and 2 tablespoons sugar until mixture thickens. Stir in mascarpone.

2. In another medium bowl, beat egg whites until stiff peaks form. Gently fold mascarpone-egg mixture into egg whites. Set aside.

3. In a medium bowl, add remaining sugar, coffee, and marsala. Stir mixture until sugar is dissolved.

4. Dip 8 ladyfingers one at a time into the coffee mixture for 1 second, then place them in a 6" × 10" × 4" baking dish. Don't leave the ladyfingers in the coffee for more than a second or they will become mushy.

5. Spread half of the mascarpone filling over ladyfingers. Dip remaining ladyfingers one at a time in the coffee mixture for 1 second, then place them in the dish over filling. Spread remaining mascarpone filling over ladyfingers. Cover and refrigerate 8 hours or overnight.

6. Sprinkle with cocoa powder before serving. Serve cold or at room temperature.

Per Serving: Calories: 201 | Fat: 11g | Protein: 5g | Sodium: 122mg | Fiber: 0.5g | Carbohydrates: 18g

Revani Syrup Cake

This simple cake is finished with syrup that soaks into the cake. Serve it with a scoop of ice cream.

INGREDIENTS | SERVES 24

1 tablespoon unsalted butter

2 tablespoons all-purpose flour

1 cup ground rusk or bread crumbs

1 cup fine semolina flour

¾ cup ground toasted almonds

3 teaspoons baking powder

16 large eggs

2 tablespoons vanilla extract

3 cups sugar, divided

3 cups water

5 (2") strips lemon peel, pith removed

3 tablespoons fresh lemon juice

1 ounce brandy

1. Preheat oven to 350°F. Grease a 13" × 9" baking pan with butter and coat with flour.

2. In a medium bowl, combine rusk, semolina flour, almonds, and baking powder.

3. In another medium bowl, whisk eggs, vanilla, and 1 cup sugar using an electric mixer on medium 5 minutes or until the eggs turn light yellow. Stir semolina mixture into egg mixture in three batches.

4. Pour batter into baking pan and bake 30–35 minutes or until a toothpick inserted into the middle of the cake comes out clean.

5. Meanwhile, make the syrup. Bring remaining sugar, water, and lemon peel to a boil in a medium pot over medium-high heat. Reduce heat to medium-low and cook for 6 minutes. Add lemon juice and cook for 3 minutes. Remove from heat and add brandy. Let syrup cool. Remove and discard lemon peel.

6. Ladle syrup over warm cake and set aside until syrup is soaked into cake, at least 15 minutes.

7. Cut cake into squares or diamond shapes. Serve at room temperature. Leftovers can be stored in the refrigerator up to 1 week.

Per Serving: Calories: 218 | Fat: 5.5g | Protein: 6g | Sodium: 142mg | Fiber: 1g | Carbohydrates: 35g

Lemon-Coconut Ice Cream   M A

For an adult treat, add a shot of lemon or coconut liqueur to the cream just before chilling it.

INGREDIENTS | SERVES 8

16 ounces coconut milk
10 ounces condensed milk
¼ cup honey
1 tablespoon vanilla extract
½ teaspoon salt
2 tablespoons grated lemon zest
5 tablespoons fresh lemon juice
1½ cups full-fat Greek yogurt
1 cup sweetened coconut flakes, toasted

1. In a large bowl, combine coconut milk, condensed milk, honey, vanilla, salt, lemon zest, lemon juice, and yogurt.

2. Cover mixture with plastic wrap and refrigerate 8 hours or overnight.

3. Add cream mixture to an ice-cream maker and process according to manufacturer's instructions.

4. Transfer ice cream to a plastic container and freeze until firm.

5. Serve the cream with a sprinkle of toasted coconut.

Per Serving: Calories: 227 | Fat: 17g | Protein: 5g | Sodium: 212mg | Fiber: 1g | Carbohydrates: 18g

Kourabiedes

These almond cookies are traditionally served at Christmas, but they are great any time.

INGREDIENTS | SERVES 20

1½ cups unsalted butter, clarified, at room temperature

2 cups confectioners' sugar, divided

1 large egg yolk

2 tablespoons brandy

1½ teaspoons baking powder

1 teaspoon vanilla extract

2¾ cups all-purpose flour, sifted

1 cup roasted almonds, chopped

Clarified Butter

Clarified butter is melted butter without the milk solids. To make clarified butter, place butter in a pan over low heat. The butter will begin to separate as it melts, and white foam will form on the surface. Remove the pan from the heat and carefully remove the white foam with a spoon. The clarified butter is what is left.

1. In a large bowl, cream butter and ½ cup sugar. Add egg and continue to beat 2 minutes.

2. In a small bowl, combine brandy and baking powder, stirring until baking powder is absorbed. Add brandy mixture and vanilla to egg mixture and continue to beat until ingredients are combined.

3. Using a large wooden spoon, slowly add flour to egg mixture to create dough. Add almonds and knead dough to incorporate flour and almonds.

4. Preheat oven to 350°F. Line a baking sheet with parchment paper.

5. Divide dough into 40 pieces. Roll each piece into a ball and then form it into a crescent shape. Place formed cookie on baking sheet. Repeat the process with remaining dough. Bake cookies in batches 25 minutes.

6. Put remaining sugar in a medium bowl. Allow cookies to cool 5 minutes. Add the cookies one at a time to sugar to coat them. Let cookies cool completely on a wire rack.

7. Sprinkle additional confectioners' sugar over cookies before serving. Store in a sealed container.

Per Serving: Calories: 210 | Fat: 15g | Protein: 2g | Sodium: 39mg | Fiber: 0.6g | Carbohydrates: 15g

Sesame Snaps

Replace the orange zest with lemon zest if you prefer a lemon flavor.

INGREDIENTS | SERVES 16

1 tablespoon unsalted butter
2 cups granulated sugar
⅓ cup water
⅓ cup honey
1 teaspoon fresh lemon juice
¼ teaspoon sea salt
1⅓ cups toasted sesame seeds
1 tablespoon grated orange zest

Toasting Sesame Seeds

Toasting sesame seeds is easy, but it requires some patience. Put the sesame seeds in a dry frying pan over medium heat. Stir them constantly with a wooden spoon until they are toasted to your liking. Toasting can take up to 10 minutes, so be patient. Don't walk away from the pan because the seeds burn very quickly.

1. Grease a medium baking sheet with 1 tablespoon butter.

2. Bring sugar, water, honey, lemon juice, and salt to a boil in a medium heavy-bottomed pan over medium-high heat. Continue cooking 10 minutes or until mixture turns into a deep amber colored syrup.

3. Stir sesame seeds and orange zest into syrup. Remove pan from the heat. Immediately pour syrup onto baking sheet. Quickly spread evenly around the pan with a greased spatula.

4. Before syrup cools completely, score the top into serving pieces (squares or diamond shapes) with a greased knife. When syrup has cooled completely, use a spatula to remove it from the pan and then cut into serving pieces.

5. Store in an airtight container.

Per Serving: Calories: 194 | Fat: 6g | Protein: 2g | Sodium: 39mg | Fiber: 1.5g | Carbohydrates: 33g

Rizogalo MA

This rice pudding is particularly good when refrigerated for a couple hours and served on sunny, warm days. The citrus zest adds a whole new dimension of flavor to the dish.

INGREDIENTS | SERVES 8

8 cups whole milk

1 cup Arborio rice

1½ cups sugar

1 teaspoon vanilla extract

1 tablespoon finely shredded citrus zest (orange, lemon, or lime)

2 large egg yolks

¼ cup cold whole milk

1 tablespoon corn flour

1 teaspoon ground cinnamon

1. In a large saucepan over medium-high heat, bring 8 cups milk to slight boil. Add rice and stir well until mixture boils. Reduce heat to medium-low and gently simmer uncovered 30 minutes, stirring regularly so milk doesn't stick to sides or bottom of the pan.

2. Add sugar, vanilla, and zest and continue to simmer and occasionally stir another 10 minutes.

3. Beat egg yolks with ¼ cup cold milk; whisk in corn flour and mix well.

4. Pour egg yolk mixture into saucepan and whisk well to incorporate. Simmer another 3–5 minutes until thick.

5. Remove from heat. Transfer mixture into 8 small bowls. Let stand 1 hour to cool. Sprinkle with cinnamon. Refrigerate or serve at room temperature.

Per Serving: Calories: 344 | Fat: 10g | Protein: 9.5g | Sodium: 126mg | Fiber: 0g | Carbohydrates: 54g

Stuffed Figs

Purchase kalamata dried string figs if you can find them, as they are larger and sweeter than most other commercially available varieties.

INGREDIENTS | SERVES 4

12 dried figs
24 walnut halves
2 tablespoons thyme honey
2 tablespoons sesame seeds

Need Calcium and Fiber?

Fresh or dried, figs are an excellent source of calcium and fiber, as well as many other nutrients. They are also rich in antioxidants and polyphenols.

1. Snip tough stalk ends off figs. Slice the side of each fig and open with fingers.

2. Stuff 2 walnut halves inside each fig and fold closed.

3. Arrange figs on platter. Drizzle with honey and sprinkle with sesame seeds to serve.

Per Serving: Calories: 216 | Fat: 12g | Protein: 4g | Sodium: 3.5mg | Fiber: 4g | Carbohydrates: 28g

254

Byzantine Fruit Medley

Feel free to experiment with the fruits you use in this recipe.

INGREDIENTS | SERVES 4

½ cup red wine

½ cup Greek anthomelo (blossom honey)

2 medium apples, peeled, cored, and diced

2 medium pears, peeled, cored, and diced

3 medium mandarins or clementines, peeled and sectioned

Seeds from 1 large pomegranate

1. In a small saucepan, bring wine and honey to a boil over high heat. Boil 3–4 minutes to evaporate most of the alcohol. Cool 20 minutes.

2. Combine apples, pears, mandarins, and pomegranate seeds in a medium bowl.

3. Pour wine mixture over fruit and refrigerate at least 1 hour. Stir fruit a few times to ensure sauce covers everything. Serve cold.

Per Serving: Calories: 287 | Fat: 0.5g | Protein: 1g | Sodium: 6mg | Fiber: 6g | Carbohydrates: 74g

Date-Almond Pie

For an added kick, use honey-flavored Greek yogurt in this tart. If you have a favorite dough recipe, you can also make this in the shape of a free form tart. Spread the dough on a baking sheet, top with the date mixture, and fold in the edges before baking.

INGREDIENTS | SERVES 6

1 cup chopped dried dates

½ cup chopped almonds

½ cup honey

1 (9") unbaked pie shell

1 cup plain nonfat yogurt

¼ cup confectioners' sugar

1. Preheat oven to 375°F.

2. Mix together dates, almonds, and honey in a medium bowl. Pour mixture into pie shell.

3. Bake 20 minutes. Cool and serve with a dollop of yogurt and a sprinkle of confectioners' sugar.

Per Serving: Calories: 429 | Fat: 15g | Protein: 5g | Sodium: 177mg | Fiber: 4g | Carbohydrates: 74g

Roasted Pears

Try your favorite light wine with this recipe. Or try it with pear cider or eau de vie.

INGREDIENTS | SERVES 6

6 medium pears
1 cup sweet white wine
1 tablespoon grated lemon zest
1 teaspoon honey
3 ounces low-fat vanilla yogurt
¼ cup chopped mint

1. Preheat oven to 375°F.

2. Peel and core pears and cut in half from top to bottom. Place pears cut-side down in a small roasting pan and pour wine over them. Sprinkle with zest and drizzle with honey.

3. Cover tightly and roast approximately 30 minutes. Then uncover and roast 10 minutes longer.

4. To serve, place a dollop of yogurt on each plate. Prop pear halves on yogurt and sprinkle with chopped mint.

Per Serving: Calories: 151 | Fat: 1g | Protein: 2g | Sodium: 17mg | Fiber: 6g | Carbohydrates: 31g

Apricot and Walnut Tart

Any type of jam can be used in this recipe. Also, try other kinds of nuts, such as almonds or pecans, to create different flavors.

INGREDIENTS | SERVES 6

1 cup flour
2 teaspoons olive oil
1 teaspoon ice water
2 cups chopped apricots
½ cup chopped walnuts
½ cup currants
¼ cup apricot jam
¼ cup light brown sugar

1. Preheat oven to 375°F.

2. In a medium bowl, mix together flour, oil, and water to form dough. On a floured surface, roll out dough into a 10" square and place on a baking sheet.

3. Arrange apricots, nuts, currants, jam, and sugar in the center of the dough and fold edges together over filling to within 2" of the center. Fold back corners to leave an opening in center. Bake 30 minutes.

Per Serving: Calories: 253 | Fat: 8g | Protein: 5g | Sodium: 9mg | Fiber: 2g | Carbohydrates: 43g

Berries and Meringue MA

A perfect ending to a picnic, this meringue provides a sweet, light finish to any summer lunch. If you like, stir a few tablespoons of sugar into the berries about 15–30 minutes before serving.

INGREDIENTS | SERVES 12

6 large egg whites

½ cup sugar

¼ teaspoon cream of tartar

2 cups fresh berries (blackberries, blueberries, raspberries, or a combination)

1. Preheat oven to 200°F. Line a baking sheet with parchment paper or spray with cooking spray.

2. In a copper or stainless steel bowl, beat egg whites, sugar, and cream of tartar until stiff. Drop egg white mixture onto baking sheet to form 12 small mounds. Bake 1½–1¾ hours, until dry, crispy, and lightly golden.

3. Place each meringue on a dessert plate. Top with berries.

Per Serving: Calories: 93 | Fat: 2g | Protein: 3g | Sodium: 28mg | Fiber: 1g | Carbohydrates: 17g

Sautéed Strawberries in Yogurt Soup

To make the most of this delectable dessert, serve with vanilla ice cream.

INGREDIENTS | SERVES 4

1 cup skim milk

1 vanilla bean

2 tablespoons sugar

2 cups nonfat plain yogurt

1 tablespoon butter

1 pint strawberries, sliced

¼ cup brown sugar

1. Combine milk, vanilla bean, and sugar in a small saucepan over medium heat. Cook 5 minutes; do not boil. Cool to room temperature and remove vanilla bean. Whisk in the yogurt.

2. Melt butter in a small skillet over medium heat. Add strawberries. Sauté, stirring constantly, 5 minutes.

3. Pour yogurt mixture into shallow bowls. Dollop with strawberry mixture and sprinkle with brown sugar.

Per Serving: Calories: 230 | Fat: 8g | Protein: 7g | Sodium: 88mg | Fiber: 1g | Carbohydrates: 34g

CHAPTER 14

Beverages

Café Frappé

Frappé is among the most popular drinks in Greece and is available at virtually all Greek cafés. Add a shot of ouzo to your afternoon frappe!

INGREDIENTS | SERVES 1

1 tablespoon instant coffee

1 teaspoon sugar

1 tablespoon room temperature water

Ice cubes

½ cup cold water

2 tablespoons evaporated milk

1. Put coffee, sugar, and water into a cocktail shaker and cover. Shake vigorously for 30 seconds.

2. Pour mixture into a tall glass with a few ice cubes. Add enough cold water to almost fill the glass.

3. Add milk and serve immediately with a straw.

Per Serving: Calories: 71 | Fat: 2.5g | Protein: 2.8g | Sodium: 35mg | Fiber: 0g | Carbohydrates: 9.5g

Instant Coffee

Instant coffee became very popular in Europe when it was brought over by U.S. troops who demanded it in their ration kits. Once Europeans began using it, they were hooked. Now instant coffee is common in places like Greece, Portugal, and Spain.

Greek Mountain Tea

Most Greek households have this tea on hand. You can buy some at any Greek grocery store.

INGREDIENTS | SERVES 4

6–8 branches Greek mountain tea (8 if branches are short, 6 if branches are longer)

5 cups water

4 tablespoons honey

½ large lemon, cut into 4 wedges

Greek Mountain Tea

Greek mountain tea is made from the leaves and flowers of Sideritis plants, also known as ironwort. These plants grow on the Greek mountainsides and the tea made from them is consumed in most Greek households. This tea is also known as "shepherd's tea" because shepherds would brew tea using the plants' leaves while tending to their flocks in the mountains.

1. Boil tea and water in a medium pot over high heat. Reduce heat to medium and simmer 5 minutes. Remove pot from heat and allow tea to steep 5 minutes.

2. Pour tea through a strainer into 4 cups and add 1 tablespoon honey per cup.

3. Serve tea hot with lemon wedges.

Per Serving: Calories: 66 | Fat: 0g | Protein: 0g | Sodium: 9mg | Fiber: 0g | Carbohydrates: 16g

Greek Coffee

Serve Greek coffee with desserts or sweets. A briki is a special one-handled pot used for making Greek coffees. It comes in various sizes and can be found in Greek or Middle Eastern shops. The grounds will remain at the bottom of the cup. Sip only until you detect a bit of the grounds.

INGREDIENTS | SERVES 1

Cold water

1 tablespoon Greek coffee

½ teaspoon sugar

Greek Coffee

Greek coffee is made by roasting a special blend of coffee beans and then grinding them into a fine powder. Visit a Greek specialty store or a Turkish or Middle Eastern shop for similar coffee.

1. Using a demitasse cup, measure the amount of cold water needed to make a serving of coffee. Put water, coffee, and sugar in a briki.

2. Place briki over medium heat. Swirl briki until coffee and sugar dissolve. As soon as coffee foams, remove from heat and pour into cup.

3. Before drinking, allow the grounds to settle to the bottom of the cup; it will take about 1 minute.

Per Serving: Calories: 8 | Fat: 0g | Protein: 0g | Sodium: 0mg | Fiber: 0g | Carbohydrates: 2g

Chamomile Tea

This soothing and delicious tea will help you relax; it can also soothe an upset stomach.

INGREDIENTS | SERVES 1

1 teaspoon dried chamomile

1½ cups water

1 tablespoon honey

1 wedge lemon

Chamomile

The word *chamomile* is derived from the Greek word meaning "earth apple." When chamomile is in bloom, it looks like a daisy and is gathered and dried to make tea. Greeks drink it to help alleviate anxiety, reduce stress, and induce sleep.

1. Boil chamomile and water in a medium pot over high heat. Reduce heat to medium and simmer 30 seconds. Take pot off heat and allow tea to steep 5 minutes.

2. Pour tea through a strainer into a cup. Add honey and serve hot with a wedge of lemon.

Per Serving: Calories: 66 | Fat: 0g | Protein: 0g | Sodium: 7mg | Fiber: 0g | Carbohydrates: 16g

Lemon Verbena Tea

Lemon verbena has a mint-lemon aroma that is very soothing. The lemon verbena plant was brought to Europe by Columbus as a gift for Spain's Queen Luisa.

INGREDIENTS | SERVES 4

½ cup loose lemon verbena leaves (dried or fresh)

5 cups water

4 tablespoons honey

½ large lemon, cut into 4 wedges

1. Boil leaves and water in a medium pot over high heat. Reduce the heat to medium and simmer tea 5 minutes. Remove pot from heat. Allow tea to steep 5 minutes.

2. Pour tea through a strainer into cups; add 1 tablespoon honey per cup.

3. Serve tea hot with lemon wedges.

Per Serving: Calories: 66 | Fat: 0g | Protein: 0g | Sodium: 6mg | Fiber: 0g | Carbohydrates: 16g

Ouzo on Ice

You need to serve ouzo over ice to bring out its cloudy color and heighten the anise flavor.

INGREDIENTS	SERVES 1

1½ ounces ouzo

Ice

Ouzo and Mezedes

Greeks eat when they drink, and they drink when they eat. Greece's national drink, ouzo, is meant to be sipped cold and always with food. Greeks do not drink shots of ouzo, rather they savor this anise-flavored aperitif with appetizers or, as Greeks call them, mezedes.

1. Pour ouzo into a highball glass with as much ice as you desire. Remember the ice will melt and dilute the ouzo.

2. Swirl glass and as soon as mixture becomes cloudy, begin sipping.

Per Serving: Calories: 97 | Fat: 0g | Protein: 0g | Sodium: 0mg | Fiber: 0g | Carbohydrates: 0g

Rakomelo M A

Rakomelo is popular in the westernmost part of Crete, in Hania. This after-dinner digestive is served cold, and it has a golden color with notes of cinnamon.

INGREDIENTS | SERVES 4

4 cups raki or tsipouro or grappa
¼ cup honey
2 cinnamon sticks
2 whole cloves

1. Heat all ingredients in a large pot over medium-low heat to a slow boil. Stir occasionally. Once the mixture boils, remove from heat.

2. Allow to cool and pour mixture into a glass bottle with a lid. Refrigerate at least 4 hours. Serve cold as a digestive after dinner.

Per Serving: Calories: 479 | Fat: 0g | Protein: 0g | Sodium: 3mg | Fiber: 0g | Carbohydrates: 17g

Mastiha on the Rocks

Mastiha liqueur is served as a digestive after a big meal.

INGREDIENTS | SERVES 1

3–4 ice cubes
1½ ounces Skinos Mastiha liqueur
Lemon wedge

1. Fill a rocks or cocktail glass with ice. Pour mastiha over ice.

2. Squeeze a lemon wedge over the glass and stir. Allow some of the ice to melt before serving.

Per Serving: Calories: 138 | Fat: 0g | Protein: 0g | Sodium: 3mg | Fiber: 0g | Carbohydrates: 20g

Windex Cocktail

The American romantic comedy My Big Fat Greek Wedding *brought the Greek immigrant experience into the mainstream. The father in the movie was convinced that Windex cured all. This cocktail is a fun drink you can make at parties.*

INGREDIENTS | SERVES 4

5 ounces ouzo

4 ounces blue curaçao liqueur

1⅓ cups lemonade

Ice cubes

1. Pour ouzo, blue curaçao, and lemonade into a large cocktail shaker with ice and shake to mix.

2. Pour into chilled martini glasses or rocks glasses filled with ice and serve.

Per Serving: Calories: 196 | Fat: 0g | Protein: 0g | Sodium: 14mg | Fiber: 0g | Carbohydrates: 19g

Mastiha Cocktail

This is the perfect summer cocktail for a Greek dinner or cocktail party.

INGREDIENTS | SERVES 1

¼ cup peeled, seeded, and chopped English cucumber

¼ large lime

⅛ teaspoon salt

½ teaspoon sugar

1½ ounces mastiha liqueur

1 ounce gin

3–4 ice cubes

2 ounces club soda, tonic water, or lemon-lime soda

1 lime wedge

1. Add cucumber, lime, salt, and sugar to a rocks glass and muddle ingredients.

2. Stir in mastiha and gin. Add ice and top with club soda. Serve with a lime wedge.

Per Serving: Calories: 220 | Fat: 0g | Protein: 0g | Sodium: 320mg | Fiber: 0g | Carbohydrates: 24g

Metaxa Mint Julep

This drink is inspired by the classic mint julep, which consists of Kentucky bourbon poured into a glass of muddled mint, lime, and sugar. Metaxa brandy replaces the bourbon in this recipe.

INGREDIENTS | SERVES 1

1 teaspoon coarse brown sugar
¼ large lime
4 fresh mint leaves
1½ ounces Metaxa brandy
Ice

Muddling

Muddling is a bartending term that refers to crushing herbs and fruit to release their oils and flavors into a drink. Muddlers are usually made of wood and come in all sizes. If you don't have one, use the handle end of a wooden spoon.

1. Put brown sugar, lime, and mint into a rocks or cocktail glass and muddle for 1 minute.

2. Add brandy to glass and fill with ice.

3. Allow ice to melt for a couple of minutes before serving.

Per Serving: Calories: 122 | Fat: 0g | Protein: 0.5g | Sodium: 10mg | Fiber: 0.5g | Carbohydrates: 7g

Greek Summer Sangria   MA

*This sangria is infused with cinnamon and cloves and has just enough sweetness
to be refreshing. This recipe can easily be doubled or tripled.*

INGREDIENTS | SERVES 10

1 cup water

½ cup sugar

2 strips lemon or orange peel,
pith removed

½ cinnamon stick

3 whole cloves

¼ cup honey

1 (25-ounce) bottle red wine

½ cup Metaxa brandy or any
other brandy

1 ripe medium peach, sliced

1 medium orange, sliced

24 ounces ginger ale

1. Bring water, sugar, lemon peel, cinnamon, and cloves to a boil in a small pot over medium-high heat. Lower heat to medium-low and cook another 5 minutes. Remove pot from heat and add honey. Allow syrup mixture to cool completely. Remove and discard peel, cinnamon stick, and cloves.

2. Pour remaining ingredients into a large pitcher. Add syrup in increments. Keep tasting after each addition of syrup until sangria reaches your desired level of sweetness. Remaining syrup can be used in another sangria.

3. Cover and refrigerate overnight. Serve cold over ice.

Per Serving: Calories: 173 | Fat: 0g | Protein: 0.5g | Sodium: 10mg | Fiber: 1g | Carbohydrates: 29g

Tsipouro

Tsipouro is a spirit enjoyed throughout Greece, although it may have a different name in other parts of the country. In Crete, it is tsikoudia; in other places, it's raki.

INGREDIENTS | SERVES 1

1½ ounces tsipouro
Ice

Tsipouro

Tsipouro is made by distilling grapes. Often it is double-distilled for a cleaner, purer product. Tsipouro is available unflavored, where the flavor of the grapes comes through in the finish. It is also flavored with anise, which makes it taste similar to ouzo but not as sweet. Although tsipouro is meant to be served after dinner as a digestive, it is gaining popularity with Greeks who prefer it to ouzo. It is now also acceptable to sip tsipouro with appetizers (mezedes).

1. Pour tsipouro into a highball glass with as much ice as you desire. Remember the ice will melt and dilute the tsipouro.

2. Swirl glass and as soon as the mixture becomes cloudy, begin sipping.

Per Serving: Calories: 97 | Fat: 0g | Protein: 0g | Sodium: 0mg | Fiber: 0g | Carbohydrates: 0g

Standard U.S./Metric Measurement Conversions

VOLUME CONVERSIONS

U.S. Volume Measure	Metric Equivalent
⅛ teaspoon	0.5 milliliter
¼ teaspoon	1 milliliter
½ teaspoon	2 milliliters
1 teaspoon	5 milliliters
½ tablespoon	7 milliliters
1 tablespoon (3 teaspoons)	15 milliliters
2 tablespoons (1 fluid ounce)	30 milliliters
¼ cup (4 tablespoons)	60 milliliters
⅓ cup	80 milliliters
½ cup (4 fluid ounces)	125 milliliters
⅔ cup	160 milliliters
¾ cup (6 fluid ounces)	180 milliliters
1 cup (16 tablespoons)	250 milliliters
1 pint (2 cups)	500 milliliters
1 quart (4 cups)	1 liter (about)

WEIGHT CONVERSIONS

U.S. Weight Measure	Metric Equivalent
½ ounce	15 grams
1 ounce	30grams
2 ounces	60grams
3 ounces	85 grams
¼ pound (4 ounces)	115 grams
½ pound (8 ounces)	225 grams
¾ pound (12 ounces)	340grams
1 pound (16 ounces)	454 grams

OVEN TEMPERATURE CONVERSIONS

Degrees Fahrenheit	Degrees Celsius
200 degrees F	95 degrees C
250 degrees F	120 degrees C
275 degrees F	135 degrees C
300 degrees F	150 degrees C
325 degrees F	160 degrees C
350 degrees F	180 degrees C
375 degrees F	190 degrees C
400 degrees F	205 degrees C
425 degrees F	220 degrees C
450 degrees F	230 degrees C

BAKING PAN SIZES

American	Metric
8 × 1½ inch round baking pan	20 × 4 cm cake tin
9 × 1½ inch round baking pan	23 × 3.5 cm cake tin
11 × 7 × 1½ inch baking pan	28 × 18 × 4 cm baking tin
13 × 9 × 2 inch baking pan	30 × 20 × 5 cm baking tin
2 quart rectangular baking dish	30 × 20 × 3 cm baking tin
15 × 10 × 2 inch baking pan	38 × 25 × 5 cm baking tin (Swiss roll tin)
9 inch pie plate	22 × 4 or 23 × 4 cm pie plate
7 or 8 inch springform pan	18 or 20 cm springform or loose bottom cake tin
9 × 5 × 3 inch loaf pan	23 × 13 × 7 cm or 2 lb narrow loaf or pate tin
1½ quart casserole	1.5 liter casserole
2 quart casserole	2 liter casserole

Index
